Table of Contents

Abbreviations Used

abbr.	abbreviation
adj.	adjective
b.	born
c.	circa; about
d.	died
Eng.	English
Fr.	French
Ger.	German
Gr.	Greek
It.	Italian
Lat.	Latin
n.	noun
Port.	Portuguese
Sp.	Spanish
v.	verb

Pronunciation Guide

CAPITAL LETTERS indicate an accented (stressed) syllable.

Short Vowels

a	short "a," as in "rat"
e, eh	short "e," as in "rent"
i	short "i," as in "rip"
o, ah	short "o," as in "rot"
u	short "u," as in "rut"

Long Vowels

ay	long "a," as in "rate"
ee	long "e," as in "reap"
ei	long "i," as in "ripe"
oh	long "o," as in "rope"
oo	long "u," as in "ruse"

Other Vowel Sounds

aw	as in "raw"
oy	as in "boy"
e[r]	as in "fern," but without pronouncing the "r"
[u]e	shaping the lips like "oo" but saying "ee"
[n]	the preceding vowel is given a nasal sound; the "n" is not pronounced

Consonants

g	as in "rig," even when preceding "e" or "i"
zh	as in "rouge"
[k]h	shaping the mouth like "k" but saying "h"
[s]h	shaping the mouth like "sh" but saying "h"

All other consonants retain their normal pronunciations.

Key to Entries

Entry Word

Language, if Other than English

Pronunciation

Literal Meaning, if Different from Common Usage

legno (*It., LEN-yoh*): "Wood." On string instruments, the stick of the *bow*. See *col legno*.

Cross-References

Definition

Dictionary of Terms

A

a, à (*It., Fr., ah*)**:** At, by, for, with.

AABA, ABA, ABC, ABCD, etc.**:** See *song forms.*

A&R (*abbr.*)**:** "Artists & Repertoire." Record company personnel responsible for the acquisition of talent and for the overseeing of their production (repertoire) and activities.

abandon, abbandono (*Fr., ah-baw[n]-DOH[N]; It., ahb-BAHN-doh-noh*)**:** Abandon, freedom, passion.

a battuta (*It., ah baht-TOO-tah*)**:** With the beat.

abbellire (*It., ahb-bel-LEE-reh*)**:** Embellish with ornaments.

abellimenti (*It., ah-bel-lee-MEN-tee*)**:** *Embellishments* or *ornaments.*

absolute music: Music without associations outside itself, in contrast to *program music.*

absolute pitch: See *perfect pitch.*

a cappella (*It., ah kahp-PEL-lah*)**:** "In the manner of the chapel." Without accompaniment.

a capriccio (*It., ah kah-PREET-choh*)**:** With a capricious style.

accelerando (*It., aht-chel-le-RAHN-doh):* Becoming faster.

accelerato (*It., aht-chel-le-RAH-toh*)**:** Accelerated.

accent, accénto (*Eng.*; *It., aht-CHEN-toh*)**:** To emphasize or stress a note. Indicated by the symbol >. There are three main kinds of accents: *agogic*, *dynamic*, and *tonic.*

accessory notes: Notes one degree above or below the principal note of a *turn.* The upper notes of a *trill.*

acciaccatura (*It., aht-chahk-kah-TOO-rah*)**:** A short grace note played simultaneously with the principal note and released immediately:

accidentals: Sharps, flats, or natural signs used to raise, lower, or return a note to its normal pitch.

accompaniment: A vocal or instrumental part that supports or is background for a solo part.

accopiato (*It., ahk-koh-PYAH-toh*)**:** Tied.

accord, accordo (*Fr., ahk-KOHR; It., ahk-KOHR-doh*)**:** Chord.

accordamento (*It., ahk-kohr-dah-MEN-toh*)**:** Harmonious, consonant.

accordare, accorder *(It., ahk-kor-DAH-ray; Fr., ahk-kor-DAY)***:** To tune.

accordion: A musical instrument in which air is pushed and pulled by a bellows across metal reeds to produce a sound (also known as a "squeeze box").

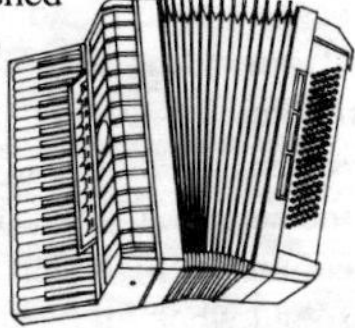

accordion

achromatic: Diatonic.

acid rock: Highly amplified music from late 1960s that attempted to simulate or strengthen the effects of narcotic use; forerunner of *heavy metal.* "Acid" coined from use of LSD by many rock artists.

acoustic: Any instrument that produces sound by means of physical vibrations, without the use of electronic amplification.

acoustics 1: The science of sound. **2:** The physical properties of an instrument or a room as they relate to sound.

action 1: On string instruments, the distance from the strings to the finger- or fretboard. **2:** The mechanism of a keyboard or other instrument that produces the sound via pressure.

active sensing: A *MIDI* message sent periodically by some equipment to notifiy other pieces of equipment that they are still connnected.

adagietto (*It., ah-dah-JET-toh*)**:** A tempo not quite as slow as *adagio.*

adagio (*It., ah-DAH-joh*)**:** "At ease." A slow tempo falling between *largo* (slower) and *andante* (faster).

adagissimo (*It., ah-dah-JEES-see-moh*)**:** Very slow tempo.

added sixth: A triad with the sixth added to the root, third, and fifth.

additive synthesis: Synthesizing sound by adding together *sine waves* at different frequencies and amplitudes.

addolorato (*It., ahd-doh-loh-RAH-toh*)**:** Sorrowfully.

à demi-jeu (*Fr., ah DEH-mee ZHE[R]*)**:** With half the power.

à demi-voix (*Fr., ah DEH-mee VWAH*)**:** With half the voice, whispered.

à deux, a due (*Fr., ah DE[R];It., ah DOO-eh*)**:** For two instruments or voices (to be played or sung in unison).

ad libitum, ad lib. (*Lat., ahd LEE-bee-toom*)**:** "At will." The performer may improvise freely, omit a part, or vary the tempo.

ADSR (*abbr.*)**:** "Attack, Decay, Sustain, Release." In synthesis, the parameters commonly used in an *envelope*.

Advent: "Arrival." The four weeks immediately preceding Christmas.

Aeolian (*ay-OH-lee-an*)**:** A medieval mode whose half- and whole-step pattern is that of playing A to A on the white keys of the piano (same as the natural minor scale). See *Scale Chart: Modes.*

aeolian harp: A musical instrument constructed of a box and strings that sound when hit by a current of air.

affábile (*It., ahf-FAH-bee-leh*)**:** Pleasing, gentle.

afflito (*It., af-FLEE-toh*)**:** Sorrowfully, sadly, mournfully.

affrettando (*It., ahf-fret-TAHN-doh*)**:** Hurrying.

A 440: The note A above middle C, whose frequency is 440 vibrations per second. The note from which orchestras and music ensembles universally tune.

aftertouch: A MIDI *continuous controller* code sent by some keyboards when pressure is exerted on a key after it has been struck.

agilità (*It., ah-jee-lee-TAH*)**:** Lightness or agility.

agilmente (*It., ah-jeel-MEN-tay*)**:** With agility; quickly and easily.

agitato (*It., ah-jee-TAH-toh*)**:** Agitated, excited, hurried, restless.

Agnus Dei (*Lat., AH-nyoos DAY-ee*)**:** "Lamb of God." In the *Mass*, the fifth part of the *Ordinary.*

agogic accent: Emphasis placed on a note by making it longer than normal. See *dynamic accent, tonic accent.*

air: A song or melody.

air guitar: An imaginary guitar played in pantomime fashion.

al, all', alla, alle (*It., ahl, ahll, AHL-lah, AHL-leh*) **1:** "To the." **2:** In the style of (e.g., *alla turca*, "in a Turkish style"; *alla marcia*, "in a march style").

Alberti bass: Accompanying bass figures consisting of broken chords, generally in the pattern low-high-middle-high:

album: A full-length recording. In pop music, it contains a number of songs.

Albumblatt (*Ger., AHL-boom-blot*)**:** A page or leaf from a book, or a short, easy piece.

al coda (*It., ahl KOH-dah*)**:** "To the coda."

aleatoric (*al-ee-ah-TOR-ic*)**:** Music where elements, such as rhythm or pitch, are chosen by chance by the performer. Used since 1945.

al fine (*It., ahl FEE-nay*)**:** To the end.

algorithm (*AL-go-rhythm*)**:** In synthesis, a method or procedure for creating sounds. In *FM synthesis,* the configuration of the operators.

alla breve (*It., ahl-lah BREH-veh*)**:** "According to the *breve*." A duple time signature, usually 2/2.

allargando (*It., ahl-lahr-GAHN-doh*)**:** Growing broader and therefore, slower.

allegretto (*It., ahl-leh-GRET-toh*)**:** A light, cheerful, fast tempo; a bit slower than *allegro*.

allegro (*It., ahl-LAY-groh*)**:** "Cheerful." A lively, fast tempo: *allegro assai,* very fast; ~ *di bravura,* fast, bright and spirited; ~ *di molto,* very fast and animated; ~ *giusto,* fast, steady and precise; ~ *moderato,* moderately fast.

allemande (*Fr., ahl-le-MAW[N]D*)**:** "German." A stately 16th-century German dance, initially in moderate duple meter. In 17th and 18th centuries it was usually the first movement of the *suite.* By 19th century it became a brisk dance in 3/4 time.

allentando (*It., ahl-len-TAHN-doh*)**:** Slower.

alphorn: A long (up to 10 feet) wooden horn from Switzerland, curved slightly at the end with an upturned bell.

al segno (*It., ahl SAY-nyoh*)**:** Return to the sign (see *dal segno*).

alt (*It., ahlt*)**:** "High." The notes, from G to F, that fall above the fifth line of the *treble clef.*

alteration: The raising or lowering of a note by means of an *accidental* (sharp or flat).

altered chord: A chord in which a note(s) has been raised or lowered chromatically.

altissimo (*It., ahl-TEES-see-moh*)**:** "Most high." The highest notes; the octave above the *alt.*

alto (*It., AHL-toh*) "High." **1:** The lowest female singing voice and highest male singing voice. The range is:

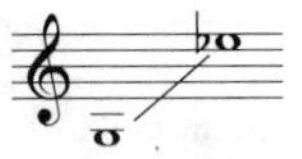

2: *Viola.*

alto clef: The C clef falling on the third line of the staff. Used almost exclusively by the *viola*:

alto flute: See *flute.*

alto saxophone: See *saxophone.*

altra, altro (*It., AHL-trah, AHL-troh*)**:** Other.

altra volta (*It., AHL-trah VOHL-tah*)**:** "Another time." Encore.

AM (*abbr.*)**:** *Amplitude Modulation.*

amabile (*It., ah-MAH-bee-leh*)**:** Amiable, gentle.

amplifier, amp: An electronic device that controls the intensity (power) or strength of a *signal.*

amplitude: In synthesis, the height of a *wave,* which corresponds to the volume (loudness) of the sound.

amplitude modulation: In synthesis, the periodic alteration of the volume of an audio signal to produce effects such as *tremolo.*

am Steg (*Ger., ahm SHTEK*)**:** On string instruments, bowing on the bridge; *sul ponticello.*

anacrusis (*Gr., ah-nah-CROO-sis*)**:** *Pickup* or upbeat.

analog: In synthesis, the use of voltages to control pitch, timbre, amplitude.

analysis: The study of the form and structure of music.

anapest: A musical or poetic foot, composed of two short notes or syllables and one long one.

anche (*Fr., aw[n]sh*)**:** A reed (for clarinet, oboe, etc.); a reed organ stop.

anche (*It., AHN-keh*)**:** Also, even, too.

ancòra (*It., ahn-KOH-rah*)**:** Repeat, again, once more.

andante (*It., ahn-DAHN-teh*)**:** "Going." A moderate, graceful tempo, between *allegretto* and *adagio.*

andantino (*It., ahn-dahn-TEE-noh*)**:** Originally, a tempo a little slower than *andante,* but now used to indicate a little faster than *andante.*

anglaise (*Fr., aw[n]-GLEZ*)**:** "English." **1:** English country dance in quick duple meter. **2:** In the English style.

anima (*It., AH-nee-mah*)**:** Life, spirit.

animato, animoso (*It., ah-nee-MAH-toh, ah-nee-MOH-zoh*)**:** Animated, engergetic or spirited.

Ansatz (*Ger., AHN-zots*)**:** The *embouchure* in wind playing; the *attack* in vocal or string playing.

answer: In the *fugue*, the second entry of the *subject.*

antecedent: The first phrase of a musical *period.* In the *fugue*, the *subject.* See *consequent.*

anthem: A choral composition, most often with religious lyric, with or without accompaniment, written for performance in church.

anticipation: Nonharmonic note or notes played prior to the chord in which it belongs.

antiphonal: Alternating singing or playing by separate groups of performers. See *responsoral.*

antithesis (*an-TI-the-sis*)**:** In the *fugue,* the *answer.*

AOR (*abbr.*)**:** "Album-Oriented Rock." A *chart* term for airplay of selections from albums on FM radio stations.

appassionato (*It., ahp-pahs-syoh-NAH-toh*)**:** Passionately.

appenato (*It., ahp-peh-NAH-toh*)**:** Distressed, grieved.

appoggiando (*It., ahp-pohd-JAHN-doh)***:** "Leaning." Emphasized.

appoggiatura (*It., ahp-pohd-jah-TOO-rah*)**:** An accented ("leaning") nonharmonic note that resolves stepwise to a harmonic note:

arabesque (*Fr., ah-rah-BESK*)**:** "Arabian." **1:** A fanciful piano piece. **2:** Ornate passage varying or accompanying a theme.

arcato (*It., ahr-KAH-toh*)**:** "Bowed." For string instruments, indicates to use the bow.
archet, archetto (*Fr., ar-SHAY; It., ahr-KET-toh*)**:** For string instruments, the bow; to bow.
archlute: A lute with two pegboxes: one for the strings to be *fretted* and one for the bass strings.
arch-top guitar: A guitar with an arched top and *f-holes* like a violin. Traditionally used for *swing* and jazz.
arco (*It., AHR-koh*)**:** "Bow." For string instruments, indicates to use the bow.
ardito (*It., AHR-dee-toh*)**:** Bold, with spirit.
aria (*It., AH-ree-ah*)**:** An air or song for solo voice within an opera or oratorio.
aria buffa (*It., AH-ree-ah BOOF-fah*)**:** A humorous or comic song.
arietta (*It., ah-ree-ET-tah*)**:** A short aria.
arioso (*It., ah-ree-OH-zoh*) **1:** A lyrical, songlike *recitative.* **2:** Lyrically.
arpa (*It., AHR-pah*)**:** Harp.
arpeggiato, arpeggiando (*It., ahr-ped-JAH-toh, ahr-ped-JAHN-doh*)**:** Arpeggiated; harp-like.
arpeggiator: In synthesis, a device that repeats notes in *arpeggio*-fashion within a defined speed, direction, and set of notes.
arpeggio (*It., ahr-PED-joh*)**:** The notes of a chord played in succession (harp-like); a broken chord.
arraché (*Fr., ahr-rah-SHAY*)**:** Strong pizzicato.
arrangement: An adaptation of a composition.
ars antiqua (*Lat., ahrs ahn-TEE-kwah*)**:** "Old art." Refers to music of the 12th and 13th centuries.
arsis (*Gr., AR-sis*)**:** The *upbeat.*
ars nova (*Lat., ahrs NOH-vah*)**:** "New art." Refers to music of the 14th century.
articulation: The degree to which notes are separated or connected, such as *staccato* or *legato.*
artificial harmonic: On string instruments, a *harmonic* played on a fingered or fretted string, as opposed to an open string. See *open harmonic.*
art song: A serious vocal composition, generally for voice and piano. Denotes a self-contained work (contrast with *aria*).

ASCAP (*abbr., AS-kap*)**:** "American Society of Composers, Authors and Publishers." A performing rights society with main offices in New York, Los Angeles, and Nashville.

assai (*It., ahs-SEI*)**:** Very, extremely.

assez (*Fr., ahs-SAY*)**:** Enough.

assoluto (*It., ahs-soh-LOO-toh*)**:** Absolute.

Atem (*Ger., AH-tem*)**:** Breath.

a tempo (*It., ah TEM-poh*)**:** Return to the original tempo.

atonal (*ay-TOH-nul, a-TOH-nul*)**:** Music lacking a tonal or key center.

attacca (*It., aht-TAHK-kah*)**:** Go on, proceed immediately to next section. *Segue.*

attack: The beginning of a note or phrase.

attendant keys: The relative keys to a scale, such as the relative major or minor, dominant, or subdominant.

attenuator: In synthesis, a device that controls the level of a signal.

a 2: *À deux, a due.*

audio: The electronic representation and manipulation of sounds.

audition: "Hearing." A trial performance in order to obtain a performing position or an award.

Auflösungszeichen (*Ger., owf-LE[R]Z-oongz-tsei-[s]hen*)**:** Natural.

Aufstrich (*Ger., OWF-shtree[s]h*)**:** Upbow.

Auftakt (*Ger., OWF-tahkt*)**:** Upbeat.

augmentation: Lengthening the duration of notes in a *theme.*

augmented: Raised, enlarged.

augmented chord: A triad composed of a root, major third, and augmented fifth.

augmented interval: A major or perfect *interval* raised by a *half step.*

augmented sixth chord: A kind of chord in which the interval of an augmented sixth resolves outward to an octave. See *French sixth, German sixth, Italian sixth.*

aulos (*OW-lohs*)**:** A double-reed wind instrument of ancient Greece.

Ausgabe (*Ger., OWS-gah-be*)**:** Edition.

ausgewählte (*Ger., ows-ge-VEL-te*)**:** Selected.

authentic cadence: A cadence with a progression from the dominant (V) chord to the tonic (I) chord.

auto-correct: In sequencing, the automatic aligning of notes to certain rhythmic subdivisions of the beat. See *quantize.*

Autoharp: Trademarked name for a kind of *zither* on which chord buttons are pressed by one hand and the strings are strummed or picked by the other hand.

auxiliary notes: See *accessory notes.*

Ave Maria (*Lat., AH-veh mah-REE-ah*)**:** "Hail Mary." A Roman Catholic prayer to the Virgin Mary, set to music by many composers, most notably *Gounod* (to a prelude by *Bach*) and *Schubert.*

axe (*slang*)**:** A musical instrument.

B

B (*Ger., beh*)**:** B-flat.

baby grand: A small grand piano.

Bach trumpet: A valveless trumpet in either C or D.

back beat: In drumming, emphasizing the second and fourth beats.

backing tracks: Recorded accompaniment for soloists.

backup group: A vocal group that sings background behind a singer.

badinage, badinerie (*Fr., bah-dee-NAHZH, bah-dee-neh-REE*)**:** The name of a playful dance or dance movement of a suite.

bagatelle (*Fr., bah-gah-TEL*)**:** A short light or whimsical piece, usually written for piano.

bagpipe: A wind instrument with one or more reed pipes attached to a windbag. Originally from Asia, now mostly associated with Scottish music.

baguala (*Sp., bah-GWAH-lah*)**:** Argentine folk song.

balalaika (*bah-lah-LEI-kah*)**:** Triangular-shaped Russian guitar, made in several sizes. It usually has three strings, tuned in fourths.

balance: The harmonious adjustment of volume and timbre between instruments or voices; it can be between players or vocalists or electronically while recording or mixing.

balancement (*Fr., bah-law[n]s-MAH[N]*)**:** Tremolo.

baldamente (*It., bahl-dah-MEN-teh*)**:** Boldly.

ballabile (*It., bahl-LAH-bee-leh*)**:** In a dance style.

ballad 1: A simple song. **2:** A song that tells a story. **3:** In popular music, usually a love song in a slow tempo.

ballade (*Fr., bahl-LAHD*) **1:** Ballad; a dance. **2:** A medieval French verse form where the *refrain* occurs at the end of the *stanza.*

Ballade (*Ger., bahl-LAHD*)**:** A lyrical instrumental piece.

ballata (*It., bahl-LAH-tah*)**:** A 14th-century Italian verse form where the *refrain* occurs at the beginning and end of the *stanza*.

ballet (*Fr., bal-LAY*)**:** A theatrical dance form with a story, sets, and music.

ballo (*It., BAHL-loh*)**:** Dance.

band 1: An instrumental ensemble, usually made up of wind and percussion instruments and no string instruments. **2:** In synthesis, a range of frequencies.

bandola (*Sp., bahn-DOH-lah*)**:** A Spanish instrument similar to a lute.

bandurria (*Sp., bahn-DOOR-ryah*)**:** A form of Spanish guitar with six double strings.

banjo: An American fretted string instrument consisting of a round wood and metal drum covered on one side with parchment or plastic. It can have four strings (tenor banjo), tuned C, G, D, A, with the following range:

banjo

or five strings, tuned G, D, G, B, D, with the following range:

bar: A *measure*; the space between two bar lines. Also, the bar line.

barbershop quartet: A male quartet (TTBB), originating in barbershops in the late 1800s, specializing in music of a sentimental style.
barcarolle (*Fr., bahr-kah-RULL*)**:** A song of the Venetian gondoliers, usually in a 6/8 or 12/8 time.
bariolage (*Fr., bah-ree-oh-LAHZH*)**:** On bowed string instruments, a technique where arpeggios are played without fingering or position changes within the groupings.
baritone: A low male singing voice (between tenor and bass) whose range is:

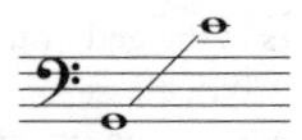

baritone clef: The C clef falling on the third line of the staff. Used for the *trombone.*
baritone horn: A brass instrument in B-flat, related to the *euphonium* with a smaller *bore* and three *valves.*

baritone horn

baritone saxophone: See *saxophone.*
bar line: A vertical line that divides the musical staff into *measures,* or bars.
baroque (*bah-ROHK*)**:** The musical era roughly from 1600 to 1750.
barre (*Fr., bahr*)**:** "Bar." In guitar playing, fretting several strings with a single finger across the fretboard.
barrel organ: Portable mechanical organ from the 19th century.
bass: "Low." **1:** The lowest male singing voice, whose range is:

2: The lowest part of the music. **3:** The lowest instrument. **4:** The *bass viol.*
bassa (*It., BAHS-sah*)**:** Low. "8va bassa"—play an octave lower than written.
bass clarinet: See *clarinet.*
bass clef: The F clef falling on the fourth line of the staff.
bass drum: A large double-sided drum used in orchestral and band ensembles, played with large padded *beaters* or *timpani* sticks.
basset horn: Alto clarinet.

bass flute: See *flute*.

bass guitar: A four- to six-string fretted instrument, generally tuned an octave lower than the guitar.

bass horn: A wind instrument related to the *serpent,* curved in a U-shape to make it easy to play on military marches.

basso (*It., BAHS-soh*) **1:** Bass, low. **2:** The lowest male voice.

basso continuo (*It., BAHS-soh kohn-TEE-noo-oh*)**:** "Continuous bass," "thoroughbass." In the baroque era, an accompaniment improvised from a bass line, usually with adjacent numbers to indicate the harmony (*figured bass*).

bassoon: "Low sound." A low double-reed woodwind instrument, with the following range:

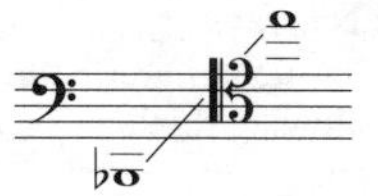

bassoon

The contrabassoon, which is the lowest-pitched bassoon and the lowest-pitched instrument in the orchestra, has the following range:

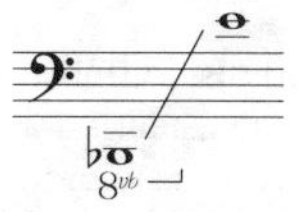

basso profundo (*It., BAHS-soh proh-FOON-doh*)**:** "Deep low." An especially low *bass* voice, extending down to C below the bass staff.

bass saxophone: See *saxophone.*

bass viol: Usually considered the lowest instrument in the violin family, although it is technically a viol.

baton: Conductor's stick.

battaglia (*It., baht-TAH-lyah*)**:** "Battle." A composition that imitates the sounds of battle and martial music.

battement (*Fr., baht-te-MAH[N]*)**:** "Beating." A 17th-century *ornament* employing an alternation of two adjacent notes, such as a *mordent* or a *trill.*

batterie, battery (*Fr., baht-te-REE; Eng.*)**:** Percussion section of an instrumental ensemble.

battuta (*It., baht-TOO-tah*)**:** Beat; the first beat of the bar. *A battuta*—in strict time.

Be (*Ger., beh*)**:** Flat sign.

beam: The horizontal line, in place of flags, that connects groups of short notes.

beat 1: *n.*—The rhythmic unit of time. **2:** *v.*—To mark time, such as a conductor does.

beater: A stick with a covering on the end used to hit percussion instruments; a *mallet*.

beats: A pulsation caused by two sound waves of slightly different frequency.

bebop: A form of jazz originating in the 1940s, characterized by solo improvisations, complex rhythms and extended harmonies.

bec (*Fr., bek*)**:** "Beak." The mouthpiece of a clarinet or a recorder.

becarre (*Fr., beh-KAHR*)**:** Natural sign.

beguine (*beh-GEEN*)**:** A sensuous Latin ballroom dance, originating in the Caribbean, with the following rhythm:

bel: A unit for measuring the relative level of power, voltage, current, or sound intensity.

bel canto (*It., bel KAHN-toh*) "Beautiful song." **1:** Brilliant Italian vocal style of the 18th and early 19th centuries. **2:** A tender, lyrical vocal style.

bell 1: Percussion instrument that vibrates when struck by either an internal *clapper* or an external hammer. **2:** The cup-shaped or flared opening of wind or brass instruments.

bellicoso (*It., bel-lee-KOH-zoh*)**:** Martial, warlike style.

bell-lyra (*BEL-lee-rah*)**:** *Glockenspiel* for marching bands, mounted on a lyre-shaped frame.

bell-lyra

bellows: An air chamber that, when pumped, supplies air to pipes or reeds in organs or accordions.

bells: *Glockenspiel* or *chimes*.

belly: The upper portion of the soundbox of a string instrument.

belly bridge: A steel string guitar bridge, deeper and thicker in the center than at the ends.

bémol (*Fr., bay-MULL*)**:** Flat sign.

bend: A smooth change in pitch, generally a half or whole step. Used on guitar, harmonica, synthesizer, and other instruments.

bend and release: On guitar, to bend the pitch up and then lower it back to normal.

bequadro (*It., beh-KWAH-droh*)**:** Natural sign.

berceuse (*Fr., behr-S[U]EZ*)**:** A lullaby.

bergamasca (*It., behr-gah-MAH-skah*)**:** An Italian country dance from the late 16th century, evolved into a 6/8 rhythmic dance similar to the *tarentella.*

betont (*Ger., be-TOHNT*)**:** Accented.

big band: Jazz band specializing in music for dancing. Most popular during the 1930s and 1940s.

Billboard: A weekly music-industry magazine important for the *charts* that track the popularity of recordings in several categories.

binary form: A compositional form in which an initial section is followed by a contrasting section (AB). See *song forms.*

bis (*Lat., beess*) **1:** Repeated, twice. **2:** Encore!

bisbigliando (*It., beez-bee-LYAHN-doh*)**:** In harp playing, a soft *tremolo.* A *tremolo* effect.

biscroma (*It., bees-KROH-mah*)**:** Thirty-second note.

bit (*abbr.*)**:** "Binary digIT." In synthesis, the smallest piece of digital information; it can have the value of either 0 or 1.

bitonal (*bei-TOHN-ul*)**:** Using two keys simultaneously.

biwa (*BEE-wah*)**:** A Japanese lute with four strings.

Blasinstrumente (*Ger., BLAHS-in-stroo-men-te*)**:** Wind instruments.

Blechinstrumente (*Ger., BLE[K]H-in-stroo-men-te*)**:** Brass instruments.

Blockflöte (*Ger., BLOK-fle[r]-te*)**:** "Block flute." Recorder.

bluegrass: A type of folk music characterized by banjo, fiddle, and quick duple meter.

blue notes: Notes sung or played below their intended pitch (most commonly the third, seventh, and sometimes fifth of the scale), creating the "blues" sound.

blues: Afro-American music form for solo voice, derived from spirituals and work songs. The basis of jazz. Characterized by the minor third and seventh of the scale; the form is 12 bars long with a specific chord progression.

blues harp: A diatonic *harmonica* and the blues style played on it.

bluette (*Fr., bl[u]e-ET*)**:** A short, sparkling piece.

BMI (*abbr.*)**:** "Broadcast Music, Inc." Performing rights society with main offices in New York, Los Angeles, and Nashville.

bocal (*BOH-kul*)**:** On bassoons, the crook-shaped metal tube that connects the reed to the instrument.

bocca (*It., BOHK-kah*) "Mouth." **1:**.The human mouth. **2:** The mouthpiece of a brass instrument.

bocca chiusa (*It., BOHK-kah KYOO-sah*)**:** "Closed mouth." Singing or humming with closed lips.

bodhran (*boh-RAHN*)**:** An Irish frame drum played with a double-ended stick.

Boehm system (*BE[R]M floot*)**:** A keying mechanism for woodwinds perfected by Theobald Boehm that allows accurate intonation and facilitates ease of playing.

Bogen (*Ger., BOH-gen*) **1:** A bow for the violin family. **2:** A slur or tie.

bois (*Fr., bwah*)**:** "Wood." Woodwind instruments.

bolero (*Sp., boh-LEH-roh*)**:** A Spanish dance in triple time, usually accompanied by castanets.

bombard 1: Bass *shawm.* **2:** A reed stop on an organ.

bones: An Afro-American instrument consisting of pairs of sticks or bones held in each hand and clicked together rhythmically.

bongo drums: Small Cuban drums in pairs, tuned differently, and played with the flat of the hand or fingers.

boogaloo: A dance popular in the 1960s and early 1970s.

boogie woogie: A jazz piano style from the mid 1930s characterized by an *ostinato* bass pattern and a 12-bar blues structure.

boot up (*slang*)**:** In synthesis, to turn on a computer or load a computerized instrument with its software.

bop: A dance popular in the 1940s and 1950s. Also see *bebop.*

bore: In wind instruments, the diameter (e.g., wide or narrow) or the shape (e.g., cylindrical or conical) of the tube.

borrowed chord: A chord from a key other than the current one.

bossa nova (*Port., BOHS-sah NOH-vah*)**:** "New trend." A popular Brazilian dance and rhythm:

bottleneck: On guitar, a tube that fits over a finger on the fretting hand, used for *slide guitar* playing.

bouche fermée (*Fr., boosh fehr-MAY*)**:** "Closed mouth." Singing or humming with a closed mouth or playing with a muted horn.

bouffe (*Fr., boof*)**:** Comical.

bourdon (*Fr., boor-DOH[N]*) **1:** Large organ pipes. **2:** A drone bass such as those produced on the lower strings of a *hurdy-gurdy.*

bourrée (*Fr., boor-RAY*)**:** A French dance, from the 17th century, in brisk duple time, starting with a pickup.

bouts: In the violin and guitar families, the curves in the ribs (sides) of an instrument, especially the C-shaped inward curves that form the *waist.*

bouzouki (*boo-ZOO-kee*)**:** Greek fretted string instrument with a long neck and four sets of strings tuned in unison or an octave apart.

bow: The device used in the string instrument family composed of a wooden stick with a pointed end, strung with horsehair. The bow is drawn across the strings to set them vibrating.

bowing: The technique of playing a stringed instrument with a bow. The instructions as to which direction (up or down) or which special technique to bow.

bpm (*abbr.*)**:** Beats per minute.

brace: In music notation, a heavy curved line used to connect the staves for a keyboard instrument or a harp.

bracket: In music notation, a heavy straight line with curved ends used to connect the staves for a group of related instruments or voices.

branle (*Fr., BRAW[N]-le*)**:** A dance from the 15th century characterized by a swaying motion.

brass band: A *band* made up of *brass* instruments. Amateur brass bands are popular in Great Britain.

brass family: Wind instruments made out of metal with either a cup- or funnel-shaped mouthpiece, such as *trumpet*, *cornet*, *bugle*, *Flügelhorn*, *trombone*, *tuba*, *baritone horn*, *euphonium*, *saxhorn*, and *French horn.*

Bratsche (*Ger., BROT-che*)**:** (From It. "braccio" ["arm"].) Viola.

bravo (*It., BRAH-voh*)**:** Good. An expression of approval at a theatre performance.

bravura (*It., brah-VOO-rah, brah-VYOO-rah*)**:** Skill and virtuosity.

break 1: The point in voices where they change from the head to chest register. **2:** In woodwind instruments, the change between the upper and lower registers. **3:** In wind instruments, an imperfectly played note that "cracks." **4:** *Caesura.*

breit (*Ger., breit*)**:** Broad.

breve (*BREH-ve, brev*)**:** Originally a short note; now it is a long note, equalling two whole notes: 𝅜

bridge 1: On string instruments, a piece of wood that supports the strings, holding them away from the body of the instrument. **2:** In music composition, a transitional passage.

brillánte (*It., breel-LAHN-teh*)**:** Brilliant.

Brill Building: Home of many music publishers' offices at 1619 Broadway in New York City. Known for the many hits born there in the early 1960s.

brio (*It., BREE-oh*)**:** Vigor, spirit.

brisé (*Fr., bree-ZAY*)**:** "Broken." On stringed instruments, detached bowing. On harp or keyboards, arpeggiated playing.

Broadway musical: A play set to music in a popular style.

broken chord: *Arpeggio*; notes of a chord played in succession rather than simultaneously.

bruscamente (*It., broo-skah-MEN-teh*)**:** Brusquely, abruptly.

brushes: Soft wire brushes used instead of drumsticks, especially in some styles of jazz.

bubblegum music: Sweet, happy pop music that appeals to preteenagers.

buffo (*It., BOOF-foh*)**:** Comical.

bugle: A brass conical horn, in many sizes, used primarily by the military and in drum and bugle corps bands. Bugles without keys or pistons sound the harmonic overtone series.

bullet: A symbol on the *charts* indicating that a song is rising rapidly in sales or radio play.

bull roarer: A primitive instrument composed of a thin piece of bone or wood tied to a string and whirled around one's head.

burden 1: The drone of a bagpipe. **2:** The return of the *refrain*.

Burgundian school: A group of composers in the early 15th century based primarily in Northeastern France and the Netherlands.

burlesque 1: A composition in a playful or satiric style. **2:** A stage show composed of various skits, some comical, some musical.

burletta (*It., boor-LET-tah*)**:** A comic operetta.

busker: A British street entertainer.

BWV (*abbr.*)**:** "Bach-Werke Verzeichnis." A catalog of the works of J.S. Bach. BWV numbers are used instead of opus numbers for Bach's compositions.

byte: In synthesis, a piece of information made up of 8 *bits*.

Byzantine chant: Christian church chants from the Eastern Roman Empire (Byzantium).

C

cabaletta (*It., kah-bah-LET-tah*) **1:** A short, simple operatic song in popular style. **2:** The final section of some arias, characterized by motoric rhythm.

cabasa (*Sp., cah-BAH-sah*)**:** A Latin American percussion instrument made up of a gourd covered with a network of beads and played by shaking the beads across the gourd.

caccia (*It., KAHT-chah*)**:** "Hunt" or "chase." A 14th-century rustic poem set to lively canonic music in which the voices "chase" each other.

cachucha (*Sp., kah-CHOO-chah*)**:** A Spanish dance in triple meter, similar to a bolero.

cacophony (*cah-CAW-foh-nee*)**:** Discordant sound; dissonance.

cadence: The melodic or harmonic ending of a piece or the sections or phrases therein. A chord progression that "feels" like a conclusion. See *authentic cadence*, *deceptive cadence*, *half cadence*, *imperfect cadence*, *perfect cadence*, *plagal cadence*.

cadenza (*It., kah-DEN-zah*)**:** A solo passage, often virtuosic, usually near the end of a piece, either written by the composer or improvised by the performer.

cadenzato (*It., kah-den-ZAH-toh*)**:** Rhythmical.

caesura (*cheh-ZOO-rah*)**:** A sudden silencing of the sound; a pause or break, indicated by the following symbol: //

caisse (*Fr., kess*)**:** A drum.

calando (*It., kah-LAHN-doh*)**:** Diminishing gradually—softer and slower.

calcando (*It., kahl-KAHN-doh*)**:** Pushing or hurrying the time.

call and response: A vocal form in which a singer a melodic question or makes a statement and an ensemble responds.

calliope (*kahl-LEI-oh-pee*)**:** An organ in which steam, rather than air, blows through the pipes. Often associated with the circus.

calma, calmando, calmato (*It., KAHL-mah, kahl-MAHN-doh, kahl-MAH-toh*)**:** Quieting, tranquilness.

calore (*It., kah-LOH-reh*)**:** Warmth.

calypso: A rhythm and song style, originally from Trinidad, that often contains satirical lyrics. It has the following rhythm:

cambia (*It., KAHM-byah*)**:** A direction found in scores to change tuning or instruments.

cambiata (*It., kahm-BYAH-tah*)**:** In counterpoint, a *nonharmonic* note inserted between a dissonance and its resolution.

camera (*It., KAH-meh-rah*)**:** "Room"; "chamber." Secular chamber music, as opposed to church music. See *chiesa*.

camerata (*It., kah-meh-RAH-tah*)**:** Small art or music schools originating in the 16th century.

camminando (*It., kahm-mee-NAHN-doh*)**:** Flowing easily and gently.

campana (*It., kahm-PAH-nah*)**:** A bell.

campanella (*It., kahm-pah-NEL-lah*)**:** A small bell.

cancan (*Fr., kaw[n]-KAW[N], KAN-kan*)**:** A late-19th-century French dance in quick 2/4 time; an offshoot of the *quadrille*.

cancel: The natural sign, used to remove the previous accidental.

canción (*Sp., kahn-SYOHN*)**:** Song.

cancrizans: *Crab canon.*

C&W (*abbr.*)**:** *Country & Western.*

canon: "Rule." In counterpoint, a melody that is repeated exactly by a different voice, entering a short interval of time after the original voice.

cantabile (*It., kahn-TAH-bee-leh*)**:** In a singing style.

cantare (*It., kahn-TAH-reh*)**:** To sing.

cantata (*It., kahn-TAH-tah*)**:** "Sung." A multi-movement vocal work for concert or church performance by chorus and/or soloists and an accompanying instrumental ensemble.

canticle: A non-metrical hymn or song.

cantilena (*It., kahn-tee-LEH-nah*)**:** A melodic song.

cantino (*It., kahn-TEE-noh*)**:** On string instruments, the highest strings.

canto (*It., KAHN-toh*)**:** Song, a melody; the highest voice.

canto fermo (*It., KAHN-toh FEHR-moh*)**:** *Cantus firmus.*

cantor (*It., KAHN-tohr*)**:** A singer, chanter; the soloist, and often director of the music, in a religious service.

cantus firmus (*Lat., KAHN-toos FEER-moos*)**:** "Fixed song." A pre-existing melody, usually an ecclesiastical chant, that serves as the theme or foundation of a polyphonic piece.

canzone, canzona (*It., kahn-TSOH-neh, kahn-TSOH-nah*)**:** A song or ballad, or "in the style of a song."

canzonet, canzonetta (*It., kahn-tsoh-NET-tah*)**:** A short song.

Capellmeister (*Ger., kah-PEL-meis-ter*)**:** *Kapellmeister.*

capo, capotasto (*It., KAH-poh* [or *KAY-poh*], *kah-poh-TAH-stoh*) **1:** The head, beginning, nut, or top. **2:** On string instruments, a device placed around the fingerboard that raises the pitch of the strings.

capo d'astro (*It., kah-poh-DAH-stroh*)**:** A corruption of *capotasto*. See *capo.*

cappella: See *a cappella.*

capriccio, caprice (*It., kah-PREET-choh; Fr., kah-PREES*)**:** Instrumental music played in a humorous or free style.

capriccioso (*It., kah-preet-CHOH-zoh*)**:** Capriciously.
carillon (*KA-ril-lon*)**:** A set of bells played from a keyboard.
carol: A joyous song, usually sung at Christmas, and usually containing verses (stanzas) and a refrain (burden).
cassa (*It., KAHS-sah*)**:** Drum.
castanets (*kas-tah-NETS*)**:** Concave, shell-shaped clappers made of wood or ivory, clapped together in the hand.
castrato (*It., kah-STRAH-toh*)**:** An adult male singer with an alto or soprano voice; a eunuch.
catch: A humorous composition for three or four voices. The parts are structured similar to a *round.*
catgut: The material, actually from the intestines of sheep or goats, used for making strings for the violin and guitar family.
cavaquinho (*kah-vah-KEEN-oh*)**:** Brazilian ukulele tuned D, G, B, D (or E).
cavatina (*It., kah-vah-TEE-nah*)**:** A short, simple song without repeats.

C clef: A clef 𝄡 usually centered on the first line (soprano clef), third line (alto clef), fourth line (tenor clef), or third space (vocal tenor clef) of the staff. Wherever it is centered, that line or space becomes middle C.
CD (*abbr.*)**:** *Compact disc.*
cédez (*Fr., say-DAY*)**:** Slow down.
cejuela (*Sp., seh-HWEH-lah*)**:** *Capo.*
celere (*It., CHEH-leh-reh*)**:** Rapid.
celesta (*It., cheh-LES-tah*)**:** A percussion instrument made up of steel bars struck by hammers via a keyboard.
cello, 'cello (*It., CHEL-loh*)**:** *Violoncello.*
cembalo (*It., CHEM-bah-loh*)**:** Harpsichord.
cent: "Hundredth." A unit for measuring intervals. There are 100 cents in an *equal-tempered semitone* (half step), 1200 cents in an octave.
cercar la nota (*It., chehr-KAHR lah NOH-tah*)**:** In singing, an anticipation of the next note.
cetera (*It., CHEH-teh-rah*)**:** Zither.
cha-cha: A Latin American dance with the basic rhythm of:

𝅘𝅥 𝅘𝅥 𝅘𝅥𝅮𝅘𝅥𝅮 𝅘𝅥

chaconne (*Fr., shah-CUNN*)**:** A slow instrumental piece, based on a Spanish dance in triple meter, constructed as a series of variations on a harmonic progression or a bass line. Similar to *passacaglia.*

chalumeau (*Fr., shah-loo-MOH*) **1:** The low register of the clarinet. **2:** A reedpipe; a clarinet.

chamber music: Music for small ensemble.

chamber orchestra: A small orchestra of about two dozen players.

chance music: Music in which the form or content depends greatly on either chance or choices made by the peformer. See *aleatoric.*

change ringing: A pattern of ringing a specific number of bells (tower bells or handbells) so that the sequence of bells changes after each time all the bells are rung.

changes 1 (*slang*)**:** *Chord* changes. The chords in a progression. **2:** The outlines of the patterns used in *change ringing.*

changko (*CHANG-koh*)**:** A two-headed Korean drum.

channel: In synthesis, a pathway over which MIDI data are transmitted or received.

chanson (*Fr., shaw[n]-SOH[N]*)**:** Song.

chant 1: *n.*—Unaccompanied sacred vocal music, usually monophonic. Often it accompanies a ritual. See *plainsong.* **2:** *v.*—To sing. **3** (*Fr., shaw[n]*)**:** Singing.

chanter 1: On a bagpipe, the pipe on which the melody is played, as opposed to the *drone.* **2** (*Fr., shaw[n]-TAY*)**:** To sing.

chanterelle (*Fr., shaw[n]-teh-REL*)**:** The E string on the violin, or the highest string on any instrument in the violin or lute family.

chantey, chanty (*SHAN-tee*)**:** A work song sung by English and American sailors.

character piece: A short instrumental piece built around a single emotion or idea.

charivari (*Fr., shah-ree-vah-REE*)**:** A noisy mock serenade for newlyweds (also *shivaree*).

chart(s) 1: Scores or parts written for an instrumental ensemble; in pop music often just the melody line and chords. **2:** In music trade magazines, the sequential lists of the most popular songs or albums.

chase chorus: In jazz, a chorus divided into segments of two to four measures played by different musicians; also called *taking fours* or *trading fours.*

chest voice: The lower register of the voice.

chiesa (*It., KYEH-sah*)**:** "Church." Church music, as opposed to chamber music. See *camera.*

chimes: Sets of bells or metal tubes. Orchestra or band chimes are the latter.

chitarra (*It., kee-TAR-rah*)**:** Guitar.

chitarrone (*It., kee-tar-ROH-neh*)**:** A lute similar to a *theorbo*, but longer.

choir: A group of singers for sacred music.

choke cymbal: *Hi-hat cymbals.*

chops (*slang*)**:** A musician's playing technique or ability.

choral (*Eng., KOR-ul*)**:** *adj.*—Pertaining to choir or chorus music.

Choral (*Ger., koh-RAHL*)**:** *n.—Chorale.*

chorale: A German Lutheran hymn tune.

chorale prelude: Organ music based on a hymn.

chord: Three or more notes sounded simultaneously.

chorister: A singer in a choir.

chorus 1: A group of singers of secular music. **2:** A piece of music sung by such a group. **3:** The *refrain* of a song. **4:** In synthesis, a *signal processor* that simulates the sound of two or more instruments playing simultaneously.

chromatic: Moving by half steps; notes foreign to a scale.

chromaticism: Use of notes outside the diatonic scale.

chromatic scale: A scale composed of twelve half steps.

cimbalom (*CHEEM-bah-lohm*)**:** A form of *dulcimer* native to Hungary made up of a box on which metal strings are strung on pegs and are struck with mallets.

cinelli (*It., chee-NEL-lee*)**:** Cymbals.

circle of fifths: The succession of keys or chords proceeding by fifths. See *Reference Charts: Circle of Fifths.*

circular breathing: A breathing technique used in playing wind instruments in which air is expelled from the mouth at the same time it is inhaled through the nose.

cittern (*SIT-tern*)**:** A 15th-century forerunner of the lute, with metal strings tuned in pairs and plucked with the fingers.

clam (*slang*)**:** A wrong note in a performance.

clapper 1: Any of a variety of percussion instruments that are clapped together, ranging from primitive *bones* and sticks to elaborate Japanese fans. **2:** The striker in the middle of a bell.

clarinet: A single-reed woodwind instrument with a cynlindrical shape (bore). The pitch is *fingered* by metal keys over holes. Clarinets in regular use are the B-flat, E-flat, and A. The most common, B-flat, has a range of:

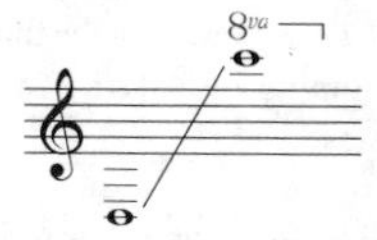

clarinet

E-flat Alto clarinet range:

B-flat Bass clarinet range:

B-flat Contrabass clarinet range:

classical 1: Music conforming to certain form and structure, considered "serious," as opposed to pop music. **2:** The time period ranging from the late 18th to the early 19th centuries.

clavecin (*Fr., klah-veh-SA[N]*)**:** *Harpsichord.*

claves (*KLAH-ves, KLAH-vayz*)**:** Cuban percussion instruments consisting of round wooden sticks that are struck together.

claves

clavichord: An early keyboard instrument in which sound is produced when a key is depressed and a brass blade at the back of the key strikes the string.

clavier (*klah-VEER*)**:** The keyboard of a piano or other keyboard instrument. See *Klavier.*

clavietta (*klah-vee-ET-tah*)**:** An keyboard instrument that's controlled by blowing into a mouthpiece.

Clavinet: Trademarked name for an amplified clavichord.

clawhammer: Banjo *fingerpicking* style using the thumb and one or two fingers.

clef: The symbol at the beginning of a staff that indicates which lines and spaces represent which notes.

cloche (*Fr., klush*)**:** Bell.

clock: In synthesis, a pulse used for setting tempos or synchronizing systems (sequencers, drum machines, digital recorders).

close harmony: Harmony in which notes of the chord are kept as close together as possible, often within an octave. See *open harmony.*

clusters: Groups of notes the interval of a second apart.

CMA (*abbr.*)**:** "Country Music Association." An organization that presents country music awards annually on network television.

coach horn: A straight horn in B-flat, 3 to 4 feet long, with a conical *bore* and a wide bell. Used on stagecoaches to announce arrivals and departures.

coda (*It., KOH-dah*)**:** "Tail." **1:** In musical form, a section at the end of a piece, which brings the piece to a close. **2:** In printed music, a separate passage to which the performer jumps after repeating from the beginning (D.C. al Coda) or the *segno* (D.S. al Coda). It is indicated by this symbol: ⊕

code: In synthesis, the computer language that makes up a program. *MIDI* messages constitute a code.

codetta (*It., koh-DET-tah*)**:** A short passage at the end of a section of a piece.

col (*It., kohl*)**:** With.

col arco (*It., kohl AHR-koh*)**:** In the violin family, playing with the bow.

coll', colla (*It., kohl, KOHL-lah*)**:** "With the."

colla voce (*It., KOHL-lah VOH-cheh*)**:** For vocal accompanists, playing with the voice.

col legno (*It., kohl LEN-yoh*)**:** In the violin family, playing with the stick (wood) part of the bow.

coll' ottava (*It., kohl oht-TAH-vah*)**:** Play the written notes and the notes an octave higher.

coloratura (*It., koh-loh-rah-TOO-rah*)**:** "Coloring." **1:** Elaborate ornamation of the melodic line, usually by a vocalist. **2:** A voice type (especially soprano) specializing in demanding vituosity.

combo (*slang abbr.*)**:** "Combination." A small group of musicians—usually from four to six.

come prima (*It., koh-meh PREE-mah*)**:** As in the first time.

come sopra (*It., koh-meh SOH-prah*)**:** "As above." Repeat the previous passage.

comic opera: An opera with light-natured music, comedy, and a happy ending.

comma 1: Breath mark (') in singing. **2:** A minute discrepancy in pitch that occurs in certain tunings.

common chord: A chord composed of a root, third, and fifth.

common time: 4/4 meter.

common tone: A note that remains constant between two chords.

còmodo (*It., KOH-moh-doh*)**:** Comfortable.

comp (*slang abbr.*)**:** "Accompany." To improvise a chordal accompaniment in jazz.

compact disc: A *digital* recording format in which information encoded on a disc is played back by (read by) laser.

compass: The complete range of an instrument or voice.

compensation: On guitar, the lengthening of a string beyond the theoretical scale length to ensure correct intonation.

complete cadence: I-IV-V-I progression.

composer: A person who creates (composes) music.

compound interval: An interval wider than an octave, e.g., a ninth, eleventh, etc.

compound meter: A time signature in which the basic pulse is divisible by three (e.g., 6/8, 9/8, 12/8). See *simple meter.*

compression: In amplification and recording, electronically restricting the dynamic range (the difference between the softest and loudest sounds) of an audio signal.

compressor: A *signal processor* that performs *compression.*

con (*It., kohn*)**:** With.

con amore (*It., kohn ah-MOH-reh*)**:** With love.
con anima (*It., kohn AH-nee-mah*)**:** With spirit.
con brio (*It., kohn BREE-oh*)**:** With animation.
concert: "Agreement." A public performance of music.
concertante (*It., kohn-chehr-TAHN-teh*)**:** A piece for two or more instruments with orchestral accompaniment.
concertato (*It., kohn-chehr-TAH-toh*)**:** A style of hymn arrangement in which the choir and congregation alternate in singing verses.
concert band: A *band* that plays concert-style pieces.
concert grand piano: The largest of the grand pianos, usually about nine feet long.
concertina (*It., kohn-chehr-TEE-nah, kon-ser-TEE-nah*)**:** A type of accordion with a hexagonal shape that uses buttons rather than a keyboard to produce sound.
concertino (*It., kohn-chehr-TEE-noh*) **1:** A short concerto. **2:** The group of soloists in a *concerto grosso.*
concertmaster: First-chair violinist in an orchestra.
concerto (*It., kohn-CHEHR-toh*)**:** A piece for a soloist and orchestra.
concerto grosso (*It., kohn-CHEHR-toh GROHS-soh*)**:** A multi-movement baroque piece for a group of soloists (*concertino*) and an orchestra (*ripieno*).
concert pitch 1: The international tuning pitch—currently A 440 or 442. **2:** The pitch for non-transposing (C) instruments.
concord: Sounds that are pleasant to the ear.
conducting: The directing of a group of musicians.
conductor: The person who directs a group of musicians.
con fuoco (*It., kohn FWOH-koh*)**:** With fire.
conga: A Latin American dance of African origin in which people dance in a line. The conga rhythm is:

conga drum: A tall, narrow Afro-Cuban drum with single heads and tuning tension rods, played with the fingers or flat of the hand.
con gusto (*It., kohn GOO-stoh*)**:** With gusto, with zest.
conjunct 1: Notes that are next to each other in succession. **2:** A second.

con lancio (*It., kohn LAHN-choh*)**:** With verve.

consecutive intervals: *Parallel intervals* between two parts, vocal or instrumental; an interval followed immediately by the same interval between the same parts.

consequent: The second phrase in a musical *period.* In the fugue, the *answer.* See *antecedent.*

conservatory: A music school.

con slancio (*It., kohn ZLAHN-choh*)**:** With vigor, dash.

console (*KON-sohl*) **1:** On organ, the portion of the instrument at which the organist sits and plays. **2:** A vertical piano between *spinet* and *upright* in height.

console (1)

consonance: Sounds that are pleasing to the ear.

con sordini (*It., kohn sohr-DEE-nee*) **1:** On string instruments, "with *mutes.*" **2:** On keyboard instruments, "with *dampers.*"

con sordino (*It., kohn sohr-DEE-noh*)**:** On string instruments, "with *mute.*"

consort: A Renaissance chamber group.

continuo (*It., kohn-TEE-noo-oh*)**:** *Basso continuo.*

continuous controllers: In electronic music, any of the MIDI codes created by moving wheels, levers, pedals, sliders, etc.

contra (*It., KOHN-trah*)**:** "Against." In the octave below normal.

contrabass: "Against the low." The double bass, lowest-pitched instrument in the violin family. Pitched E, A, D, G.

contrabass clarinet: See *clarinet.*

contrabassoon: See *bassoon.*

contractor: The person responsible for hiring professional musicians for a performance or recording session.

contralto: "Against the high." The lowest female voice; *alto.* The range is:

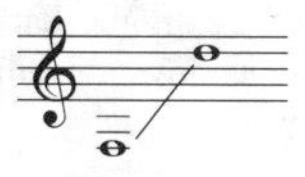

contrapuntal: Using *counterpoint.*

contrary motion: In *counterpoint*, two voices moving in opposite directions.

cor (*Fr., kor*)**:** Horn.

cor anglais (*Fr., kor aw[n]-GLEH*)**:** English horn.
corda, corde (*It., KOHR-dah; Fr., kord*)**:** String.
cor de chasse (*Fr., kor de SHAHSS*)**:** Natural hunting horn in E-flat or D.
cornet, cornetta: A B-flat brass instrument with three valves, similar to a trumpet. The range is:

cornett, cornetto: A curved wind instrument made of wood or ivory with holes that are stopped by the fingers and a cup-shaped mouthpiece.
corno (*It., KOHR-noh*)**:** Horn.
cornopean (*kor-NOH-pee-an*)**:** Late-19th-century brass instrument, similar to a trumpet.
coro (*It., KOH-roh*)**:** Choir or chorus.
corona (*koh-ROH-nah*)**:** *Fermata.*
corps style: Marching band performance in the lively and flamboyant style of a drum and bugle corps.
corrente (*It., kohr-REN-teh*)**:** *Courante.*
cotillon (*Fr., koh-tee-YOH[N], koh-TIL-yon*)**:** A lively French dance; a *quadrille.*
count: The beat or pulse.
counterpoint: "[Note] against note." The combination of two or more melodic lines played simultaneously. A horizontal structure of melody against melody rather than chords.
countertenor: "Against the tenor." The highest male voice. The range is:

country: Music characterized by simple harmonies and lyrics that often speak of good times, hard times, love, or unfaithfulness.
country & western: *Country.*
coupler: A device on an organ or harpsichord that enables the player to connect two or more manuals or pedals or to double at an octave.
courante (*Fr., koo-RAW[N]T*): "Running." A rapid French dance in triple meter.

course: On string instruments, a group of strings tuned in unison or an octave apart and plucked together.

cover (*slang*)**:** A new recording of a previously recorded song.

cowbell 1: A metal bell with a clapper, originally hung around the neck of a cow. **2:** A metal bell without a clapper, struck with a drumstick.

crab canon: A contrapuntal piece in which one part is identical to another, but backwards.

crash cymbal: A single cymbal suspended from a stand and struck with a drumstick or mallet.

Credo (*Lat., KREH-doh*)**:** "I believe." In the *Mass*, the third part of the *Ordinary*. The Creed.

Cremona: The Italian city that was home to violin makers such as Amati, Guarneri, and Stradivari.

crescendo (*It., kreh-SHEN-doh*)**:** Gradually growing louder:

crook: A tube that is inserted into a brass instrument to change its pitch. Various sized crooks are used primarily on non-valve instruments.

crossover: In music business, when a song "crosses over" from one popularity chart to another, e.g., from the country chart to the pop chart.

cross rhythm: Different rhythm patterns played simultaneously.

crotales (*kroh-TAH-layz*)**:** Tuned cymbals.

crotchet: Quarter note: ♩

crumhorn: *Krummhorn.*

csárdás, czardas (*CHAR-dahss*)**:** A Hungarian dance in two sections—slow and melancholy, quick and lively.

cue 1: Indication by the conductor or a spoken word or gesture for a performer to make an entry. **2:** Small notes that indicate another performer's part. **3:** Music occurrence in a film.

cue sheet: A list of music cues (occurrences) in a film.

cut (*slang*)**:** In the music business, **1:** *n.*—A recording or one song on an album. **2:** *v.*—To record a song.

cut time: 2/2 meter.

cycle 1: A set of songs meant to be performed as a whole. **2:** In synthesis, one complete occurrence of a *waveform.*

cyclic, cyclical 1: Compositions made up of several complete movements or forms in contrast to each other, such as sonata, symphony, cantata. **2:** Various movements with recurring thematic material.

cymbals: In the percussion family, circular brass plates held in the hand(s) and struck together. They come in varying sizes and can also be crashed mechanically (see *hi-hat*) or suspended individually and hit with a mallet or stick.

D

D: For "Deutsch," the cataloguer of Schubert's works. D numbers are used instead of opus numbers for Schubert's compositions.

da capo (*It., dah KAH-poh*)**:** "From the beginning." Indicates to return to the beginning of a piece.

da capo al coda (*It., dah KAH-poh ahl KOH-dah*)**:** Indicates to return to the beginning of a piece and play to the "To Coda" indication, then to skip to the *Coda* to finish the piece.

da capo al fine (*It., dah KAH-poh ahl FEE-neh*)**:** Indicates to return to the beginning of a piece and play to the "Fine" sign.

da capo aria (*It., dah KAH-poh AH-ree-ah*)**:** A vocal form popular in baroque opera, with the form *ABA*.

dal (*It., dahl*)**:** "From the," "by the."

dal segno (*It., dahl SAY-nyoh*)**:** "From the sign." Indicates to return to the sign 𝄋 .

dal segno al coda (*It., dahl SAY-nyoh ahl KOH-dah*)**:** Indicates to return to the *D.S.* sign and play to the "To Coda" indication, then to skip to the *Coda* to finish the piece.

dal segno al fine (*It., dahl SAY-nyoh ahl FEE-neh*)**:** Indicates to return to the *D.S.* sign and play to the "Fine" sign.

damper 1: On a piano, the felt piece that damps the vibration of the string until the key (or the damper pedal) is depressed. **2:** Mute.

damper pedal: On pianos, the pedal that lifts the dampers from the strings.

damping: On guitar or string instruments, to press down on the strings to stop their vibrations.

dance 1: *v.*—To move rhythmically to music. **2:** *n.*—A musical piece with a rhythm that invites dancing.

danse, danza (*Fr., daw[n]s; It., DAHN-tsah*)**:** *Dance.*

darbuk (*dar-BOOK*)**:** Goblet-shaped Slavic drum.

DAT (*abbr.*)**:** "Digital Audio Tape." A trademarked name for a certain kind of two-track digital audio tape recording.

dB (*abbr.*)**:** *Decibel.*

D.C. (*abbr.*)**:** *Da capo.*

decay: The fading out of a note or phrase.

deceptive cadence: A cadence with a progression where the dominant chord (V) resolves into a chord other than the tonic (I). Especially the progression V-vi.

decibel: A unit for measuring the relative level of power, voltage, current, or sound intensity. A tenth of a *bel.*

deciso (*It., deh-CHEE-zoh*)**:** Bold, forceful.

decrescendo (*It., deh-kreh-SHEN-doh*)**:** Gradually growing softer:

degree: A note of a scale, identified by number.

delay: In synthesis, a unit that produces sound effects such as an echo.

delicato (*It., deh-lee-KAH-toh*)**:** Delicately.

demi- (*Fr., DEH-mee*)**:** "Half."

demiquaver: Sixteenth note:

demisemiquaver: Thirty-second note:

demo (*slang abbr.*)**:** "Demonstration." A recording used by songwriters and music publishers to sell their songs to artists or producers.

descant 1: Soprano or tenor voice. **2:** A melodic line or counterpoint accompanying an existing melody. **3:** The upper part of a polyphonic composition.
descriptive music: *Program music.*
desk (*British slang*)**:** *Mixing console.*
destra (*It., DEH-strah*)**:** Right.
détaché (*Fr., day-tah-SHAY*)**:** In string playing, short detached bowing strokes.
detune: To tune two sound sources a few *cents* different from each other to produce harmonic beating.
development: The elaboration of thematic, melodic, harmonic, or rhythmic material.
di (*It., dee*)**:** Of, with.
diapason (*Gr., dei-ah-PAY-sun*) **1:** The pipes that form the foundation for the sound on the organ, also called principal. **2:** The range of an octave. **3:** The normal range of the human voice.
diatonic: The notes indigenous to a key in a major or minor scale.
didgeridoo: Native Australian primitive horn made of wood or bamboo, with a straight, cylindrical shape.
dièse, diesis (*Fr., dee-EZ; Gr., dee-EH-sees*)**:** Sharp sign ♯, a half step.
Dies Irae (*Lat., DEE-es EE-ray*)**:** "Day of wrath." The *Sequence* for the *Requiem Mass.*
digital: In synthesis, the numeric representation of data. To produce sound, digital data must be converted to *analog.*
digital piano: An electronic piano making use of digital *sampling* to provide the sound.
diluendo (*It., dee-loo-EN-doh*)**:** Fading.
diminished: Lowered.
diminished interval: A minor or perfect *interval* lowered by a half step.
diminished seventh chord: A chord made up of a root, minor third, diminished fifth, and diminished seventh.
diminished triad: A triad made up of a root, minor third, and diminished fifth.
diminuendo (*It., dee-mee-noo-EN-doh*)**:** Gradually getting softer.
diminution: Shortening the duration of note values in a *theme.*
direct: A symbol at the end of a *staff* or page that indicates the next note.
dirge: A piece that is performed at a funeral or memorial service.

disco, discothèque (*Fr., dis-koh-TEK*)**:** A lively dance; a dance club.
discord: Sounds that are dissonant or unpleasant to the ear.
disinvolto (*It., dee-zeen-VOHL-toh*)**:** Easily, freely.
disjunct: Moving by skips—intervals larger than a second.
disposition: On an organ, the organization of the stops, manuals, pedals, etc.
dissonance: Sounds that are unpleasant to the ear.
distortion: For guitar, electronic effects (or the devices that produce them) that alter the sound, such as *fuzz tone, overdrive, wah-wah.* See *effects.*
divertimento (*It., dee-vehr-tee-MEN-toh*)**:** An entertaining instrumental piece of short movements.
divertissement (*Fr., dee-vehr-tees-MAH[N]*)**:** A dance or ballet, with or without lyric, included in an opera or play to add variety.
divisi, div. (*It., dee-VEE-see*)**:** "Divided." Indicating separate parts written on one staff are to be played by separate performers.
Dixieland: A New Orleans jazz style developed in the early 1900s, characterized by group improvisation over a steady two-beat ragtime rhythm.
DJ (*slang abbr.*)**:** "Disc Jockey." One who plays recordings at a disco or on the radio.
do (*doh*)**:** The first (tonic) note of the *diatonic* scale. "C" in the *fixed-do* system.
Dobro: Trademarked name for a guitar with a circular metal resonator on the belly and an internal tone chamber. Often played with a *bottleneck.*
dodecaphonic (*doh-dek-ah-FON-ic*)**:** Twelve-tone music.
doit (*doyt*)**:** A jazz technique on brass or wind instruments where a note is sounded and then "glissed" upwards from one to five steps:

dolce (*It., DOHL-cheh*)**:** Sweet.
doloroso (*It., doh-loh-ROH-zoh*)**:** Sorrowful.
dominant: The fifth *degree* of the *diatonic* major or minor scale.
domra (*DOHM-rah*)**:** A type of early *balalaika* with a round body and two or three metal strings tuned a fourth apart.
doo wop: A type of close harmony singing developed in pop music of the late '50s that incorporates the use of nonsense syllables as rhythmic background or punctuation.

doppio (*It., DOHP-pyoh*)**:** Double.

Dorian: A medieval mode whose half- and whole-step pattern is that of playing D to D on the white keys of the piano. See *Scale Chart: Modes.*

dot 1: Written after a note, a dot increases the length of the note by one half of its original value. **2:** Written above or below a note, a dot indicates *staccato*.

double 1: To play the same part. **2:** To play a second instrument.

double bar: Two lines on a staff that indicate the end of a section or the entire piece.

double bass: The lowest member of the violin family, tuned E, A, D ,G (sounds an octave lower than written), with a range of:

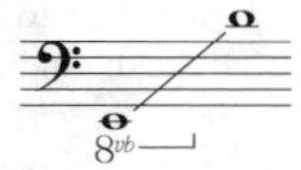

It can also have five strings by adding a low C.

double concerto: A *concerto* for two solo instruments and ensemble.

double counterpoint: *Invertible counterpoint.*

double croche (*Fr., DOO-ble KRUSH*)**:** Sixteenth note (*semiquaver*).

double dot: Written after a note, a double dot increases the length of the note by three-fourths of its original value.

double flat: Written before a note 𝄫, lowers the pitch of that note one whole step.

double fugue: A *fugue* with two themes that occur simultaneously.

double horn: A French horn that essentially combines two horns (in F and B-flat) by means of an additional valve, for better intonation and a wider range:

double reed: Two thin pieces of cane bound together at their thicker ends. These vibrating mouthpieces are used on the *oboe, English horn, heckelphone, sarrusophone,* and the *bassoon family.*

double sharp: Written before a note 𝄪, raises the pitch of that note one whole step.

double stem: When a note is stemmed both up and down, it indicates that two parts share that pitch.

double stop: In the violin family, playing two notes simultaneously.

doublet: *Duplet.*

double time 1: *Duple meter.* **2:** Twice as fast as before.

double tonguing: On flute and brass instruments, the technique of rapidly articulating notes by using the front and the back of the tongue in alternation ("t-k-t-k-t-k").

downbeat: The first beat; given by the conductor with a downward stroke.

down bow: In the violin family, drawing the bow downward from its *frog* (*nut*). The symbol is: ⊓

doxology (*Gr., dox-OL-o-jee*)**:** "Expression of glory." A song of praise, usually heard at the end of a church service or close of a hymn or prayer. In Protestant services, the hymn "Praise God from Whom All Blessings Flow."

drag: A drum rudiment. A sticking pattern consisting of two grace notes followed by two eighth notes, the second accented:

dramatic soprano: A female singer with a slightly lower range than a *lyric soprano*:

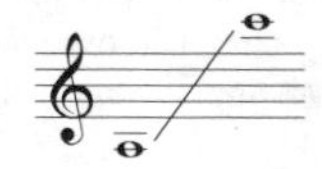

dramatic tenor: A male singer with a slightly lower range than a *lyric tenor*:

drawbars: On some electric and electronic organs, the replacements for *stops.*

Dreadnought guitar (*DRED-nawt*)**:** A large-bodied steel-stringed guitar with very little S-curve and a propensity toward bass resonance.

droite (*Fr., drwaht*)**:** Right.

drone: A note that continues at the same pitch for an extended time. Instruments with built-in drones include *bagpipes* (the lower pipes), five-string *banjo*, Appalachian *dulcimer*, and *hurdy-gurdy*.

drum: Percussion instruments made up of stretched skin or membrane over a cylinder on which sound is produced by the vibration of the head after it is struck.

drum and bugle corps: A marching ensemble of percussion and brass instruments, assisted by choreographed flag and rifle drill teams.

drum kit, drum set: A set of drums and cymbal organized so that one person can play them.

drum kit

drum machine: An electronic box that offers digitally sampled percussion sounds, which can be arranged into rhythmic patterns.

drumstick: Cylindrical stick of wood or plastic used to strike a drum.

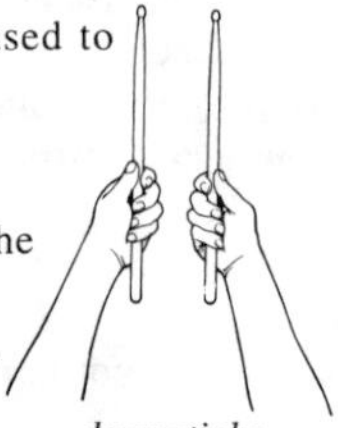

D.S. (*abbr.*)**:** *Dal segno.*

du (*Fr., d[u]e*)**:** "From the," "of the."

dub (*slang abbr.*)**:** "Double." **1:** *n.*—A copy of the *master* recording. **2:** *v.*—To record from a *master***.**

duet (*doo-ET*) **1:** A piece for two performers. **2:** On piano, two performers at one instrument. Compare *duo.*

drumsticks

dulcimer (*DUL-si-mer*)**:** "Sweet song." An instrument of English origin with strings stretched over a box that are plucked with a plectrum (Appalachian dulcimer) or hammered (*cimbalom*).

dumka (*DOOM-kah*)**:** A melancholy Slavonic folk ballad.

dump: A melancholy elegy, lament, or slow dance from the 16th century.

duo (*DOO-oh*) **1:** *Duet.* **2:** On piano, two performers at separate instruments. Compare *duet.*

Appalachian dulcimer

duple meter (*DOO-pl*)**:** A time signature with two beats to a measure.

duplet (*DOO-plet*)**:** Two notes played in the time of three notes of equal value.
dur (*Ger., door*)**:** Major.
duramente (*It., doo-rah-MEN-teh*)**:** Harshly.
duration: The length of a note or a rest.
dynamic accent: Emphasis placed on a note by giving it a louder attack than those around it. See *agogic accent*, *tonic accent.*
dynamic allocation: In synthesis, when *voices* are assigned to different parts (sounds) as needed while the instrument is being played.
dynamic markings: The symbols indicating the varying degress of loudness or softness (*volume*). See *Reference Charts: Dynamic Signs and Symbols.*
dynamics: The degrees of loudness or softness; their symbols.

E

ear training: An instructional course that teaches how to hear music and write it down.
ebollimento (*It., eh-bohl-lee-MEN-toh*)**:** Sudden passion.
échappée (*Fr., ay-shahp-PAY*)**:** *Escape tone.*
échelle (*Fr., ay-SHEL*)**:** The scale.
echo, eco (*Eng., It., EH-koh*) **1:** Imitation of a previous passage, usually softer. **2:** An electronic device (*signal processor*) that produces an echo effect.
écossaise (*Fr., ay-kohs-SEZ*)**:** A lively dance of Scottish origins in 2/4 time.
effects: Changes in the characteristics of an audio signal, or the electronic devices that produce them, such as *chorus*, *compression*, *delay*, *distortion*, *echo*, *equalization*, *flanging*, *limiting*, *reverb*, etc.
eighth: Octave.

eighth note/rest: A note/rest half the length of a quarter note and an eighth of the length of a whole note: ♪ 𝄾

eight to the bar: A repeated bass pattern that has eight eighth notes to a *measure.*

8va, 8vb: See *ottava alta, ottava bassa.*

Einhalt (*Ger., EIN-hahlt*)**:** A pause.

Einklang (*Ger., EIN-klahng*)**:** Unison, harmonious.

Einsatz (*Ger., EIN-zots*)**:** An entrance or attack.

electric bass: An electric solid-body guitar strung like a string bass with a range of:

electric guitar: A guitar that has either an electronic attachment or built-in electronics that serve to amplify and modify the sound.

electric guitar

electric instruments: Instruments in which either physical vibrations or mechanical motion are amplified electronically to produce sound, such as electric bass, electric guitar, electric piano, and "*tone wheel*" electric organs. See *electronic instruments.*

electric piano: An amplified keyboard instrument in which the sound is produced by hammers striking metal strings, bars, or reeds.

electromagnetic pickup: A *pickup* producing a magnetic field that reacts to vibrations from ferrous-based strings.

electronic instruments: Instruments in which the sound originates in electronic circuits, such as synthesizers, electronic drums, and digital pianos. See *electric instruments.*

electronic music: Music performed solely on synthesizers, computers, or via tape recordings of electronically produced sound.

elegy: A melancholy piece.

eleventh: The diatonic interval from the first to the eleventh note.

embellishment: *Ornaments* added to music.

embouchure (*Fr., AHM-boo-shoor*)**:** On wind and brass instruments, **1:** The shape of the mouth and lips. **2:** The mouthpiece.

ému (*Fr., ay-M[U]E*)**:** With feeling.

encore (*ON-kor*)**:** "Again." To repeat a piece or play an additional piece at the end of a performance.

end-blown flute: Recorder family.

English flute: Recorder.

English horn: An alto *oboe*, pitched a fifth lower and having a conical shape and a bulbous bell. Its range is:

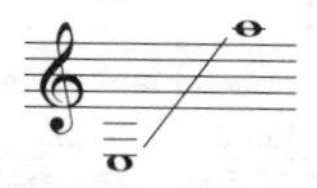

enharmonic: Two notes that are the same pitch but "spelled" differently, e.g., F-sharp and G-flat.

ensemble (*on-SOM-bl*)**:** A group of instrumentalists or singers.

entr'acte (*Fr., ah[n]-TRAHKT*)**:** A piece played between acts of an opera or ballet.

entrada (*Sp., en-TRAH-dah*)**:** Prelude.

entrée (*Fr., ah[n]-TRAY*) **1:** Opening piece for entry of characters in a ballet or opera. **2:** A scene or section in an opera or ballet.

envelope: In synthesis, the shape of some aspect of the sound (such as volume) over time.

envelope generator: In synthesis, a device that controls the shape of the volume, *filter*, or other parameters of sound.

Epiphany: "Appearing." The church season between Christmas and Lent, beginning on January 6th.

episode: In the *fugue*, a section that does not contain the main theme or *subject*.

EQ (*slang abbr.*)**:** *Equalizer*, *equalization*.

equalization: In amplification and recording, the process of setting a tonal balance.

equalizer: In amplification and recording, a device that raises or lowers a sound signal within certain *frequencies*.

equal temperament: Any tuning system that divides the octave into a number of equal intervals.

erleichterte (*Ger., ehr-LEI[S]H-ter-te*)**:** Simplified.

escape note/tone: In harmony, nonharmonic note between two notes that takes a step in one direction and then and then moves by at least a third in the opposite direction.

espressivo (*It., es-pres-SEE-voh*)**:** Expressive, emotional.

estampe (*Fr., eh-TAW[N]P*)**:** A 13th- and 14th-century dance form with various sections that have first and second endings.

estinto (*It., es-TEEN-toh*)**:** Soft, almost inaudible.

ethnomusicology: The study of various types of music in relation to their racial and cultural context.

ethos (*Gr., EE-thohs*)**:** The character and variables of specific scales.

étouffé (*Fr., ay-toof-FAY*)**:** Muted, damped.

-etto (*It., ET-toh*)**:** "Little." A diminutive, which, when ending a word, makes it "little."

étude (*Fr., ay-T[U]ED, AY-tood*)**:** A study or exercise piece written to improve technique.

etwas (*Ger., ET-vahss*)**:** Somewhat.

euphonium (*yoo-FOH-nee-um*)**:** A large brass instrument related to the *baritone horn* (*saxhorn*) but with a larger bore; played primarily in brass bands.

eurhythmics (*yoo-RITH-miks*)**:** A system of teaching rhythm through body movement.

evaded cadence: A *cadence* that implies one type of *resolution* but resolves in another direction.

exercise: A short study written to improve technique.

exposition 1: In the *sonata form,* the first section that contains the *statement* of the themes. **2:** In the fugue, the introduction of the *subject* in all parts.

expressionism: Early 20th-century musical style employing a subjective and abstract approach, in opposition to *impressionism.*

expression marks: Symbols or explanations for musical interpretation such as *dynamics, tempi,* mood, *articulation.*

F

f (*abbr.*)**:** *Forte.*

fa (*fah*)**:** The fourth degree (note) of the *diatonic* scale.

facile (*It., FAH-chee-leh*)**:** Light, easy.

fado (*Port., FAH-doh*)**:** A Portugese street song and dance, usually accompanined by guitar.

Fagott (*Ger., fah-GOHT*)**:** Bassoon.

fake (*slang*)**:** To improvise.

fake book: A book containing the melody lines, lyrics, and chords of songs.

false cadence: *Deceptive cadence.*

falsetto (*It., fahl-SET-toh*)**:** A high artificial voice used for notes that lie above the normal register.

fandango (*Sp., fahn-DAHN-goh*)**:** A lively Spanish dance in triple meter, usually accompanied by castanets and guitar.

fanfare: A *prelude* or opening, a *flourish*, usually played by brass instruments.

fantaisie, fantasia, fantasy (*Fr., faw[n]-teh-ZEE; It., fahn-tah-ZEE-ah* [or *fan-TAY-zhah*]*; Eng.*)**:** A piece in free style and form.

farandole (*Fr., fah-raw[n]-DUL*)**:** A French line dance in 6/8 time.

fastoso (*It., fahs-TOH-zoh*)**:** Pompous.

F clef: A clef 𝄢 usually centered on the fourth line of the staff (bass clef), designating that line as the note F below middle C.

feedback: In amplification, the inadvertent return of the output of a sound system (e.g., a loudspeaker) to the input (e.g., a microphone), resulting in a harsh squeal. Also purposely set on electronic guitars to produce a distorted sound.

feminine cadence: A *cadence* ending on a weak beat.

fermata (*It., fehr-MAH-tah*)**:** A hold or pause 𝄐.

festoso (*It., fes-TOH-zoh*)**:** Merry.

ff (*abbr.*)**:** *Fortissimo.*

fff (*abbr.*)**:** *Fortississimo.*

f-hole: On the instruments of the violin family (and some guitars), the *f*-shaped sound holes located on the top of the instrument.

fiato (*It., FYAH-toh*)**:** Breath.

fiddle 1: In general, a bowed member of the lute family. **2:** A violin used to play bluegrass or folk music, often refitted with all metal strings and a *tuner* on each string.

field holler: A Southern Afro-American unaccompanied worksong, highly embellished, loosely structured and rhythmically free.

fiero (*It., FYEH-roh*)**:** Bold.

fife: A small high flute, often without keys, a tone lower than the piccolo.

15ma: See *quindicesima.*

fifth: The interval of five diatonic degrees.

figuration: The consistent use of a specific melodic or harmonic figure.

figure: Small group of notes or a phrase. See *motif.*

figured bass: The bass part with numbers written adjacent to it to indicate the intervals or harmonies to be played above it:

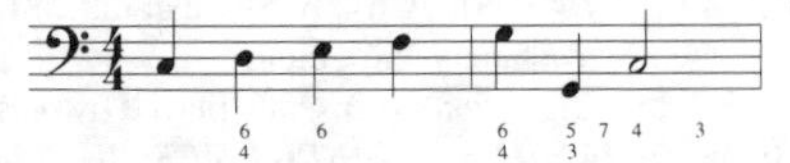

figured chorale: A setting for a *chorale* in which a specific figure is used throughout.

figured melody: A highly ornamented melody.

filter: In synthesis, a device that boosts or cuts certain audio frequencies of *waveforms.*

finale (*It., fee-NAH-leh*)**:** The last movement of a symphony or sonata, or the last section of an opera.

fine (*It., FEE-neh*)**:** End.

fingerboard: On string instruments, the top surface of the neck where the fingers press down on the strings.

finger cymbals: Small pairs of metal cymbals that slip over the thumb and forefinger; used primarily in Middle Eastern music.

fingering, finger 1: *n.*—The notation written on music to indicate where to place the fingers. **2:** *v.*—The act of placing the fingers.

fingerpicking: On guitar or banjo, plucking the strings with each individual finger, with or without fingerpicks. See *flatpicking.*

first-movement form: *Sonata form.*

five-string banjo: See *banjo.*

fixed do: The system in which the note C is always "do," in contrast to *movable do.*

flag: A line or lines extending from the right side of a stem of a note. Indicates an eighth note or smaller.

flageolet (*fla-joh-LET, fla-joh-LAY*)**:** A small type of recorder.

flam: A drum rudiment; a small grace note played softly before the written note with alternate sticking:

or

L R   R L

flamenco (*Sp., flah-MEN-koh*)**:** "Flemish [gypsy]" or "flamingo." A Spanish song and dance form, often performed on guitar.

flanging (*FLANJ-ing*)**:** In recording and synthesis, a hollow, metallic, or "whooshing" effect achieved with extremely short signal delays.

flat 1: *n.*—The flat symbol ♭, indicating to lower a note one half step. **2:** *adj.*—Below normal pitch.

flatpicking: On guitar or banjo, plucking the strings with a teardrop-shaped pick held between the thumb and forefinger. See *fingerpicking.*

flauto (*It., FLAHW-toh*)**:** Flute.

flauto dolce (*It., FLAHW-toh DOHL-cheh*)**:** "Sweet flute." Recorder.

flebile (*It., FLEH-bee-leh*)**:** Plaintive, mournful.

Flex-a-tone: Trademarked name for a percussion instrument made up of an S-shaped steel blade, a metal handle, and two clappers; it can be shaken, struck with a mallet, or bowed.

flip: A jazz technique on brass or wind instruments where a note is raised in pitch and then "glissed" down to the following note:

flourish 1: A fanfare. **2:** An ornamented passage.

flue pipes:.Organ pipes, other than reed pipes, in which air passes through a narrow aperture.

flue stop: On organs, a device that controls the air to a rank of *flue pipes*.

Flügel (*Ger., FL[U]E-gel*)**:** "Wing." Grand piano, so called for its winglike shape.

flugelhorn (*FLOO-gl-horn*)**:** A brass instrument in the cornet family, but with a wider *bore* and a larger bell, resulting in a mellower tone. It has the following range:

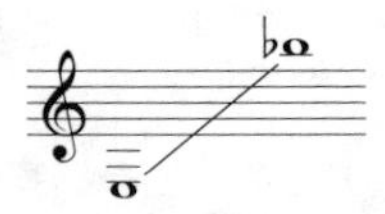

flute: A woodwind instrument made of a wood or metal cylindrical tube closed at one end. Sound is produced by blowing into a hole near the closed end. The range is:

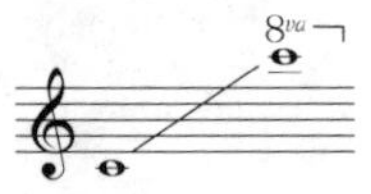

flute

The alto flute has the following range:

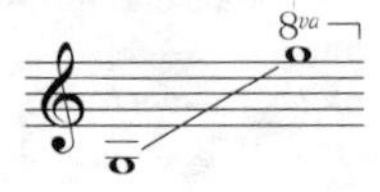

The bass flute has the following range:

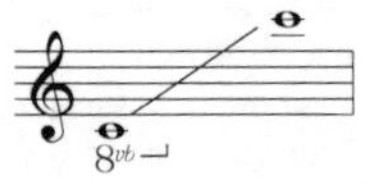

See *piccolo*.

flûte à bec (*Fr., fl[u]et ah BEK*)**:** "Beak flute." Recorder.

Flutophone: In the wind family, a wood or plastic end-blown flute with finger holes.

flutter tonguing: On wind instruments, a rapid *tremolo* produced by rolling the tongue saying "drr."

FM (*abbr.*)**:** *Frequency modulation.*

FM synthesis: A type of synthesis in which *waveforms* interact with each other to produce complex *timbres.*

folio: Songbook.

folk music: Originally songs and music passed down through oral tradition. Traditional music that reflects a locale or a national feeling.

foot: On organs, a measure of the pitch of a rank of organ pipes.

for free, for nothing (*slang*)**:** Beats or measures given as a count-off before the music begins; e.g., "I'll give you four beats for free."

form 1: The shape and order of music. **2:** See *song forms.*

forte (*It., FOHR-teh*)**:** "Strong." Loud (*f*).

fortepiano (*It., FOHR-teh-PYAH-noh*)**:** A historic name applied to the early *pianoforte*.

fortissimo (*It., fohr-TEES-see-moh*)**:**.Very loud (*ff*).

fortississimo (*It., fohr-tees-SEES-see-moh*)**:**.Very very loud (*fff*); the loudest common dynamic marking.

45: In recording, a small record for individual songs (*singles*) that revolved at 45 revolutions per minute.

forzando, forzato (*It., fohr-TSAHN-doh, fohr-TSAH-toh*)**:** "Forced." Strongly accented.

four-part harmony: A conception of harmony stemming from the 18th century, working with the basics of four melodic lines horizontally and four-part chords vertically.

fourth: The interval of four diatonic degrees.

fourth chord: A chord consisting of intervals of a fourth.

fox trot: A ballroom dance in duple time, using both fast and slow steps.

frailich (*Yiddish, FRAY-lu[k]h*)**:** A lively Eastern European Jewish dance in 2/4 time with a steady eighth-note bass line.

française (*Fr., fraw[n]-SEZ*)**:** "French." A French country dance in 3/4 time.

free reed: A reed that vibrates freely in an aperture, such as in a reed or pipe organ, pitch pipe, or accordion.

French harp: Harmonica.

French horn: A brass instrument with a funnel-shaped mouthpiece, a coiled *bore* (tubing) and a flared bell and is controlled by valves. It has the following range:

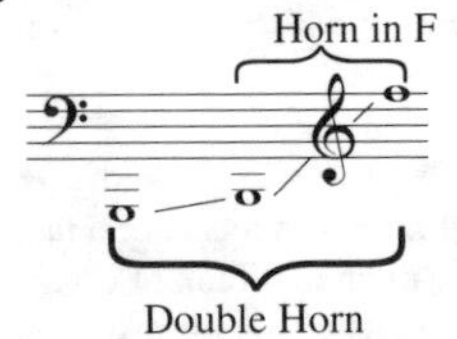

French horn

French overture: A baroque instrumental form that featured a slow first section with (double-) dotted rhythms, followed by a fast section with a fugal texture.

French sixth: A type of *augmented sixth chord* with a major third, augmented fourth, and augmented sixth above the bass.

frequency: The rate of fluctuation in an electrical voltage or the changes in air pressure of an acoustic sound.

frequency modulation: In synthesis, the periodic alteration of the frequency of an audio signal to produce effects such as *vibrato.*

fret 1: *n.*—On guitars, banjos, mandolins, viols, and electric basses, a thin strip of wood, ivory, gut, or metal that's placed across the fingerboard to indicate a specific position of a note. **2:** *v.*—To press the strings against the *fretboard* with one's fingers.

fretboard: On certain string instruments, a *fingerboard* with frets on it.

frog: On bowed string instruments, the end of the bow that is held in the hand.

fuga (*FOO-gah*) **1:** (*Lat.*) A fugue. **2:** (*It.*) A canon.

fugato (*It., foo-GAH-toh*)**:** A section of a piece that is treated as a fugue.

fughetta (*It., foo-GET-tah*)**:** A short fugue.

fugue (*fyoog*)**:** "Flight." A *contrapuntal* piece in which two or more parts are built (layered) on a recurring *subject* (theme) that is introduced alone and followed by an *answer* (which is the *subject* at a different pitch).

full score: An instrumental score in which all the parts for the instruments appear on their own staves in standard instrumental family order.

fundamental: The lowest note in a *harmonic series.*

funk: A rhythm and blues sound, usually lowdown, rhythmic, and rough.

furioso (*It., foo-ree-OH-zoh*)**:** Furiously, wildly.
fusion: A combination of jazz and rock dating from the early 1970s.
fuzz pedal, fuzz tone: An electronic distortion device that modifies the *signal* from an electric guitar or bass pickup and gives it a rasping tone.
fz (*abbr.*)**:** *Forzando, sforzando.*

G

gallant: A style of 18th-century music that was elegant, light, noncontrapuntal, and highly ornamented.
galliard (*gahl-LYARD*)**:** A lively 16th-century dance in triple time.
galop: A spirited 19th-century round dance in 2/4 time.
gamba (*GAHM-bah*)**:** "Leg." *Viola da gamba.*
gamelan (*GAM-e-lon*)**:** An Indonesian orchestra made up of pitched *gongs*, *drums*, various *xylophone*-type instruments, and a *spike fiddle*.
gapped scale: Scale constructed from a complete scale by leaving some notes out, such as the *pentatonic* scale.
gavotte (*gah-VOT*)**:** An elegant and graceful late-17th-century dance in 4/4 time; generally begins on the third beat.
G clef: A clef 𝄞 usually centered on the second line of the staff (treble clef), designating that line as the note G above middle C.
Gebrauchsmusik (*Ger., ge-BROW[K]HS-moo-zik*)**:** "Utility music." Music for daily living or educational purposes.
Geige (*Ger., GEI-ge*)**:** Violin.
gekkin (*GEK-kin*)**:** A Japanese lute.
gemendo (*It., jeh-MEN-doh*)**:** Lamenting.

General MIDI: A recommended specification for consumer electronic *MIDI* instruments that includes a uniform numbering of instrumental and drum sounds.

general pause: *Grand pause*.

genre (*ZHAHN-re*)**:** A distinct type of composition, such as a symphony, opera, string quartet, pop song.

German flute: A standard flute.

German scale: A scale using natural notes employing the note H, which in German stands for B-natural, instead of B, which stands for B-flat.

German sixth: A type of *augmented sixth chord* containing a major third, perfect fifth (or doubly augmented fourth), and augmented sixth above the bass.

Gesang (*Ger., ge-ZAHNG*)**:** Singing; song; voice part.

Gestopft (*Ger., ge-SHTOHPFT*)**:** "Stopped." Muting a horn with one's hand.

ghost bend: A guitar technique, a note that is bent upward before it is played; notated:

ghost note: A guitar technique, a note that is barely played; notated:

gig (*slang, gig*)**:** A job for a musician.

gigue (*Fr., zheeg*)**:** A jig; a lively dance popular from the late 17th to mid 18th centuries, generally in 6/8. In a *suite*, the last of the four dances (see *allemande, courante, sarabande*).

giocoso (*It., joh-KOH-zoh*)**:** Humorous.

gioioso (*It., joh-YOH-zoh*)**:** Joyful.

gitana (*It., jee-TAH-nah*)**:** A Spanish (gypsy) dance.

glass harmonica: An 18th-century instrument made up of various-sized glass bowls that were played by rubbing a wet finger around the rims.

glee: Vocal music for three or four parts, unaccompanied and homophonic, popular in 18th-century England.

glee club: The group that sings *glees*.

glide: A *portamento*—changing the pitch smoothly from one note to another.

glissando (*It., glees-SAHN-doh*)**:** A rapid scale produced by sliding the fingers or hand from one note to another.

Glocke (*Ger., GLOH-ke*)**:** A bell.

glockenspiel (*Ger., GLOK-en-shpeel*)**:** "Bell-play." A percussion instrument made up of steel bars arranged like a keyboard and played with mallets.

glockenspiel

Gloria (*Lat., GLOH-ree-ah*)**:** "Glory [to God in the highest]." In the *Mass*, the second part of the *Ordinary*.

gold record: A recording that has sold half a million copies.

gong: A percussion instrument from the Orient made up of a circular metal plate that is struck by a wooden mallet with a wrapped head.

gospel: Christian music in a popular style.

G.P. (*abbr.*)**:** *Grand pause.*

grace note: An ornamental note, usually played quickly before the beat: 𝆔

gran (*It., grahn*)**:** Great, large.

gran cassa (*It., grahn CAHS-sah*)**:** Bass drum.

grandioso (*It., grahn-dee-OH-zoh*)**:** Grand, grandiose.

grand opera: Opera on a large scale, usually entirely sung, in contrast to *comic opera.*

grand pause: A rest for the entire ensemble.

grand piano: A piano with a winglike shape and a horizontal frame, strings, and soundboard.

grand staff: The combination of the treble and bass staves.

grand piano

grave (*It., GRAH-veh*) **1:** Grave, slow. **2:** Deep, low in pitch.

grazia, grazioso (*It., GRAH-tsee-ah, grah-tsee-OH-zoh*)**:** Grace, graceful.

great pause: *Grand pause.*

Gregorian chant: A body of chants of the Roman Catholic Church, most of which are part of two liturgical rites—the *Mass* and the Offices. Origins traditionally are ascribed to the period of Pope Gregory I (590–604).

groove (*slang*)**:** When music comes together for the players or listeners.

grosse caisse (*Fr., grus kes*)**:** Bass drum.

grosso, grosse (*It., GROHS-soh; Ger., GROHS-se*)**:** Great, large.

ground bass: A bass line that is repeated constantly throughout a piece; an *ostinato.*

growl 1: A rough sound produced on brass instruments. **2:** In amplification, a distorted low bass sound.

gruppetto, groppo, gruppo (*It., groop-PET-toh, GROHP-poh, GROOP-poh*)**:** "Group." Ornamental group of notes such as a *turn*, *shake*, or *trill.*

guaracha (*gwah-RAH-chah*)**:** A Latin American dance rhythm:

♩ ♩ ♪♩ ♪

guida (*It., GWEE-dah*)**:** The *subject* of a fugue.

guiro (*GWEE-roh*)**:** A Latin American percussion instrument made up of a large notched gourd over which a stick is "scraped."

guitar: A string instrument from Spain, with a large flat-backed sound box, violin-like curved shape, a *fretted* neck and six strings. It is played by strumming, plucking, or picking with metal or plastic *picks*. It is tuned E, A, D, G, B, E. Its range is:

guitarrón (*gee-tar-ROHN*)**:** Bass guitar used primarily in *mariachi* bands.

gusto (*It., GOO-stoh*)**:** Style, enjoyment.

Gypsy scale: *Hungarian minor scale.*

H

H 1: (*Ger.*) B-natural. **2:** For "Hoboken," the cataloguer of Haydn's works. H numbers are used instead of opus numbers for Haydn's compositions.

habanera (*Sp., hah-bah-NEH-rah*)**:** "From Havana." A slow, gliding 19th-century Cuban dance in 2/4 time, similar to a tango, with a rhythm of:

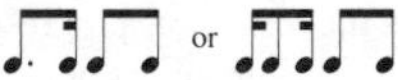

half cadence: *Imperfect cadence.*

half note/rest: A note/rest equal to two quarter notes/rests or one half the length of a whole note/rest.

half step: The smallest *interval* in common use; there are twelve half steps in an *octave*.

hammer: In pianos, the felt-covered part of the *action* that strikes the strings.

hammer-on: On string instruments, sounding a note by quickly and percussively *fretting* (or fingering) a string to the next note above. See *pull-off.*

Hammond organ: An electric organ developed by Laurens Hammond in the 1930s. The first instrument to incorporate *drawbars* and *tone wheels*.

handbell: A hand-held bell with a handle, made in graduated sizes. Sets of chromatically tuned handbells, spanning up to six octaves or more, are played in ensembles called choirs or bands.

hand organ: Portable *barrel organ*.

Harfe (*Ger., HAR-fe*)**:** Harp.

harmonica: A mouth organ with free reeds that are activated by a blowing or drawing action. The *diatonic harmonica* is made in several different keys and plays only a diatonic scale (no chromatics). A *chromatic harmonica* has a side button that can be pushed to sound *chromatic* notes. Also see *glass harmonica.*

harmonica

harmonic minor: See *minor scale.*

harmonic progression: Movement from one chord to another chord.

harmonic rhythm: The rate of movement from one chord to the next.

harmonics 1: The individual, pure tones that make up a complex tone. **2:** On string instruments, sound produced by touching the string lightly at certain points; *natural harmonics* are on *open strings, artificial harmonics* are played on a fingered (stopped) string.

harmonic series: A series of notes produced above a *fundamental* (the series includes the fundamental), and sounded in a definite order.

harmonium: A *free-reed* instrument resembling a small organ.

Harmonizer: In synthesis, a trademarked name of a *signal processor* that shifts the pitch of sound.

harmony 1: The study of the structure, progression and relationships of *chords*. **2:** When pitches are in agreement or *consonance*.

harp 1: A triangular-shaped string instrument with the strings strung vertically; the standard orchestra harp also has seven pedals that raise the pitch of a note a half or whole step. There are many types of harps dating back 2000 years B.C. **2** (*slang*)**:** *Harmonica.*

harpsichord: A keyboard instrument from the 14th to the 18th centuries; the forerunner of the *piano*. When a key is struck it sets in motion a mechanism that plucks a string with a quill.

hastig (*Ger., HAHS-tee[s]h*)**:** Hastily.

haut, haute (*Fr., oh, oht*)**:** High.

hautbois, hautboy (*Fr., oh-BWAH; Eng., HOH-boy*)**:** "High wood [-wind]." Oboe.

Hawaiian guitar 1: *Steel guitar.* **2:** *Ukulele.*

head 1: The membrane stretched over the top of a drum, tambourine, or banjo. **2:** The beginning of the music. **3:** In the violin family, **a:** the scroll and peg box; **b:** the tip of the bow.

head voice: The upper *register* of the voice.

heavy metal: Highly amplified rock with a hard-edged sound and a heavy, rapid, rhythmic beat.

heckelphone (*HEK-el-fohn*)**:** A double-reed, baritone oboe with a conical *bore* and bulbous bell.

heel: On a guitar, the part of the neck that extends down the sides at the junction between the neck and body.

Heldentenor (*Ger., HEL-den-ten-or*)**:** "Heroic tenor." A tenor with a strong, robust voice.

helicon (*HEL-i-con*)**:** A tuba with a circular construction for marching bands.

hemidemisemiquaver: Sixty-fourth note:

hemiola (*hee-mee-OH-lah*) **1:**The rhythmic relation of three notes in the time of two, especially as follows:

2: The interval of a perfect fifth (which has the vibration ratio of 3:2).

hemitonium (*hem-ee-TOHN-ee-oom*)**:** Half step.

herald trumpet: A Renaissance trumpet used to play *fanfares*. Constructed with a long cylindrical tube and flaring bell, with or without valves.

Hertz: A unit of measurement for frequency equal to one complete *waveform* cycle per second.

heterophony (*Gr., het-er-AH-foh-nee*)**:** The simultaneous performance of two or more slightly different versions of the same melody.

hexachord: A scale of six notes.

hidden fifths, hidden octaves: *Parallel fifths, parallel octaves.*

high fidelity: The electronic reproduction of sound with minimal distortion.

high stringing: On guitar, replacing low strings with ones tuned an octave higher. Used in country music.

hi-hat cymbals: A pair of cymbals mounted face to face (the lower is fixed) on a stand and controlled by a foot pedal. Part of the *drum kit.*

hip hop: *Rap* music.

hold 1: A *fermata,* a pause. **2:** In the music business, when a song is being considered for recording.

hold bend: On string instruments, *bending* the note and playing the string while the string is still bent.

hold pedal: On electronic instruments, a controller that sustains or holds notes even after the player releases them.

homophony (*hoh-MAH-foh-nee*)**:** Music in which one voice has the melody with a chordal accompaniment.

homorhythmic: Music in which all parts move in the same rhythm.

honky-tonk 1: A style of piano playing related to *stride* and *ragtime*. **2:** A tinny, out-of-tune piano sound. **3:** In country songs, a bar.

hook: A repetitive phrase, usually in the *chorus* of the song, that catches the listener's attention.

hora (*HOR-ah*)**:** A quick Israeli circle dance.

horn: A brass instrument with a connical-shaped tube wound into a spiral that ends in a flared bell; played with a funnel-shaped mouthpiece.

hornpipe 1: A Celtic wind instrument with a single reed and a horn end **2:** A dance in triple time.

humbucking pickup: On electric guitars and basses, a double-coil *pickup* developed to negate the hum generated by power sources and to produce a fuller sound.

Hummel (*Ger., HOOM-ml*)**:** A Swedish zither.

humoresque (*Fr., [u]e-mor-ESK*)**:** "Humorous." A humorous or capricious instrumental piece.

Hungarian minor scale: Harmonic minor scale with a raised fourth degree. See *Scale Chart: Other Scales*.

hurdy-gurdy: A medieval string instrument in which the sound is produced by the friction of a hand-cranked wooden wheel and the pitch is determined by stopping the strings with keys.

huruk (*hoo-ROOK*)**:** An hourglass-shaped Indian drum.

hymn (*Gr., him*)**:** A song or poem that praises God.

hyper-: Above, over.

hypo-: Below, beneath.

Hz (*abbr.*)**:** *Hertz*.

I

iambic (*ei-AM-bik*)**:** A pattern in music or poetry (lyrics) consisting of a short syllable or note followed by a long; or an unstressed syllable or note followed by a stressed.

ictus (*Lat., IK-toos*)**:** A stress or accent.

imitation: In *counterpoint*, the restatement of a *theme, motif,* or *phrase* in another part.

imperfect cadence: A *cadence* usually found in the middle of a piece since the *progression* moves from the *tonic* to *dominant.*

impresario (*im-pre-SAH-ree-oh*)**:** An agent, manager, or promoter of performers, orchestras, or opera companies.

impressionism: A stylistic period in music that coincides with the period of impressionistic painting, from the 1870s to early 1900s. Claude *Debussy*, Frederick *Delius*, and Maurice *Ravel* were considered impressionistic composers. The music avoided traditional harmonic progressions, employing 9th, 11th, and 13th chords, often doubling the melody in parallel "chord streams."

impromptu (*Fr., a[n]-proh[n]p-T[U]E, im-PROMP-too*)**:** A short, improvisational-sounding piece.

improvisation: Spontaneous composition.

incidental music: Short pieces that accompany a play.

incomplete cadence: A *cadence* in which a note other than the *key note* is in the soprano of the *tonic* chord.

indeterminacy (*in-dee-TER-min-a-see*)**:** *Chance music.*

inflection: Any alteration in the pitch or tone of the voice. Also see *psalmody.*

instrument: Any device that produces a musical sound.

instrumentation: The art of composing, *orchestrating,* or arranging for an instrumental ensemble.

interlude: A short piece that is used to bridge the acts of a play or verses of a hymn.

intermezzo (*It., een-tehr-MED-zoh*) **1:** An instrumental interlude used in the course of an opera or play. **2:** A short, simple opera performed between the acts of a larger one.

interpretation: An expression of one's own character and style in a work.

interrupted cadence: A *cadence* in which the progression moves from the *dominant* to a chord other than the *tonic*.

interval: The distance between two notes.

intone, intonation 1: Chanting. **2:** In *plainsong*, the opening phrase to establish the key or mode. **3:** The accuracy of pitch.

intrada (*It., een-TRAH-dah*)**:** The opening movement of a *suite* or a short *prelude*, homophonic and in a marchlike style.

introduction: The preparatory section, movement, or phrase of a piece.

Introit (*Fr., a[n]-TRWAH; Lat., EEN-troh-eet*)**:** "Entrance." A psalm (or psalm verses) sung at the beginning of the Roman Catholic *Mass*.

invention: A short contrapuntal piece.

inversion 1: Chordal—A chord that has as its bass a tone other than its *root*. **2:** Melodic—The change of each ascending interval into the corresponding descending interval. **3:** Intervallic—Transferring a lower note of an interval an octave higher, or a higher note an octave lower.

inverted canon: A *canon* in which there is a *melodic inversion,* or imitation by contrary motion.

inverted mordent: An *ornament* where the written note ascends and returns a *second* in a rapid *trill*.

invertible counterpoint: *Counterpoint* in which two or more voices can be interchanged.

Ionian (*ei-OH-nee-an*)**:** A medieval mode whose half- and whole-step pattern is that of playing C to C on the white keys of the piano (same as the major scale). See *Scale Chart: Modes.*

Irish harp: A small harp without pedals, held in the lap.

isometric: In polyphonic music, when the same rhythmic pattern is applied throughout the parts.

istesso (*It., ee-STES-soh*)**:** The same.

Italian sixth: A type of *augmented sixth chord* containing a major third and an augmented sixth above the bass.

J

jack 1: On a harpsichord or a piano, the upright lever in the *action*. **2:** On electric or electronic devices, a socket into which a cord or a cable is plugged.

jam (*slang*)**:** A loose gathering of musicians to play, improvise, or rehearse.

Janissary/Janizary music: Highly percussive music of, or in the style of, Turkish military bands.

jarabe (*hah-RAH-beh*)**:** A type of Spanish tap dance.

jazz: A style of music of Afro-American roots characterized by a strong rhythmic understructure, *blue notes*, and *improvisation* on melody and chord structure.

jazz combo: A small *jazz ensemble*, consisting of at least piano, drums, and bass, and often a reed soloist.

jazz ensemble: A group made up of wind instruments, drums, bass, guitar, and keyboard, which plays a variety of jazz styles.

jeté (*Fr., zheh-TAY*)**:** "Flung." A bowing technique wherein upper part of the bow is bounced on the string on a *down bow* stroke (can be heard in the *William Tell Overture*).

jew's harp: A keyhole-shaped folk instrument consisting of a metal frame surrounding a strip of metal fastened at one end. The frame is held between the teeth and the strip is twanged with the fingers.

jig: A lively folk dance, usually in 6/8 time, with origins in Great Britain.

jingle 1: Music composed for a commercial. **2:** Circular pieces of metal such as on a *tambourine*.

jive: To swing with a combo.

joropo (*hoh-ROH-poh*)**:** A Latin dance in rapid 3/4 time.

jota (*HOH-tah*)**:** A Spanish dance in fast 3/4 time accompanied by castanets.

Jubilate (Lat., *yoo-bee-LAH-teh*)**:** A hymn of praise, usually based on Psalm 100.

jubiloso (*It., yoo-bee-LOH-zoh*)**:** Jubilant.

jug band: A folk group consisting of a jug (played by blowing across the mouth), accompanied by guitar, banjo, fiddle, or bass.

just intonation: Any system of tuning in which all intervals are *pure* (represented by ratios of small whole numbers) rather than *tempered.*

K

K: Used instead of "Opus" in numbering compositions of two composers. **1:** For "Köchel," the cataloguer of Mozart's works. **2:** For "Kirkpatrick," the cataloguer of Domenico Scarlatti's works.

Kalimba (*kah-LIM-bah*)**:** *M'bira.*

Kanon (*Ger., KAH-nohn*)**:** *Canon.*

Kapellmeister (*Ger., kah-PEL-meis-ter*)**:** "Master of the chapel." Director of music for a church or royalty.

karaoke (*Japanese, ka-ray-OH-kee*)**:** "Empty orchestra." Singing along with recorded accompaniment.

kazoo: A horn-shaped folk instrument with a vibrating membrane; played by humming into it.

kettledrum: A percussion instrument made of a kettle-shaped shell with a skin or plastic *head* held by an iron ring and tuning screws. Also called *timpani.*

key 1: The tonal center based on the tonic note of the scale. **2:** On keyboard instruments, a lever that controls the sound mechanism. **3:** On woodwind instruments, a metal lever that opens or closes a tone hole.

keyboard: A set of keys on a piano, organ, harpsichord, or synthesizer.

keynote: The first note of the scale of a *key*; the *tonic.*

key signature: The sharps or flats written on the staff at the beginning of a piece to indicate the key. See the *Key Signature Chart.*

kicks: In jazz, accents supplied by drums, piano, or bass.

kin: A small *koto.*

kit 1: A pocket-sized violin. **2:** A *drum kit.*

kithara (*KITH-ah-rah*)**:** An ancient, but sophisticated, Greek *lyre.*

Klavier (*Ger., klah-VEER*).**1:** Keyboard. **2:** Keyboard instrument (with strings).

klein (*Ger., klein*)**:** Small, little.

klingend (*Ger., KLING-ent*)**:** Ringing.

Knollhorn (*Ger., NOHL-horn*)**:** Soft-sounding herald horn from the midwestern region of the U.S.

koto (*KOH-toh*)**:** A Japanese instrument with seven to 13 silk strings plucked by the fingers.

kräftig (*Ger., KREFT-i[k]h*)**:** Forcefully, vigorously.

krakowiak (*kra-KOH-vyak*)**:** Brisk Polish dance in 2/4 time.

Kreuz (*Ger., kroyts*)**:** A *sharp.*

Krummhorn (*Ger., KROOM-horn*)**:** A family of Renaissance double-reed instruments, shaped like a "J."

kujawiak (*koo-YAH-vyak*)**:** A Polish couple dance, a slower variant of the *mazurka.*

Kyrie (*Gr., KEE-ree-eh*)**:** "Lord [have mercy]." In the *Mass*, the first part of the *Ordinary.*

L

la: The sixth note (degree) of the *diatonic* scale.

lacrimoso (*It., lah-kree-MOH-zoh*)**:** Tearful, mournful.

laissez vibrer (*Fr., les-say vee-BRAY*)**:** Let vibrate, let sound.

lament, lamento (*Eng.; It., lah-MEN-toh*)**:** A mournful piece, either meant to be played at a funeral or commemorating a death.

lamentoso (*It., lah-men-TOH-zoh*)**:** Mournful.

Landini cadence: The melodic *cadence* "ti-la-do," found in the music of Francesco *Landini*, among others.

Ländler (*Ger., LEND-ler*)**:** A slow Austrian dance similar to a waltz.

langsam (*Ger., LAHNG-zahm*)**:** Slowly.

lap steel guitar: An amplified *steel guitar* that is held in the lap or on a tabletop.

lap steel guitar

largamente (*It., lahr-gah-MEN-teh*)**:** Broadly.

largando (*It., lahr-GAN-doh*)**:** Slowing down.

larghetto (*It., lahr-GET-toh*)**:** A slow tempo, a little faster than *largo*.

largo (*It., LAHR-goh*)**:** Slow and broad.

layering: In synthesis, two or more voices combined to sound together when a note is played.

LCD (*abbr.*)**:** "Liquid Crystal Display." A type of display used in some synthesizers, which produces dark symbols against a light background.

leader: Conductor. *Concertmaster* in an ensemble.

leading note/tone: The seventh degree of the *diatonic* scale; called "leading" because it gives the feeling of wanting to move to the *tonic*.

lead sheet (*leed*)**:** The melody line, lyrics, and chords for a song. Originally used for copyright purposes.

leap: A *skip*.

lebendig (*Ger., leh-BEN-di[k]h*)**:** Lively.

lebhaft (*Ger., LEHP-hahft*)**:** Lively.

LED (*abbr.*)**:** "Light-Emitting Diode." A type of display used in some synthesizers, which produces light symbols (usually red) against a dark background.

ledger lines, leger lines: Short lines written above or below the staff for notes pitched outside the staff.

legato (*It., leh-GAH-toh*)**:** Smooth.

legato slide: On guitar, a long descending slide to the next fret.

leggero, leggiero (*It., led-JEH-roh*)**:** Lightly.

legno (*It., LEN-yoh*)**:** "Wood." On string instruments, the stick of the *bow*. See *col legno*.

leicht (*Ger., lei[s]ht*)**:** Light.

leise (*Ger., LEI-ze*)**:** Soft.

leitmotif, Leitmotiv (*Ger., LEIT-moh-teef*)**:** "Leading theme." Recurring theme written for a specific character or event in opera or television and film music.

leno (*It., LAY-noh*)**:** Faint.

Lent: The season of the church year from Ash Wednesday to Easter (40 days not counting Sundays).

lento (*It., LEN-toh*)**:** Slow.

Leslie speaker: A rotating loudspeaker developed by Don Leslie for use with the *Hammond organ*.

lesto (*It., LEH-stoh*)**:** Lively.

LFO (*abbr.*)**:** "Low-Frequency Oscillator." In synthesis, a device or function that repeatedly raises and lowers an aspect of a sound, such as for vibrato and tremolo effects.

L.H. (*abbr.*)**:** "Left Hand." Indication for keyboard players.

liberamente (*It., lee-beh-rah-MEN-teh*)**:** With liberty.

libretto (*It., lee-BRET-toh*)**:** The text (lyrics and any spoken parts) of an *opera*, *oratorio*, or *musical.*

licks (*slang*)**:** Short melodic musical phrases that sometimes can become musical "signatures" for jazz and pop artists.

lieblich (*Ger., LEEP-lee[s]h*)**:** Sweet, melodious.

Lied, Lieder (*Ger., leet, LEED-er*)**:** Song, songs. Especially German songs of the *romantic* period.

lieto (*It., lee-EH-toh*)**:** Joyful.

lift: On brass instruments, to approach a note from below via a *chromatic* or *diatonic* scale. A long lift starts a fifth below the note; a short lift starts a third below the note:

ligado (*It., lee-GAH-doh*)**:** In *flamenco* guitar playing, a technique whereby passages of notes are played with the left hand alone.

ligature 1: In the clarinet and saxophone families, the adjustable band that holds the reed against the mouthpiece. **2:** A *slur* or *tie* over a group of notes indicating that they are to be sung to the same syllable.

limiter: A *signal processor* that performs *limiting*.

limiting: In amplification and recording, electronically keeping an audio signal from exceeding a certain level.

lip: The *embouchure*; to adjust the *embouchure* ("lipping").

lip trill: On brass instrumentes, an ascending *trill* similar to a *shake,* but slower and with more lip control:

lira (*It., LEE-rah*)**:** A 16th-century string instrument with *drones,* played with a bow.

liscio (*It., LEE-shoh*)**:** Smooth.

l'istesso (*It., lee-STES-soh*)**:** The same.

litany (*LIT-a-nee*)**:** A set of prayers recited by a leader alternating with responses by the congregation, often set in *plainsong* form.

liturgy (*LIT-er-jee*)**:** A prescribed order of worship in a church, usually applied to the *Mass.*

loco (*It., LOH-koh*)**:** "Place." Return to the normal place (usually after playing one or more octaves above or below written pitch).

Locrian (*LOK-ree-an*)**:** A medieval mode starting on the seventh degree of the diatonic scale, with half steps between the first and second degrees and fourth and fifth degrees. See *Scale Chart: Modes.*

looping, loops 1: In synthesis, the electronic repetition of a musical phrase or portion of a *sample.* **2:** (*slang*) In recording, the process of re-recording singers' voices to synchronize with a picture. **3:** In recording, continuous sounds (special effects such as crickets) used in film tracks.

loudness: Volume; intensity of sound.

lourd, lourde (*Fr., loor, loord*)**:** Heavy.

loure (*loor*) **1:** A French bagpipe. **2:** A slow rustic dance with bagpipe accompaniment.

louré (*Fr., loo-RAY*)**:** On string instruments, *legato* bowing.

Lp (*abbr.*)**:** "Long-playing." In recording, a large record with several *cuts* that revolves at 33 1/3 *rpm.*

luftig (*Ger., LOOF-ti[k]h*)**:** Light.

Luftpause (*Ger., LOOFT-pow-ze*)**:** A pause for a breath.

lullaby: A cradle song.
lungo (*It., LOON-goh*)**:** Long.
lustig (*Ger., LOOS-ti[k]h*)**:** Cheerful, merry.
lute: A plucked string instrument with a half-pear-shaped body, fretboard and pegbox set at an angle. In the 17th century, after a thousand years of development, the lute settled into a form with six pairs of strings.
lutherie (*Fr., l[u]e-teh-REE*)**:** "Lute making." The art of making string instruments such as lutes, guitars, and the violin family.
luthier (*Fr., l[u]e-TYAY*)**:** "Lute maker." One who makes string instruments.
l.v. (*abbr.*)**:** *Laissez vibrer.*
Lydian (*LID-ee-an*)**:** A medieval mode starting on the fourth degree of the diatonic scale, with half steps between the fourth and fifth and seventh and eighth degrees. See *Scale Chart: Modes.*
lyra, lyre (*LEE-rah, leir*)**:** An ancient Greek instrument with a four-sided frame, encompassing strings attached from a soundbox to a cross bar. Played like a harp.
lyric 1: The words to a song. **2:** In a singing and melodious manner.
lyric soprano: A female singer with a range between a *colouratura* and a *dramatic soprano*:

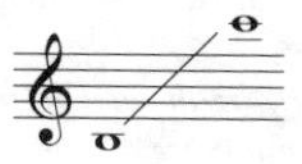

lyric tenor: A male singer with the highest tenor range:

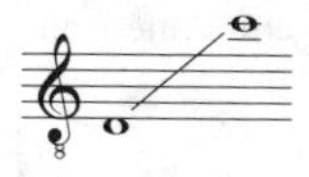

M

ma (*It., mah*)**:** But.
machete (*mah-CHEH-teh*)**:** A Portuguese four-string folk guitar.
madrigal: A Renaissance choral piece, usually unaccompanied.
maestoso (*It., mah-es-TOH-zoh)*)**:** Majestically, stately.
maestro (*It., mah-ES-troh*)**:** Master, teacher, conductor.
maggiore (*It., mahd-JOH-reh*)**:** Major mode.
main (*Fr., meh[n]*)**:** Hand.
mainstream: Music that goes along with a prevailing current trend.
majeur (*Fr., mah-ZHER*)**:** Major.
major: "Greater." Used in music theory to describe *intervals*, *chords*, and *scales*.
major chord: A triad composed of a root, major third, and perfect fifth.
major scale: A *diatonic* scale in which the *half steps* occur between the third and fourth, and seventh and eighth degrees. See *Scale Chart.*
malagueña (*mah-lah-GEH-nyah*)**:** An Andalusian folk dance from Spain.
malincolico, malinconico (*It., mah-leen-KOH-lee-koh, mah-leen-KOH-nee-koh*)**:** Melancholy.
mallet: A drumstick with a large tip.
mambo (*MAHM-boh*)**:** A Latin American ballroom dance with the following rhythm:

or

mallet

mancando (*It., mahn-KAHN-doh*)**:** Fading away.
mandocello (*man-doh-CHEL-loh*) ("mando[lin]" + "cello")**:** Bass mandolin.
mandola, mandora (*man-DOH-lah, man-DOR-ah*) ("mando[lin]" + "[vio]la")**:** Tenor mandolin.

mandolin (*man-doh-LIN*)**:** An instrument in the lute family, fretted and with eight wire strings tuned in four pairs (G, D, A, E) like a violin, and played with a *plectrum* (*flatpick*).

Mannheim school (*MON-heim, MAN-heim*)**:** Preclassical group of German symphonic composers whose style included extended crescendos (called "steamrollers") and melodies that arpeggiated upward dramatically (called "rockets").

mandolin

mano (*It., MAH-noh*)**:** Hand.

manual: A keyboard of the organ or harpsichord to be played by the hands.

maracas (*mah-RAH-cahs*)**:** Latin American percussion instruments consisting of seed-filled gourds with handles attached to shake them.

marcato (*It., mar-KAH-toh*)**:** "Marked." Stressed, accented. In the violin family, marcato bowing calls for decisive attack strokes.

maracas

march: Music for marching, such as in a parade or procession, in duple or quadruple time.

marching band: A *band* that plays while marching in parades or performing in choreographed field shows.

marcia (*It., MAR-shah*)**:** March.

mardakion (*Gr., mar-DAK-ee-on*)**:** A sleek accordion-like instrument from the midwest U.S.

mariachi (*mah-ree-AH-chee*)**:** A Mexican folk group, usually containing two violins, guitar, *guitarron,* and rhythm instruments.

marimba (*mah-RIM-bah*)**:** A tuned percussion instrument from Africa via Latin America; a deeper-pitched version of the *xylophone* with metal *resonators.*

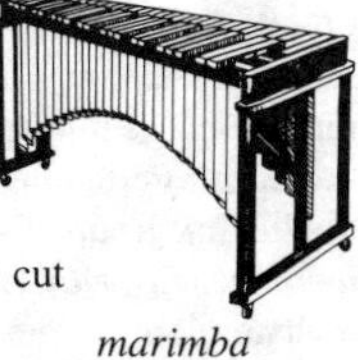

marimba

mark tree: A wind chime made out of brass tubes cut and graduated in size to form a series of microtonal pitches.

marqué (*Fr., mar-KAY*)**:** Marked, accented.

martelé, martellato (*Fr., mar-teh-LAY; It., mar-tel-LAH-toh*)**:** "Hammered." In the violin family, playing with short detached strokes, never lifting the bow from the strings.

marziale (*It., mar-TSYAH-leh*)**:** Martial.

masculine cadence: A *cadence* in which the final chord occurs on the strong beat.

masque (mask): A musical entertainment from the 16th century combining poetry, singing, dancing, music, and elaborate costumes and scenery.

Mass: The musical setting of the Roman Catholic church service—usually the *Ordinary,* but sometimes also the *Proper.*

mässig (*Ger., MES-si[s]h*)**:** Moderate.

master 1: *n.*—A final, completed recording from which copies can be made. **2:** *v.*—To make a final recording.

matching folio: A songbook containing all the songs from an *album.*

Matins (*Fr., mah-TA[N], MAT-inz*)**:** "Mornings." In liturgical churches, the daily morning service. See *Vespers.*

mazurka (*mah-ZOOR-kah*)**:** A Polish folk dance in moderately fast triple time, often strongly accented on the third beat.

m'bira (*um-BEE-rah*)**:** An African "thumb piano" made up of a number of metal or cane tongues held in position with a bar attached to a box or board. The free ends are "twanged" with the thumbs.

m.d. (*abbr.*)**:** *Main droite, mano destra.*

mean-tone tuning: A system of *tempering pure intervals* for the sake of playing in different keys on keyboard instruments. Used primarily from the mid-1500s to the early 1800s.

measure: A *bar*; the space between two *bar lines.*

medesimo (*It., meh-DEH-see-moh*)**:** The same.

mediant: The third *degree* (note) of the scale.

medieval: Pertaining to the *Middle Ages.*

medley: A group of songs linked together muscially.

mélange (*Fr., may-LAW[N]ZH*)**:** "Mixture." Medley.

melisma: Several notes sung to one syllable.

mellophone: A variation of the *French horn* (orchestral horn) constructed for marching.

melodeon (*meh-LOH-dee-on*)**:** A *free-reed* instrument related to the *concertina,* with 10 treble keys on the right, a bellows, and four bass keys on the left.

Melodica (*meh-LOD-i-kah*) ("melod[y] + "[harmon]ica")**:** Trademarked name for a wind instrument with a keyboard.

melodic minor: See *minor scale.*

melody: An organized sequence of single notes.

melos (*Gr., MEH-lohs*)**:** Song.

meno (*It., MEH-noh*)**:** Less.

mensural notation: The system of notation from the 13th century that began to express notes and rests with more exact time values; used prior to *metrical notation* with bar lines.

menuet (*Fr., meh-n[u]e-AY*)**:** *Minuet.*

merengue (*meh-REN-geh*)**:** Latin American ballroom dance with the following rhythm:

messa di voce (*It., MES-sah dee VOH-cheh*)**:** "Placing of the voice." In singing, a crescendo and decrescendo on a sustained note.

mesto, mestoso (*It., MES-toh, mes-TOH-zoh*)**:** Sad, sadly.

metallophone: Similar to a *xylophone,* but with metal bars instead of wood.

meter 1: A framework for rhythm determined by the number of beats, the time value of those beats, and the accents thereof. In *simple meters,* the beats are divisible by two; in *compound meters,* they are divisible by three. **2:** The division of music into measures, bars, or phrases. **3:** In verse (lyrics), the pattern of long and short syllables.

method: A course of instruction for an instrument or voice.

metronome: A mechanical device that can be adjusted to indicate the exact tempo of a piece. Invented around 1812.

mezza voce (*It., MED-zah VOH-cheh*)**:** "Half voice." Quietly.

mezzo (*It., MED-zoh*)**:** Half, medium.

mezzo forte (*It., MED-zoh FOHR-teh*)**:** Moderately loud (*mf*).

mezzo piano (*It., MED-zoh PYAH-noh*)**:** Moderately soft (*mp*).

mezzo soprano (*It., MED-zoh soh-PRAH-noh*)**:** A female voice between soprano and alto.

mf: *Mezzo forte.*

m.g. (*abbr.*)**:** *Main gauche.*

mi (*mee*)**:** The third degree of the *diatonic* scale.

microtonal, microtone: *Intervals* lying outside the *twelve-tone equal temperament.*

Middle Ages: European historical period between roughly A.D. 500 and 1450.

middle C: The note C (C 256) in the middle of the *grand staff* and near the middle of the keyboard.

MIDI (*abbr., MID-ee*)**:** "Musical Instrument Digital Interface." The means by which musical performance and other information is transmitted and received by electronic instruments using a common serial interface.

MIDI channel: On electronic instruments and computers, a pathway over which *MIDI* data are transmitted or received.

MIDI controllers: See *continuous controllers.*

MIDI In, Out, Thru: On *MIDI* instruments, ports (receptacles for cables) that receive MIDI messages (In), transmit MIDI messages (Out), or pass through MIDI messages (Thru).

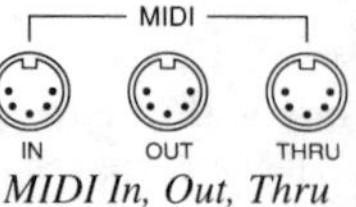

MIDI In, Out, Thru

mineur (*Fr., mee-NER*)**:** Minor.

miniature score: A small-sized score containing the vocal or instrumental parts of a piece; used for study or concert attendence.

minim: Half note: 𝅗𝅥

minimalism: A contemporary musical style that makes use of simple musical materials, repetition, and slow or no variation.

minim rest: Half rest.

minor: "Lesser." Used in music theory to describe *intervals*, *chords*, and *scales.*

minor chord: A triad composed of a root, minor third, and perfect fifth.

minor scale: A *diatonic* scale in which the *half steps* occur between the second and third, and fifth and sixth *degrees* (*natural minor*). In the *harmonic minor scale,* the seventh *degree* is raised one half step. In the *melodic minor scale,* the sixth and seventh *degrees* are raised one half step in the ascending version only. See *Scale Chart: Scale Construction.*

minstrel: Wandering musician from the Middle Ages; in the late 19th century, applied to black-face singers.

minuet: A French dance from the mid-1600s in slow 3/4 time. A movement (usually the third) in sonatas and symphonies of the Classical period.

mirliton (*Fr., meer-lee-TOH[N]*)**:** Kazoo.

mirror canon: A *canon* in which the *consequent* is either the *inversion* or the *retrograde* of the *antecedent.*

missa (*Lat., MEES-sah*)**:** Mass.

misterioso (*It., mees-teh-ree-OH-zoh*)**:** Mysteriously.

misura (*It., mee-ZOO-rah*)**:** Measure, bar. "Time" in the sense of regular beat.

mit (*Ger., mit*)**:** With.

mix: To combine and balance several *tracks* of a recording.

mixed folio: A songbook containing songs of many artists.

mixer 1: A small *mixing console.* **2:** One who operates a *mixing console* and balances *tracks* of a recording.

mixing console: An electronic device with which one can combine and balance *tracks* of a recording. Also called a mixing board.

Mixolydian (*mix-oh-LID-ee-an*)**:** A medieval mode starting on the fifth *degree* of the *diatonic scale* with *half steps* between the third and fourth, and sixth and seventh degrees. See *Scale Chart: Modes.*

M.M.: "Maelzel's metronome" (Johann Nepomuk Maelzel patented the metronome). The double "m"s, followed by a note and its beats per minute, indicate tempo.

mobile (*It., MOH-bee-leh*)**:** Changeable.

modal (*MOHD-l*)**:** Pertaining to *modes.*

mode: A type of scale with a specific arrangement of intervals (see *Aeolian, Dorian, Ionian, Locrian, Lydian, Mixolydian, Phrygian*).

moderato (*It., moh-deh-RAH-toh*)**:** Moderate tempo.

modern: Music written in the 20th century or contemporary music.

modulate, modulation (*v., n.*) **1:** To change keys; the transition from one key to another within a piece. **2:** In synthesis, using the level of an output (which usually changes over time) to control the operation of a function.

moll (*Ger., mohl*)**:** Minor.

molto (*It., MOHL-toh*)**:** Very.

monochord: An instrument composed of a single string stretched over two fixed bridges on a resonating box and moveable bridges to measure intervals of a scale. Used by Pythagoras to explain *tuning* according to mathematical ratios.

monody: A solo or unison song with accompaniment.

monophonic, **monophony** (*adj., mon-oh-FON-ic; n., mon-AH-foh-nee*): Music with a single melody line only.

monothematic: Music based on one theme.

monotone: A single, unvaried *pitch*. Reciting words on one pitch.

Moog synthesizer (*mohg*): The earliest commercial *voltage-controlled synthesizer*, designed by Robert Moog starting in the mid 1960s.

MOR: "Middle Of the Road." A music business term for ballad and easy listening music.

morceau (*Fr., mor-SOH*): "Morsel." A musical piece or composition.

mordent (*MOR-dnt*): "Biting." An ornament consisting of an alteration (once or twice) of the written note by playing the one immediately below it (lower mordent), or above it (upper, or inverted, mordent) and then playing the note again:

morendo (*It., moh-REN-doh*): "Dying." Fading away.

mosso (*It., MOHS-soh*): Moved, lively.

motet (*moh-TET*): A choral composition, generally on a sacred text.

motif, motive (*moh-TEEF, MOH-tiv*): A short melodic pattern or musical idea that runs throughout a piece.

moto (*It., MOH-toh*): Motion.

Motown sound: Music of the Black musicians of the 1960s and 1970's emanating from the Detroit-based Motown Record Corp. ("Motown" = "Motor Town" [Detroit]).

moustaches 1: On string instuments, the decorative designs on the bridge. **2:** In music engraving, the brackets that indicate the grand staff, or that indicate that several lines of lyrics are uniting into one.

mouth harp 1: *Jew's harp*. **2:** *Harmonica*.

mouth organ: *Harmonica.*

mouthpiece: On brass and wind instruments, the part of the instrument placed to a players lips.

movable do (*doh*)**:** The system of syllables in which the first note of each diatonic scale is "do." See *fixed do.*

movement: A self-contained section of a composition, such as a *symphony, suite, concerto, sonata,* etc.

mp (*abbr.*)**:** *Mezzo piano.*

m.s. (*abbr.*)**:** *Mano sinistra.*

multitimbral (*mul-tee-TAM-brul*)**:** In synthesis, capable of playing more than one tone color at a time.

multitracking: Recording each voice or instrument on a separate track to eventually *mix* them together.

musetta, musette (*It., moo-SET-tah; Fr., m[u]e-ZET*) **1:** An early French bagpipe. **2:** A dance with a drone bass accompaniment.

music: The organization of sounds with some degree of rhythm, melody, and harmony.

musical saw: A handsaw that is held between the knees; sound is produced via a violin bow or mallet, with pitch being changed by bending the saw.

music box: A mechanical device with a revolving disk or cylinder that has protruding pins. When the disk or cylinder rotates, the pins pluck a row of pitched steel "teeth" that produce a melody.

music drama: Opera, especially that of Richard *Wagner.*

musicology (*myoo-zi-KOL-o-jee*)**:** The study of musical composition and history.

music theory: The study of how music is put together.

music therapy: The use of music as part of a medical or psychological and social treatment.

musique concrète (*Fr., m[u]e-ZEEK koh[n]-KRET*)**:** Music composed by manipulating recorded sounds—specifically "concrete," real-world sounds (noises, nature sounds, etc.) rather than sounds that are generated electronically.

muta (*It., MOO-tah*)**:** A direction to change keys, frequently found in timpani and horn parts.

mute 1: A device that softens or muffles an instrument's sound. **2:** Brass instrument mutes: cup—conical with a donut on the end; straight—conical with smooth sides; wow-wow—short, light-bulb shaped.
muting: A guitar technique, wherein one "stops" the string with the picking or fretting hand to prevent it from ringing.
m.v. (*abbr.*)**:** *Mezza voce.*

N

nach (*Ger., nah[k]h*)**:** After (as "in the manner of"); behind.
Nachschlag (*Ger., NAH[K]H-shlahk*)**:** An ornament consisting of an unaccented note or notes at the end of the main note, or at the end of a trill

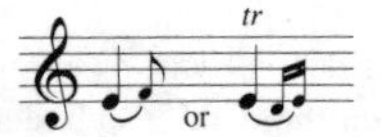

Nachtmusik (*Ger., NAH[K]HT-moo-zik*)**:** "Night music." A serenade.
nach und nach (*Ger., NAH[K]H oont NAH[K]H*)**:** Little by little.
naked fifth: Open fifth.
NARAS (*abbr.*)**:** "National Academy of Recording Arts and Sciences." The organization that presents the Grammy Awards and provides services for musicians and recording personnel.

natural: The music symbol ♮ that indicates that a note that is neither sharp nor flat. When the symbol is placed to the left of the note, it cancels a previous accidental.
natural harmonic: *Open harmonic.*
natural horn: A horn without valves or slides.
natural minor: See *minor scale.*

N.C. (*abbr.*)**:** No Chord.
Neapolitan sixth: A chord constructed on the fourth degree of a *diatonic* scale with a minor third and a minor sixth above the bass.
neck: On string instruments, the long, slender part where the fingerboard or fretboard is affixed.
neighboring note: A *nonharmonic* note on a weak beat that moves a half or whole step above or below another note and returns to that note.
neoclassicism: A 20th century movement that revolted against romanticism and reached back to the classical traditions, especially in compositional structures and genres.
neumes (*nyoomz, noomz*)**:** The signs and symbols used for notation in the *Middle Ages.*
New Age: A style of textural and atmospheric music, primarily instrumental, that grew out of meditative music of the early 1970s.
new jack swing: A type of funk dance, often with rap.
ninth: The interval of nine *diatonic degrees* (an octave and a second).
ninth chord: The third, fifth, seventh, and ninth above the root.
nobilmente (*It., noh-beel-MEN-teh*)**:** Nobly, stately.
nocturne, notturno (*Fr., nohk-T[U]ERN, NOK-turn; It., noht-TOOR-noh*)**:** A night-piece, a serenade.
node: A point of minimal amplitude in a wavelength. On string instruments, these stationary places on the string are where *harmonics* are produced by lightly touching the string.
noël, nowell (*Fr., Eng., noh-EL*)**:** Christmas carol.
non (*Fr., noh[n]; It., nohn*)**:** No; not.
nonet 1: A piece for nine instruments or voices. **2:** Nine performers.
nonharmonic notes: Notes that are not part of the chord structure around them.
non-transposing: Label given to an instrument that is pitched in the key of C.
nose flute: Wooden, bamboo, or plastic flutes blown via the nose; most are from Polynesia.
notation: Written music indicating pitch and rhythm.
notehead: The main part (round portion) of the note.
note on/note off: On synthesizers, the MIDI codes that command an instrument to play a note and to stop a note that is playing.
notes: The written symbols of music.

novelty song: A song with humorous lyrics or music.

nuance: The subtle shading of *tempo*, *phrasing*, *articulation*, *dynamics*, and *intonation.*

nut On string instruments, **1:** The strip at the end of the neck next to the *pegbox* that raises the strings above the fingerboard. **2:** The base of the *bow* that is held in the hand and from which the bow hair is tightened by means of the *screw*; the *frog*.

O

O 1: The symbol for an open string. **2:** The symbol for "diminished." **3:** Triple time in medieval notation.

obbligato (*It., ohb-blee-GAH-toh*)**:** Originally meant an obligatory (essential) part; now means a solo or contrasting melody that is optional.

ober, obere (*Ger., OH-ber, OH-ber-e*)**:** Upper, higher, above.

oblique motion: Two melodic lines where one moves while the other is stationary.

oboe: A *double-reed* woodwind instrument with a conical *bore* in C (*non-transposing*) and a natural scale of D. It has the following range:

oboe

oboe d'amore (*OH-boh dah-MOH-reh*)**:** An oboe slightly bigger than the normal oboe with a pear-shaped bell, and pitched a minor third lower.

ocarina (*It., oh-kah-REE-nah, ok-uh-REE-nuh*)**:** "Little goose." A small round wind instrument with finger holes, made out of clay or plastic; also called *sweet potato.*

octave: The interval between the first and eighth *degrees* of the *diatonic* scale.
octavo (*ohk-TAH-voh*)**:** Individual copy of choral music or band music, roughly 6"x 9".
octet 1: A piece for eight instruments or voices. **2:** Eight performers.
odd meters: Meters that are groupings of an odd number and an even number of beats, such as 5/4 (3+2) or 7/8 (3+4).
ode: A lyrical poem set to music in honor of a person or occasion.
oeuvre (*Fr., e[r]v*)**:** *Opus*.
Offertory 1: A part of the *Roman Catholic Mass* (*Proper*), following the *Credo* and sung during the offering. **2:** In Protestant church services, any music sung or played during offering.
oliphant: A small medieval horn made from an elephant's tusk.
Op., Opp. (*abbr.*)**:** *Opus*, *opera* (2).
open: Not stopped, *fingered*, *muted* or *fretted*.
open fifth: A *triad* without the third.
open harmonic: On string instruments, a harmonic played on an *open string*.
open harmony: When notes of a chord are not played in their closest positions (*close harmony*), but every other note is transposed by an octave, so there are "spaces," usually of a fifth or a sixth, between notes.
open notes 1: On string instruments, *open strings*. **2:** On brass or wind instruments, notes produced without *valves*, *keys*, *slides*, or *crooks*.
open strings: Strings that are not *stopped, fingered*, or *fretted*.
open triad: *Open fifth*.
opera 1: A dramatic work set to music in which all or most of the text is sung with instrumental accompaniment, costumes and sets. **2:** The plural of *opus*.
opéra bouffe, opera buffa (*Fr., oh-pay-RAH BOOF; It., OH-peh-rah BOOF-fah*)**:** Comic opera.
opéra comique (*Fr., oh-pay-RAH kuh-MEEK*)**:** Comic opera.
opera seria (*It., OH-peh-rah SEH-ree-ah*)**:** Serious opera.
operetta (*It., oh-peh-RET-tah*)**:** Light opera.
ophicleide (*AW-fi-kleid*)**:** In the brass family, a large, keyed bass bugle played in the upright position.
Op. Posth. (*abbr.*)**:** Posthumous opus—a work published after the death of the composer.

opus (*Lat., OH-poos, OH-puhs*)**:** "Work." With a number, used to show the order in which pieces were written or published.

oratorio (*It., oh-rah-TOH-ree-oh*)**:** A musical setting for voices and orchestra of a text based on the Scriptures or an epic theme. Essentially an opera without staging, scenery, or costumes.

orchestra: A large group of musicians, made up of string, brass, woodwind, and percussion instruments.

orchestration: The art of writing, arranging, or scoring for the orchestra.

Ordinary: The parts of the *Mass* that remain the same from day to day, as distinct from the *Proper*. The Ordinary consists of the *Kyrie*, *Gloria*, *Credo*, *Sanctus*, and *Agnus Dei*.

organ 1: A keyboard instrument made up of manual and pedal keyboards, which, when depressed, send air supplied by bellows through a reservoir and into pipes. **2:** An electric or electronic instrument patterned after the pipe organ.

organetto (*It., ohr-gahn-ET-toh*)**:** A portable organ from the 14th century.

organum (*Lat., OHR-gahn-oom*) **1:** Organ. **2:** Earliest polyphonic music.

Orgel (*Ger., OR-gl*)**:** Organ.

ornamentation: To add *ornaments* to a melody.

ornaments: Melodic embellishments, either written or improvised. See *acciaccatura, appogiatura, arpeggio, grace notes, mordent, Nachschlag*, *springer, trill, turn.*

oscillator: In synthesis, the device that generates the electrical *waveforms.*

ossia (*It., ohs-SEE-ah*)**:** "Or." Indicating an alternative passage or version.

ostinato (*It., ohs-tee-NAH-toh*)**:** A repeated musical figure, rhythmic pattern, or *motive*, most often occurring in the bass.

ottava (*It., oht-TAH-vah*)**:** Octave.

ottava (*8va*) **alta** (*It., oht-TAH-vah AHL-tah*)**:** An octave higher.

ottava (*8va*) **bassa** (*It., oht-TAH-vah BAHS-sah*)**:** An octave lower. Also notated *8vb.*

ottavino (*It., oht-tah-VEE-noh*) **1:** *Piccolo.* **2:** A small *virginal.*

oud, ud (*ood*)**:** A short-necked, unfretted, double-strung lute played with a *plectrum.*

overblow: On wind instruments, a hard-blowing technique employed to produce *harmonics* instead of *fundamentals.*

overdrive: In electronic effects, *distortion* produced by high signal levels.

overdub, overdubbing: To record a *track* on top of another track.

overtone series: Same as the *harmonic series*, except it does not include the *fundamental*.

overture: The introductory music for an opera, oratorio or ballet. A concert overture is an independent work.

P

p 1: (*It.*) *Piano* (soft). **2:** (*Fr.*) Pedal. **3:** (*Sp.*) Thumb.

pacato (*It., pah-KAH-toh*)**:** Calm, quiet.

pad (*slang*)**:** A part in an arrangement that produces soft, sustained background chords.

panning: In amplification, the movement of an audio signal between two or more speakers.

panpipes: An ancient wind instrument, consisting of several pipes of graduated lengths bound together in a row.

pantomime: A play in which the story is conveyed only by gestures and movement with musical accompaniment.

paradiddle (*pa-rah-DID-dl*)**:** On drums, a repeated *sticking pattern* where the strong beats are played with alternate hands:

parallel chords: The movement of specific chords or chord combinations up and down the scale.

parallel fifths, parallel octaves: The movement of two parts in *parallel motion* a fifth or an octave apart.

parallel intervals: The movement in two or more parts of the same interval in the same direction.

parallel keys: Major and minor keys having the same key note (tonic). See *relative keys.*

parallel motion: The movement in two or more parts in the same direction with the same intervallic separation.

parameter (*puh-RAM-e-ter*)**:** In synthesis, a variable that can be changed, such as a *waveform* or an *envelope* setting.

parlando, parlante (*It., par-LAHN-doh, par-LAHN-teh*)**:** A declamatory style of singing that sounds close to speaking.

part 1: The music for an individual voice or instrument. **2:** A single melodic line in counterpoint.

partials: *Harmonics* and *overtones* of the *harmonic series.*

partita (*It., par-TEE-tah*) **1:** A set of *variations.* **2:** A *suite.*

partition, Partitur, partitura (*Fr., par-tee-SYOH[N]; Ger., par-TEE-toor; It., par-tee-TOO-rah*)**:** Score (*not* "parts").

part song: An unaccompanied *homophonic* composition for three or more voices.

paso doble (*Sp., PAH-soh DOH-bleh*)**:** A Spanish dance with double steps in rapid 2/4 time.

passacaglia (*It., pahs-sah-KAH-lyah*)**:** A slow, stately dance in triple meter, often with a repetitive theme or bass line. Similar to *chaconne.*

passage: A section of a piece.

passepied (*Fr., pahs-se-PYAY*)**:** A French dance in quick triple time.

passing notes: Scalewise notes that are not part of the harmony, but serve to connect two notes that are.

Passion: An *oratorio* on the the suffering and death of Jesus Christ.

pastorale (*It., pahs-toh-RAH-leh*)**:** "Shepherdly." **1:** An instrumental movement in 6/8 or 12/8 time, often with a long bass drone. Originally intended to depict the music of shepherds. **2:** A musical play based on a rustic subject.

patch 1: *n.*—In synthesis, a set of *parameters* for a specific sound. **2:** *v.*—To connect pieces of equipment together.

patch bay: In recording, the device into which the *patch cords* are plugged and routed.

patch cords: In recording, wires that route the *signals* from synthesizers, tape recorders, mixers, etc.

patch editor: In synthesis, a computer program for designing and modifiying *patches*.

patch librarian: In synthesis, a computer program that organizes or rearranges the *patches*.

pathétique (*Fr., pah-tay-TEEK*)**:** With great emotion.

patter song: A rapid, sometimes tongue-twisting, song often found in comic opera and now in pop music.

pausa (*It., POW-sah*)**:** A rest.

pause 1: A rest of indefinite length. **2:** A hold, *fermata.*

pavane (*pah-VAHN*)**:** A slow dance in duple time from the 16th century.

PCM: "Pulse Code Modulation." The most common technique of digital *sampling.*

peal 1: A set of tuned bells or chimes. **2:** Nonmelodic patterns of sounds that the set emits when rung.

pedal 1: A mechanism controlled by the foot, such as on a piano or organ. **2:** The *fundamental* (lowest note) on a brass instrument.

pedal keyboard: On organs, the pedals used for playing bass notes.

pedal point: A sustained note, usually in the bass, about which other voices move.

pedal steel guitar: An amplified *steel guitar* mounted on a stand, with pedals and knee levers for changing the pitches of individual strings.

pedal tone: *Pedal point.*

peg: On string instruments, the mechanism, around which a string is wound, that tightens or loosens the string.

pegbox: On string instruments, the box at the end of the neck into which the pegs are inserted.

pentachord: The first five notes of the diatonic scale.

pentatonic scale 1: Any scale made up of five notes. **2:** The scale corresponding to a *major scale* without the fourth and seventh degrees, which can be played on the black keys of the piano. See *Scale Chart: Other Scales.*

percussion family: Instruments made of sonorous material that produce sounds of definite or indefinite pitch when shaken or struck, including drums, rattles, bells, gongs, and xylophones.

perfect cadence: A *cadence* in which the progression moves from the dominant (V) chord to the tonic (I) chord (also see *authentic cadence*).

perfect interval: Interval of an octave, fifth, or fourth without alteration.

perfect pitch: The ability to hear and identify a note without any other musical support.

performing rights society: In the music business, an organization (ASCAP, BMI, SESAC, etc.) for composers and publishers that surveys and collects royalties from television and radio stations, convention halls, stadiums, nightclubs, and any venue where music is performed either live or prerecorded (except movie theatres).

period: A musical statement, made up of two or more *phrases* and a *cadence*.

perpetual canon: A *canon* with no ending; i.e., it leads back to the beginning.

personality folio: A songbook containing songs by a single artist.

pesante (*It., peh-SAHN-teh*)**:** Heavy.

petit (*Fr., puh-TEE*)**:** Little.

peu à peu (*Fr., PE[R] ah PE[R]*)**:** Little by little.

pezzo (*It., PED-zoh*)**:** Piece.

pf (*abbr.*) **1:** Pianoforte. **2:** Soft, then loud.

phrase: A musical idea; a natural unit of a melodic line.

phrasing 1: In classical music, "punctuating" a melodic line. Often used as a synonym for *articulation.* **2:** In popular music, "delivering" a melodic line, including all facets of *nuance,* as well as departures from the original melody.

Phrygian (*FRIJ-ee-an*)**:** A medieval mode, starting on the third degree of the diatonic scale, whose half steps fall between the first and second degrees and fifth and sixth degrees. See *Scale Chart: Modes.*

piacere (*It., pyah-CHEH-reh*)**:** "Pleasure." At the performer's discretion.

pianissimo (*It., pyah-NEES-see-moh*)**:** Very soft (*pp*).

pianississimo (*It., pyah-nees-SEES-see-moh*)**:** Very very soft (*ppp*); the softest common dynamic marking.

piano (*It., PYAH-noh*) **1:** Soft (*p*). **2:** *Pianoforte.*

pianoforte (*It., pyah-noh-FOHR-teh*)**:** "Soft-loud." A keyboard instrument, the full name for the piano, on which sound is produced by hammers striking strings when keys are pressed. It has 88 keys, with the following range:

piano quartet: Piano, violin, viola, and cello.

piano roll: For *player pianos,* a paper roll with perforations that correspond to the pitch and length of the notes to be produced.

piano score: A *score* arranged for playing on piano.

piano trio: Piano, violin, and cello.

piatti (*It., PYAHT-tee*)**:** Cymbals.

picado (*Sp., pee-KAH-doh*)**:** In *flamenco* guitar playing, a fast run picked with two fingers of the right hand.

Picardy third: A major third in the final chord of a piece in a minor key.

piccolo (*It., PEEK-koh-loh*)**:** "Little [flute]." In the *flute* family, a small flute that sounds an octave higher than written (piccolo in C) or, less often, a minor ninth higher than written (piccolo in D-flat). The written range is as follows:

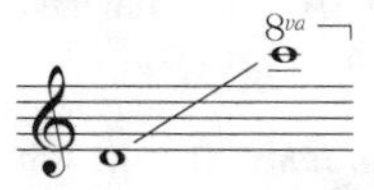

pick: On string instruments, a device for strumming or plucking the strings made out of ivory, horn, wood, or plastic. A fingerpick fits over an individual finger; the triangular-shaped flatpick is held between the thumb and index finger.

pick scrape: On guitar, a right-hand technique of scraping along a wound string with the edge of the pick.

pickup 1: Introductory note or notes preceding the first strong beat of a new measure. See *anacrusis.* **2:** An electrical device that, when attached to an instrument, converts vibrations into electrical impulses.

piezo-electric transducer (*pee-e-zoh-e-LEK-trik*)**:** On guitars, a *pickup* with a piezo-electric crystal that converts vibrations in the guitar to electrical impulses.

pin bridge: On guitars and electric basses, a bridge with holes through which the strings are inserted and held in place with pins on their ends.

pipe 1: Any hollow tube made out of reed, wood, metal, or plastic that, when blown, produces a musical note, such as organ pipes. **2:** Instruments made from these tubes. **3:** *v.*—To play a pipe.

pipe organ: In the keyboard family, an organ played with the hands and feet controlled by *manuals* and *pedals* which when depressed send air under pressure through a series of pipes to sounds the notes. See *coupler, manual, pipe, stop.*

pitch: The highness or lowness of a note, as determined by its frequency.

pitch bend: In synthesis, continuous (sliding) control over pitch, usually controlled by a wheel, knob or slider.

pitch pipe: A small wind instrument with one or several reeds, used for tuning.

più (*It., pyoo*)**:** More.

pivot chord: When modulating, a chord that is common to both the old and new keys.

pizzicato (*It., peed-zee-KAH-toh*)**:** "Pinched." On string instruments, plucking the string.

placido (*It., PLAH-see-doh*)**:** Calm.

plagal cadence: A *cadence* in which the progression moves from the subdominant (IV) chord to the tonic (I) chord. It is typically used as the "amen" of hymns.

plainchant, plainsong: *Monophonic* chant, unaccompanied and unmeasured.

player piano

plainte (*Fr., plent*)**:** A 17th and 18th century French ornament. See *Nachschlag.*

platinum record: A recording that has sold a million copies.

player piano: A piano with a mechanical or electro-mechanical apparatus that plays back prerecorded performances.

plectrum: On string instruments, a pick made out of ivory, horn, wood, or plastic.

plectrum banjo: A four-string banjo with a long neck, tuned C, G, B, D.

plein-jeu (*Fr., ple[n]-ZHE[R]*)**:** Full organ.

plop: On brass or wind instruments, a rapid slide down the scale before sounding a note:

pluck: On string instruments, to sound the string by pulling it with the finger.

poco a poco (*It., POH-koh ah POH-koh*)**:** Little by little.

poi (*It., poy*)**:** "Then." After, afterwards.

point: In the violin family, the tip of the bow.

polka: A Bohemian dance in moderately quick duple time, characterized by a hop on the first beat.

polonaise (*Fr., poh-loh-NEZ*)**:** A stately Polish dance in moderate triple time, often with a repeated rhythmic pattern.

polychoral (*pol-ee-KOR-ul*)**:** A style in which an ensemble is divided into groups that may perform individually, alternately, or together.

polychords (*POL-ee-kordz*)**:** Chords that result from two separate triadic units.

polymetric (*pol-ee-MET-rik*)**:** The simultaneous use of different meters.

polyphony (*po-LI-fuh-nee*) **1:** Music that combines two or more melodic lines simultaneously. **2:** In synthesis, the number of notes that an instrument can play at one time.

polyrhythm (*POL-ee-rith-m*)**:** Contrasting rhythms played simultaneously.

polytonal (*pol-ee-TOHN-ul*)**:** The simultaneous use of different tonal centers (keys).

pomposo (*It., pohm-POH-zoh*)**:** Pompous, majestic.

ponticello (*It., pohn-tee-CHEL-loh*)**:** The bridge of a stringed instrument. *Sul ponticello,* bowing at (on) the bridge.

port: In synthesis, the place on an electronic instrument or computer where a cable is connected for transmitting or receiving information.

portable keyboard: An electronic keyboard, with built-in speakers, that can be carried easily.

portamento: A smooth glide from one note to another.

portative organ (*por-tah-TEEF*)**:** A small portable organ from the Middle Ages.
portato (*It., por-TAH-toh*)**:** Half *staccato*; halfway between *staccato* and *legato*:

position, pos. 1: On string instruments, the placement of the left hand on the finger- or fretboard. **2:** On trombone, the placement of the slide to produce notes. **3:** The inversion of a chord.
positive organ (*poh-zee-TEEF*)**:** A medieval flue-pipe organ of moderate size with one *manual*, no *pedals*, and *bellows* that required a second person to pump them.
posthorn: In the bugle family, a cylindrical straight horn without valves used by coach horseriders and mailcarriers to announce their arrival.
postlude "Play after." **1:** The final piece in a multi-movement work. **2:** Organ piece played at the end of a church service.
potentiometer, pot: In synthesis, a knob or *slider*.
poussé, poussez (*Fr., poos-SAY*)**:** "Pushed." On string instruments, up-bow.
pp (*abbr.*)**:** *Pianissimo*.
ppp (*abbr.*)**:** *Pianississimo*.
praeludium (*Lat., pray-LOO-dee-oom*)**:** Prelude.
Pralltriller (*Ger., PRAHL-tril-ler*)**:** A short trill.
prebend: On guitar, to bend a string before picking it.
preciso (*It., preh-SEE-zoh*)**:** Precise, exact.
prélude (*Fr., pray-L[U]ED, PRAY-lood*)**:** "Play before." An introductory movement or piece.
première (*Fr., preh-MYEHR, pre-MEER*)**:** First performance.
preparation: The introduction of a consonant note prior to the playing that same note as part of a discord.
prepared piano: A piano whose sound has been altered by means of objects placed on the strings.
presets 1: On synthesizers, preprogrammed sounds; see *patch*. **2:** On pipe organs, pistons that allow combinations of stops to be recalled with a single press. **3:** On electronic organs, standard settings that produce various instrumental sounds.

pressure, pressure sensitivity: In synthesis, a feature in some instruments where various controls can be accessed (such as *vibrato, pitch bend,* volume changes) by applying pressure to a key. See *aftertouch.*

prestissimo (*It., pres-TEES-see-moh*)**:** Very, very fast; the fastest tempo.

presto (*It., PRES-toh*)**:** Fast.

prima donna (*It., PREE-mah DOHN-nah*)**:** "First lady." The most important female singer in an opera. Also implies a vain or difficult person.

primary chords: The tonic, subdominant, and dominant chords of a key.

prime 1: Unison. **2:** The first note of scale.

primo (*It., PREE-moh*)**:** "First." **1:** The first part. **2:** The upper part of a piano duet.

principal 1: Instrumental section leader. **2:** *Diapason* (1).

processional: Music performed for an entrance.

program 1: *n.*—Instructions given to a computer to perform a certain task. **2:** *v.*—In synthesis, to set the *parameters* of a device.

program music: A piece that conveys a picture or story. In contrast to *absolute music.*

progression: Movement from one chord to another chord.

progressive jazz: Jazz from the 1950s, smooth and cool in contrast to *bebop.*

prologue (*PRO-lawg*)**:** An introductory piece that presents the background for an opera.

pronto (*It., PROHN-toh*)**:** Prompt, quick.

Proper: The parts of the *Mass* whose texts change from day to day, as distinct from the *Ordinary.* The Proper consists of the *Introit,* Gradual, Alleluia or Tract, *Offertory,* and Communion.

proposta (*It., proh-POHS-tah*)**:** The subject of a *fugue.*

psalm (*sahlm, sahm*)**:** A sacred song or hymn, usually sung in *plainsong* form. Specifically, one of the 150 psalms in the Bible.

psalmody (*SAHL-moh-dee*)**:** The singing of psalms.

psalter (*SAHL-ter*) **1:** The Old Testament Book of Psalms. **2:** The Books of Psalms of the Reformed churches in poetic verse settings suitable for congregational use.

psaltery (*SAHL-ter-ee*)**:** An ancient string instrument, similar to the dulcimer; the strings are plucked with the fingers or a *plectrum.*

pulgar (*Sp., pool-GAR*)**:** Thumb.

pull-off: On string instruments, sounding a note with the fretting finger after plucking the string, sounding the open string or fretted note below it.
pulse: A beat.
punk rock: An aggressive, deliberately offensive style of rock music (and fashion) emerging from the late 1970s.
punta (*It., POON-tah*)**:** "Point." The point of the bow.
purfling: On string instruments, a decorative strip inlayed around the edges of the instrument.
PV, PVG: "Piano/Vocal," "Piano/Vocal/Guitar." A standard sheet music arrangement.
pyiba (p'i p'a) (*PEE-bah, PEE-pah*)**:** Pear-shaped, four-stringed Chinese lute.
Pythagorean scale (*pi-thag-oh-REE-an*)**:** The earliest known scale of an octave. The arrangement of whole steps and half steps is the same as the major scale; the ratios of whole and half steps differ.

Q

Q: *Regeneration* setting on a *filter*.
Quadrat (*Ger., kwahd-RAHT*)**:** A natural sign.
quadrille (*Fr., kwah-DREE, kwah-DREEL*)**:** An early 19th-century French dance in five movements, which are alternately in 6/8 and 2/4 time.
quadruple meter: A *time signature* with four beats to a measure.
quadruplet: Four notes played in the time of three notes of equal value.
quantize: In synthesis, aligning notes to precise rhythmic values to correct for human inaccuracies.
quartal harmony: *Harmony* based on the *interval* of a *fourth*, rather than thirds. See *tertian harmony*.

quarter note/rest: A note/rest one half the length of a half note and one quarter the length of a whole note.

quarter tone: The *interval* of one half of a *half step.*

quartet 1: A piece for four instruments or voices. **2:** Four performers.

quasi (*It., KWAH-zee*)**:** Almost, nearly, as if.

quaver: Eighth note: ♪

quickstep: A fast march.

quill: On a harpischord, the portion of the *action* that plucks the strings.

quindicesima (*15ma*) (*It., kween-dee-CHEH-zee-mah*)**:** "Fifteenth." Two octaves; play two octaves higher than written.

quintal harmony: *Harmony* based on the *interval* of a *fifth*, rather than thirds. See *tertian harmony.*

quintet 1: A piece for five instruments or voices. **2:** Five performers.

quintuple meter: A *time signature* with five beats to a *measure*; e.g., 5/4.

quintuplet: Five notes to be played in the time of four notes of equal value.

quodlibet (*Lat., kwohd-lee-BET, KWAHD-li-bet*)**:** "That which pleases." A group of pieces or songs, often humorous, played simultaneously or successively.

R

rabab (*rah-BOB*)**:** *Rebab.*

racket: A Renaissance double-reed wind instrument consisting of a short, thick cylinder of wood with a tubular air channel pierced with holes, giving it a limited scale and a deep sound.

raga (*RAH-gah*)**:** An Indian classical music, an organized collection of tones that sets the melodic and rhythmic framework for a piece.

ragtime: The earliest form of jazz, from the early 1900s. Features "ragged" syncopated rhythms against a regular rhythmic background of 2/4 or 4/4.

rake: On guitar, dragging the pick across muted strings in an arpeggiated fashion, either ascending or descending, and unmuting the last string so it sounds.

rallentando (*It., rahl-len-TAHN-doh*)**:** Becoming gradually slower.

RAM (*abbr.*)**:** "Random-Access Memory." On computers and synthesizers, a digital storage medium for sound and other data to be added, changed, or retrieved. See *ROM*.

R&B (*abbr.*)**:** *Rhythm & Blues.*

range: The notes, from the lowest to the highest, that a voice or instrument may be capable of producing.

rap: In pop music, a rhyming half-sung, half-spoken style, often enhanced by electronic effects.

rasgado, rasgueado (*Sp., rahz-GAH-doh, rahz-geh-AH-doh*)**:** In guitar playing, a right-hand flamenco technique where the fingers, from the little finger to the index finger, strum the strings quickly.

raspa (*Sp., RAHS-pah*)**:** A Cuban percussion instrument made out of a gourd with notches cut into it across which a stick is scraped. See *guiro.*

ratamacue (*RAT-a-mah-kyoo*)**:** A drum rudiment. An alternating-hand *sticking* pattern:

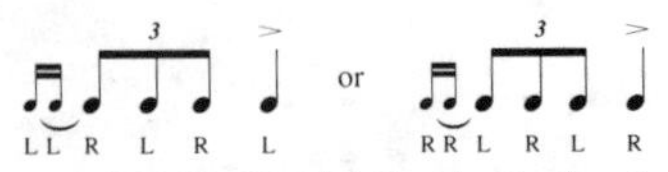

rattenuto (*It., raht-teh-NOO-toh*)**:** Holding back, slowing down.

rattle: In the percussion family, **1:** A gourd or other container filled with seeds, stones, pieces of clay or wood that is shaken with a handle. **2:** A notched cogwheel turned by a handle against a flexible piece of wood or metal.

re (*ray*)**:** The second note of the *diatonic* scale. D in the *fixed-do* system.

realization: The notation or performance of a part that originally was not notated in detail (for example, *figured bass*).

real-time mode: In synthesis, relying on the timing of events as they occur when performing an operation (such as recording). See *step-time mode.*

rebab (*re-BOB*)**:** An ancient Northern African and Middle Eastern short-necked fiddle with two strings.

rebec (*REH-bek*)**:** A small, pear-shaped medieval bowed string instrument with a short neck and three or four strings.

recapitulation 1: The final section in *sonata form*, in which the themes are restated. **2:** Return to, or repetition of, a theme or passage.

recessional: A hymn or music played at the close of a church service, as the celebrants or worshipers exit.

recital: A performance by one or more performers.

recitative (*re-chi-tah-TEEV, re-si-ta-TEEV*)**:** A vocal number that mimics the inflections of speech, found primarily in operas and oratorios.

recorder: An end-blown wooden flute without keys, with a tapering *bore*. The most common sizes are the soprano:

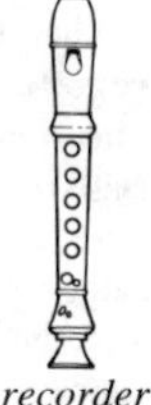
recorder

alto:

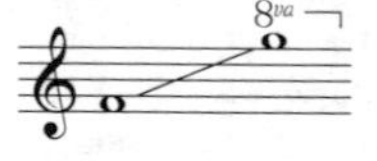

tenor:

bass:

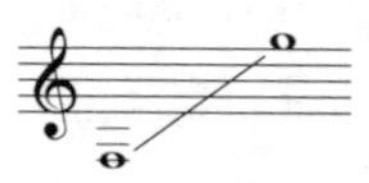

reduction: An arrangement of a piece for a smaller number of parts.

reed: A vibrating strip of metal or cane, which when activated by air, produces a tone. Single reeds are found on clarinets and saxophones, double reeds on oboes and bassoons. See *free reed, fixed reed.*

reel: A lively Celtic dance in 4/4 or 6/8 time with regular four-bar phrases.

refrain: The chorus of a song, usually repeated. See *burden.*

regal: A portable reed organ from the 16th century.

regeneration: In synthesis, when an output is fed back into an input, causing a special effect. Used in *delay, echo, flanging,* and *filter* effects.

reggae (*REG-gay*)**:** A Jamaican pop music style, a combination of West Indian (*ska, rock steady*) and Afro-American music styles with a hypnotic, heavy bass sound.

register 1: A specific area of the range or *compass* of a voice or instrument. **2:** On the organ, a set of pipes controlled by a single *stop.*

registration: On the organ, the organization of *stops* and *registers* to produce a specific sound.

relative keys: Major and minor keys that share the same key signature. See *parallel keys.*

relative pitch: The ability to recognize or produce a note based on its relationship to notes heard previously.

religioso (*It., reh-lee-JOH-zoh*)**:** Sacred, religious.

Renaissance: "Rebirth." The era from the mid 15th century to the end of the 16th century. The music was characterized by freer forms, and a progression from modes toward major and minor scales and harmony.

repeat The restatement of a passage. See *Reference Charts: Repeat Signs and Symbols.*

replica (*It., REH-pli-kah*)**:** Repeat.

reprise (*re-PREEZ*) **1:** *Repeat.* **2:** *Recapitulation* (2). **3:** In a piece in binary form, the return of the first section as the latter part of the second section.

Requiem Mass: A mass for the dead, the sections being: *Introit*, *Kyrie*, Gradual and Tract, *Sequence* (*Dies Irae*), *Offertory*, *Sanctus*, *Agnus Dei*, Communion, and Responsory.

resolution: The progression of chords or notes from the dissonant to the consonant or point of rest.

resonance 1: The transmission of vibrations from one vibrating object to another vibrating object. **2:** *Regeneration* setting on a *filter.*

resonator: Any instrument or part of an instrument (body, sounding board) that reinforces sound by resonance.

resonator guitar: See *Dobro.*

response 1: In the fugue, the *answer.* **2:** An answer by a group to a musical *call* or question, such as in gospel music.

responsoral: Alternating singing or speaking between a soloist and a group. See *antiphonal.*

rest 1: A period of silence. **2:** Symbols that indicate silence:

whole rest	𝄻
half rest	𝄼
quarter rest	𝄽
eighth rest	𝄾
sixteenth rest	𝄿
thirty-second rest	𝅀

retardation: Gradually slowing, holding back.

retrograde: Playing a melodic line backwards.

reveille (*Fr., reh-VAY, REH-vi-lee*)**:** "Reawakening." Military wake-up call played by a bugle.

reverb, reverberation 1: An electronic effect that imitates the persistence of sound in a room. **2:** The rebounding of sound.

rf, rfz (*abbr.*)**:** *Rinforzando.*

R.H. (*abbr.*)**:** "Right Hand." Indication for keyboard players.

rhapsody: A free-style instrumental piece characterized by dramatic changes in mood.

Rhodes piano: An electric piano developed by Harold Rhodes.

rhumba (*ROOM-bah*)**:** *Rumba.*

rhythm: The pattern of long and short note values in music.

rhythm & blues: A form of pop music that evolved in the 1940s, characterized by heavily syncopated dance rhythms and blues scales. The roots of *rock 'n' roll.*

rhythm section: In jazz and pop music, the instruments—piano, guitar, bass, and drums—that play rhythm and harmony in accompaniment to a soloist.

ribs: On string instruments, the strips joining the back and front of the instrument.

ricercar, ricercare (*It., ree-chehr-KAR, ree-chehr-KAH-reh*)**:** "To seek again." A 16th- and 17th-century instrumental piece in imitative contrapuntal style.

ride cymbal: On a jazz drum set, the main cymbal, 16"–24".

riff: A repeated melodic pattern.

rigadoon, rigaudon (*Eng., rig-a-DOON; Fr., ree-goh-DOH[N]*)**:** In the 16th century, a study. Afterwards, a French dance in 2/2 time that became part of the *suite.*

rinforzando (*It., reen-for-TSAHN-doh*)**:** A reinforced accent.

ripieno (*It., ree-PYEH-noh*)**:** In a *concerto grosso*, the full orchestra, as opposed to the *concertino.*

riposato (*It., ree-poh-ZAH-toh*)**:** Relaxed, quiet.

ritardando (*It., ree-tar-DAHN-doh*)**:** "Delaying." Becoming gradually slower.

ritenuto (*It., ree-teh-NOO-toh*)**:** "Held back." Immediately slower.

ritmo (*It., REET-moh*)**:** Rhythm.

ritornello (*It., ree-tor-NEL-loh*) **1:** A *refrain.* **2:** The return to the *tutti* (full orchestra) in a baroque concerto.

rock, rock 'n' roll (*slang*)**:** A form of pop music that evolved in the mid 1950s from *rhythm & blues*, characterized by strongly accented *back beats* and youth-oriented lyrics.

rock steady: A Jamaican pop music style, a combination of West Indian and Afro-American music styles.

rococo (*roh-koh-KOH, roh-KOH-koh*)**:** A highly ornamented style of music and decorative arts in the mid 18th century.

roll: On percussion instruments, a sticking technique consisting of a rapid succession of notes:

Drum *rudiments: closed roll*—a series of fast, tight indiscernable strokes; *buzz roll*—a short series of fast, tight, strokes; *long roll*—a series of double strokes.

rolled chord: A chord in which the notes are played consecutively, rather than struck simultaneously; an *arpeggio.*

ROM (*abbr.*)**:** "Read-Only Memory." On computers and synthesizers, a memory chip with permanent information. See *RAM.*

romance, romanza (*Eng.; It., roh-MAHN-tsah*)**:** A short vocal or instrumental piece with a lyrical, romantic flavor.

romantic: The era roughly from 1820 to 1900, in which music progressed to a freer, more subjective form with increasing chromaticism, the use of folk themes, the introduction of more virtuostic solo music, and larger orchestras.

ronde (*Fr., rohnd*)**:** Whole note.

rondeau (*Fr., rohn-DOH*) **1:** A *rondo.* **2:** A form of medieval French poetry set to music, usually with a *refrain* and a *verse.*

rondo (*It., ROHN-doh*)**:** A musical *form* characterized by a recurring theme in alternation with contrasting themes; often the form is ABACADA or ABACABA.

root: The *fundamental* note (I) of a chord or a scale.

rosin: For string instruments, a block of hardened tree resin that is rubbed across the bow hairs to enhance the friction of the bow hairs on the strings.

rote, rotta (*Eng.; It., ROHT-tah*)**:** A plucked lyre-type instrument from the Middle Ages.

roulade (*Fr., roo-LAHD*)**:** An ornamental vocal phrase.

round: A vocal *canon* for two or more voices, sung in unison or octaves. Each part enters in succession with the same music and lyric, and upon reaching the end can start over, continuing indefinitely.

rounded binary form: A compositional form in which an initial section is followed by a contrasting section, which ends with a return of material from the initial section (AB[A]). See *binary form, ternary form, song forms.*

roundelay: *Rondeau.*

row: See *tone row.*

rubato (*It., roo-BAH-toh*)**:** "Robbed." Freely slowing down and speeding up the tempo without changing the basic pulse.

rudiments: On drums, the basic *sticking* patterns. See *drag, flam, paradiddle, ratamacue, roll, ruff.*

ruff: On drums, a *rudiment*, a *sticking* technique consisting of a note preceded by two grace notes:

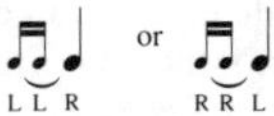

L L R or R R L

rumba (*ROOM-bah*)**:** An Afro-Cuban dance in rapid, syncopated 2/4 time, with the following rhythm:

run: A rapid scale passage.
rustico (*It., ROOS-tee-koh*)**:** Rustic, rural.

S

S. (*abbr.*)**:** *Segno, senza, sign, sinistra, sol, solo, soprano, sordini, subito.*
SA (*abbr.*)**:** In choral music—soprano, alto.
SAB (*abbr.*)**:** In choral music—soprano, alto, baritone.
sackbut: A brass instrument, forerunner of the trombone with a smaller *bell* and cylindrical *bore.*
sacred music: Music for worship, religious concerts, or devotional use.
saddle: On guitar, a thin strip of ivory, bone, or plastic set into the *bridge.*
Saite (*Ger., ZEI-te*)**:** String.
salsa: A Latin American pop music and dance style combining Latin rhythms with rock.
saltato, saltando (*It., sahl-TAH-toh, sahl-TAHN-doh*)**:** "Jumping." On string instruments, a bowing technique where the bow is bounced lightly on the string.

samba: A Brazilian dance in 2/4 time, with the following rhythm:

samisen (*SAH-mee-sen*)**:** A flat-backed, long-necked lute from Japan with a skin-covered belly and three strings.

sample, sampling 1: In synthesis, a digital recording of a sound. **2:** In pop music, a small portion of an existing recording that is *mixed* into a new recording—a technique used primarily in *rap* music.

sampler: In synthesis, a digital device that records sound as *digital* information that can be manipulated and played back.

sämtliche (*Ger., ZEMT-lee-[s]heh*)**:** Complete.

Sanctus (*Lat.*)**:** "Holy [, Holy, Holy]." In the *Mass*, the fourth part of the *Ordinary.*

sanft (*Ger., zahnft*)**:** Soft, gentle.

sans (*Fr., saw[n]*)**:** Without.

sansa (*SAHN-sah*)**:** See *m'bira.*

saraband(e) (*Fr., sah-rah-BAW[N], sah-rah-BAW[N]D*)**:** A slow, sensuous dance in triple time, often with an accent on the second beat. In time it became faster and more dignified, and was incorporated into the *suite.*

sarangi (*sah-RAHN-jee*)**:** A Northern Indian fiddle with a short thick neck and three to four bowed strings plus sympathetic strings.

sarrusophone (*sah-ROO-soh-fohn*)**:** A double-reed military band instrument made of brass with a wide conical *bore;* uses the same fingering as a bassoon.

SATB (*abbr.*)**:** In choral music—soprano, alto, tenor, bass.

Satz (*Ger., ZOTS*)**:** A *movement.*

sautillé (*Fr., soh-tee-YAY*)**:** See *saltato.*

saw: See *musical saw.*

sawtooth wave: In synthesis, a *waveform* in which the voltage alternately changes slowly in one direction and quickly in the other. It produces a bright, buzzy sound.

saxhorn: In the brass family, a group of valved bugles invented by Adolphe Sax.

saxophone: In the woodwind family, a group of keyed, brass instruments with conical *bores* and single-reed, clarinet-type mouthpieces. The written ranges (three octaves) on all are from B-flat below middle C to F above the staff; but they sound different since each is a transposing instrument. Following are their names and the ranges of notes as they sound:

saxophone

E-flat sopranino saxophone (straight):

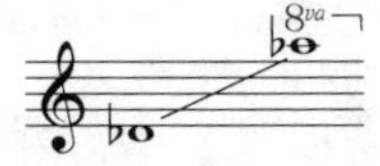

B-flat soprano saxophone (straight and curved):

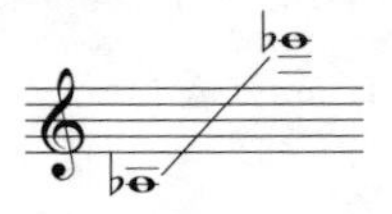

E-flat alto saxophone:

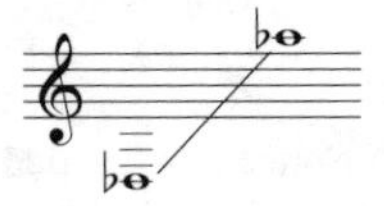

B-flat tenor saxophone:

E-flat baritone saxophone:

B-flat bass saxophone:

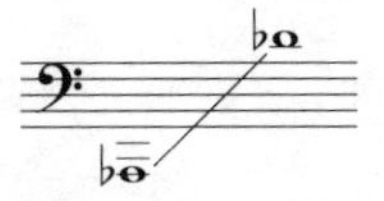

scale 1: A progression of notes in a specific order. See *Scale Chart.* **2:** The proportions of lengths or widths of strings or pipes in polyphonic instruments such as guitar, piano, and pipe organ.

scale degrees: The names and numbers for each note in the scale.

scaling: In synthesis, the degree to which a *parameter* (e.g., key number, or velocity) influences a function (e.g., *pitch*, or *envelope* times).

scat singing: A form of improvisational jazz singing using nonsense syllables.

schalmey (*SHAL-mee*)**:** See *shawm.*

scherzando, scherzhaft (*It., skehr-TSAHN-doh; Ger., SHEHRTS-hahft*)**:** Playful, light-hearted.

scherzo (*It., SKEHR-tsoh*)**:** "Joke." **1:** A piece in a lively tempo. **2:** A movement of a symphony, sonata, or quartet in quick triple time, replacing the minuet.

schmaltz (*Yiddish, shmahlts*)**:** "Fat"; "melted grease." Extreme sentimentality.

schnell (*Ger., shnel*)**:** Fast.

Schneller (*Ger., SHNEL-ler*)**:** *Inverted mordent.*

schola cantorum (*Lat., SKOH-lah kahn-TOH-room*)**:** A school of Roman monks that helped popularize Gregorian chant in the empire.

Schottische (*Ger., SHOHT-ti-sheh*)**:** "Scottish." A round dance similar to a polka, but slower.

sciolto (*It., SHOHL-toh*)**:** Easy, free.

scordatura (*It., skohr-dah-TOO-rah*)**:** On string instruments, changing the tuning of one or more strings from their standard pitch.

score: The written depiction of all the parts of a musical ensemble with the parts stacked vertically and rhythmically aligned.

scoring 1: Organizing the various instrumental parts of a piece into a score form. **2:** The art of composing a score for a film.

Scotch snap: A sixteenth note followed by a dotted eighth note: ♬.

scraped instruments: Percussion instruments with notched or ridged surfaces over which a stick is scraped to produce sound.

screw: In the violin family, the mechanism that tightens the bow hair.

scroll: In the violin family, the ornamental curled portion at the end of the *pegbox.*

Scruggs picking: Banjo *fingerpicking* style developed by Earl Scruggs, using the thumb and two fingers to play even note values with syncopated accents.
secco (*It., SEK-koh*)**:** "Dry." Unornamented.
second: The *interval* between two consecutive *degrees* of the *diatonic* scale.
secondary dominant: A dominant chord built on the fifth *degree* of a chord other than the tonic.
secondo (*It., seh-KOHN-doh*)**:** "Second." **1:** The second part. **2:** The lower part of a piano duet.
secular music: Any music that is not *sacred music.*
segno (*It., SAY-nyo*)**:** "Sign" 𝄋
segue (*It., SAY-gway*)**:** "Follows." **1:** Continue to the next movement or section without a break. **2:** Continue in the same fashion.
sehr (*Ger., zehr*)**:** Very.
semibreve: Whole note: 𝅝
semiquaver: Sixteenth note: 𝅘𝅥𝅯
semitone: One half step.
semplice (*It., sem-PLEE-cheh*)**:** Simple.
sempre (*It., SEM-preh*)**:** Always.
senza (*It., SEN-tsah*)**:** Without.
septet 1: A piece for seven instruments or voices. **2:** Seven performers.
septolet: *Septuplet.*
septuplet. Seven notes played in the time of four or six notes of equal value.
sequence 1: Repetition of the same melodic or chordal pattern at a different pitch. **2:** In synthesis: *v.*—to record incoming performance data on a *sequencer. n.*—That which is recorded by a *sequencer.* **3:** A type of *Gregorian chant* with nonbiblical texts, lines grouped in rhymed pairs, and one note per syllable. See *Requiem Mass.*
sequencer: In synthesis, a device that records and plays back incoming *MIDI* information in the order it occurs.
serenade: A love song or piece, usually performed below someone's window in the evening.
serenata (*seh-reh-NAH-tah*)**:** An 18th-century *cantata* or short *opera.*

sereno (*It., seh-REH-noh*)**:** Serene, peaceful.
serial music: A type of composition based on *twelve-tone technique*. Some such music applies this technique to dimensions other than pitch (e.g., note values, dynamic markings).
serpent: In the horn family, an S-curved wooden horn with a conical *bore,* finger holes, and a cup-shaped mouthpiece.
SESAC (*abbr., SEE-sak*)**:** Originally "Society for European Stage Authors & Composers." A performing rights society.
sestetto (*It., ses-TET-toh*)**:** *Sextet.*
seven-string guitar: A specially built guitar with a high A string.
seventh: The *interval* between the first and seventh *degrees* of the *diatonic* scale.
seventh chord: A chord built from the *root, third, fifth,* and *seventh degrees.*
sextet 1: A piece for six instruments or voices. **2:** Six performers.
sextolet: *Sextuplet.*
sextuplet: Six notes played in the time of four notes of equal value.
sforzando, sfz (*It., sfor-TSAHN-doh*)**:** A strong accent on a note.
shake: A fast *trill* upward:

shaker: A percussion instrument made up of a gourd or can filled with pebbles, seeds or beans and shaken to produce sound.
shakuhachi (*shah-koo-HAH-chee*)**:** An end-blown bamboo flute from Japan.
shanty: *Chantey, chanty.*
shape-note: A system that indicates the *degrees* of the scale by differently shaped *noteheads*, used primarily in hymnals in 18th- and 19th-century America and England.

sharp 1: *n.*—The sharp symbol ♯, indicating to raise a note one half step. **2:** *adj.*—Above normal pitch.
shawm: High-pitched double-reed, woodwind instrument from the Middle Ages and Renaissance with a *conical bore;* a forerunner of the oboe.
sheet music 1: An individually printed song, most often for voice, piano, guitar, or a combination of the three. **2** (*slang*)**:** Any printed music.

sheng: A Chinese mouth organ made up of a wind chamber fitted with pipes containing *free reeds* that vibrate when air is introduced into the chamber.

shift, shifting: On string instruments, to change the position of the fingering hand.

shivaree (*shiv-a-REE*)**:** A corruption of *charivari.*

shofar (*SHOH-far*)**:** An ancient Hebrew instrument made of a ram's horn, which may have a separate mouthpiece.

shuffle: A "skipping" rhythm, in which subdivisions of the beat are performed as long-short, rather than as equal values.

si (*see*) **1:** The seventh *degree* of the *diatonic* scale. The same as *ti.* **2:** The fifth degree of the diatonic scale (*sol*) raised a half step.

side drum: *Snare drum.*

sideman (-person): A musician who is part of a group or combo, but not the leader or soloing musician.

sightreading: Playing a piece of music at first reading.

sightsinging: Singing a piece of music at first reading.

signal: In synthesis, an electrical impulse or a *digital* representation of one.

signal processor: An electronic device that changes the characteristics of an audio signal that passes through it; an *effects* device.

signature: Signs, symbols, or numbers placed at the beginning of a staff or piece. See *key signature, time signature.*

signs: Symbols that indicate articulation, blowing, bowing, breathing, dynamics, fingering, ornamentation, pitch changes and various other effects in music.

Simandl bow (*si-MAHN-dl*)**:** For string basses, a bow configured to be held with the palm up.

similar motion: The movement of two or more parts in the same direction.

simile, sim. (*It., SEE-mee-leh, SIM-i-lee*)**:** "Like." Continue in a similar manner.

simple meter: A time signature in which the basic pulse is divisible by two (e.g., 2/4, 3/4, 4/4). See *compound meter.*

sin' (*seen*)**:** *Sino.*

sin' al fine (*It., seen-ahl-FEE-neh*)**:** To the end.

sine wave: In synthesis, a *waveform* that produces a simple, flutelike sound, having no overtones.

sinfonia (*It., seen-foh-NEE-ah, seen-FOH-nyah*) **1:** *Symphony*. **2:** A small orchestra. **3:** An overture to a *cantata, opera,* or *suite.*

sinfonietta (*It., seen-fo-NYET-tah*) **1:** A short symphony. **2:** A small symphony orchestra.

single: A recording of a one song; a *45* or a "*cassette* single." Actually contains two songs—one on each side.

single-coil pickup: An electromagnetic *pickup* with one coil wound around a single pole.

single-reed instruments: Instruments characterized by a single vibrating reed attached to or cut out of a cylindrical tube forming a mouthpiece (e.g., *clarinet*, *saxophone*).

Singspiel (*Ger., ZING-shpeel*)**:** "Sing-play." A light German opera with spoken dialogue.

sinistra (*It., SEEN-ees-trah*)**:** Left hand.

sino (*It., SEE-noh*)**:** Until.

sistrum: Ancient percussion instrument made up of metal disk rattles threaded on rods.

sitar (*si-TAR*)**:** A long-necked Indian lute with movable arched frets and three to seven strings, below which are sympathetic strings, often as many as twelve.

six-four chord: A triad of the second inversion, with a sixth and a fourth above the bass note.

sixteenth note/rest: A note/rest half the length of an eighth note and a sixteenth the length of a whole note:

sixth chord 1: A triad of the first inversion, with a sixth and a third above the bass note. **2:** An *added sixth* chord.

ska (*skah*)**:** A Jamaican pop music style, a combination of West Indian and Afro-American music styles that led into *reggae.*

Skala (*Ger., SKAH-lah*)**:** *Scale.*

skiffle: A British pop music style from the late 1950s that combined traditional jazz and blues with a simplified jug-band style of music.

skip: Melodic movement of more than a whole step.

skirl: On bagpipe, the sounds made by the upper pipes.

slave: In synthesis, *n.*—A device controlled by or operated from another device; *v.*—The act of controlling one device from another.

sleigh bells: Small notched metal bells containing steel balls, a group of which are afixed to leather straps or steel frames and shaken.

slentando (*It., slen-TAHN-doh*)**:** Gradually slower.

slide 1: To move smoothly from one note to another without the cessation of sound; *portamento.* **2:** An *ornament* consisting of two grace notes moving stepwise quickly to the principal note. **3:** The movable tube on the trombone that alters the length of the air column.

slide guitar: A technique of guitar playing in which strings are stopped by a *bottleneck* or a ring placed over one of the fretting fingers, which can slide freely along the strings.

slider: A knob on an electronic instrument that moves by means of sliding, providing continuous control over a parameter.

slit drum: A drum made from a length of wood or bamboo that is hollowed out through cuts or slits.

slur: A curved line connecting two or more notes, indicating that they are to be played *legato*.

smear: On wind instruments, a slide into a note from below. The slide is completed just prior to proceeding to the next note:

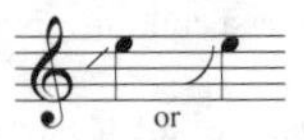

smorzando (*It., smor-TSAHN-doh*)**:** Fading away.

SMPTE (*abbr., SIMP-tee*) **1:** "Society of Motion Picture and Television Engineers." **2** (*slang*)**:** SMPTE Time Code, the standard *synchronization signal* used for television and motion picture sound.

snare drum: A small cylindrical drum with two heads. Several gut, steel or nylon wires (snares) are stretched across the bottom head, which vibrate when the top head is struck with wooden drumsticks or brushes.

so: *Sol.*

soave (*It., soh-AH-veh*)**:** Sweet, mild.

sock cymbal: *Hi-hat.*

soft pedal: On the piano, the left pedal, which softens the tone. (Also called *una corda* pedal.)

sol: The fifth note of the *diatonic* scale. G in the *fixed-do* system.

solfège, solfeggio (*Fr., sohl-FEZH; It., sohl-FED-joh*)**:** For eartraining and sightsinging, singing the degrees of the scale with syllables (do, re, mi, etc.).

solmization: The method of teaching scales and intervals using solfège.

solo (*It., Lat., Sp., SOH-loh*)**:** "Alone." To perform alone or as the predominant part.

sonare (*It., soh-NAH-reh*)**:** To sound; to ring.

sonata (*It., soh-NAH-tah*)**:** "Sounded." An instrumental piece, often in several movements.

sonata (allegro) form: The form used in the first movement of sonatas (symphonies, concerti, quartets): *exposition, development, recapitulation.*

sonatina (*It., soh-nah-TEE-nah*)**:** Short *sonata.*

song 1: A piece for voice. **2:** A piece in a lyrical style.

song cycle: A group of related songs unified by theme or lyric.

song forms: The organization of sections of a song, represented by letters that depict similar and contrasting sections: ABA, AABA, ABC, etc.

songplugger: In the music business, a person employed by a publisher who promotes songs for recording or performance.

song position pointer: In synthesis, a *MIDI* command that tells a sequencer or drum machine where to begin playing.

song select: In synthesis, a *MIDI* command that tells a sequencer's or drum machine which song in memory to play.

sopra (*It., SOH-prah*)**:** Above, over.

sopranino saxophone: See *saxophone.*

soprano: The highest female voice. The range is

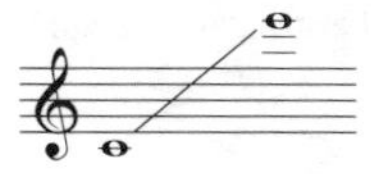

soprano clef: The C clef that places middle C on the first line of the staff:

soprano saxophone: See *saxophone.*

sordini (*It., sor-DEE-nee*)**:** The *dampers* on a piano.

sordino (*It., sor-DEE-noh*)**:** Mute.
sostenuto (*It., sohs-teh-NOO-toh*)**:** Sustained.
sotto voce (*It., SOHT-toh VOH-cheh*)**:** "Under the voice." Quietly; in soft voice.
soubrette (*Fr., soo-BRET*)**:** In opera, a soprano comedienne.
soul: In the music business, the name for Afro-American music of *rhythm and blues* origin.
soundboard: On string instruments, the top (*belly*) of the instrument, over which the strings are stretched, which serves to amplify the sound.
sound hole: On string instruments, the round or c- or *f*-shaped holes cut into the *belly*.
soundpost: In the violin family, a wooden post positioned under the *bridge*, from the *belly* to the back, that supports the belly and carries the vibrations.
Sousaphone: A tuba, made specifically for John Philip *Sousa*'s band, that encircles the body and projects the sound horizontally.
space: The interval between two lines of a *staff* or between *ledger lines*.
spacing: The vertical placement of the notes of a chord.
Spanish guitar: The traditional classical guitar, flat both front and back, with six gut or nylon strings and a standard waist.
species: A method of teaching *counterpoint* with five basic processes.
spezzato (*It., sped-ZAH-toh*)**:** Divided.
spiccato (*It., speek-KAH-toh*)**:** "Demarcated." On string instruments, a bowing technique wherein the bow (at mid bow) is bounced on the string at a moderate speed.
spike fiddle: A Middle Eastern/Asian fiddle in which the neck pierces the body and projects through the base. Held vertically, and played braced on the lap.
spill (long, short): On wind instruments, a rapid *diatonic* or *chromatic* drop:

spinet 1: A small Renaissance keyboard instrument with a plucking action like a *harpsichord*. **2:** The smallest of the upright pianos.
spirito, spiritoso (*It., SPEE-ree-toh, spee-ree-TOH-zoh*)**:** Spirit; witty.
spiritual: An Afro-American religious song.
splash cymbal: A cymbal 3" to 6" in diameter, on a stand. Its short ring is used for effect.

split keyboard: In synthesis, a keyboard that can be divided into two parts that produce different sounds.

split point: In synthesis, the point on a *split keyboard* that divides one sound from another.

spoons: Percussion instruments made of two spoons that are clapped together rhythmically.

Sprechstimme (*Ger., SHPRE[K]H-shtim-me*)**:** "Speech-voice." Half spoken, half sung.

Springer (*Ger., SHPRING-er*)**:** An *ornament* wherein the note above is played quickly following the principal note.

square wave: In synthesis, a *waveform* where the voltage is alternately high and low, which produces a hollow, reedy sound.

sringara (*srin-GAH-rah*)**:** A deep-bodied Indian fiddle with a skin *belly*, medium-length neck, and three to four bowed strings plus *sympathetic strings.*

SSA (*abbr.*)**:** In choral music—soprano, soprano, alto.

SSAA (*abbr.*)**:** In choral music—soprano, soprano, alto, alto.

staccato (*It., stahk-KAH-toh*)**:** "Detached." Short, separated notes indicated by this symbol:

staff, staves: The horizontal lines upon which music is written.

stage band: *Jazz ensemble.*

standard: In the music business, a long-lasting song that receives many *covers* over the years.

stanza (*It., STAHN-tsah, STAN-zuh*)**:** A section of a song, two or more lines long, characterized by a common meter, rhyme, and number of lines.

stationary do: *Fixed do.*

steel drums: Drums made out of various-sized oil cans. The heads are deeply incised with specific patterns that provide different pitches.

steel guitar: A guitar, positioned horizontally, whose strings are stopped by sliding a steel bar along them, rather than by fretting them with the fingers.

steel strings: Guitar or electric bass strings made out of steel.

stem: The vertical line extending from a *notehead.*

step: Melodic movement of one or two semitones.

step-time mode: In synthesis, programming each event and its timing individually, rather than performing a series of events with the desired timing. See *real-time mode.*

stesso (*It., STES-soh*)**:** Same.

stick: On string instruments, the wooden part of the bow.

Stick (Chapman): An electric 10-stringed (5 bass, 5 guitar) instrument, with a range of 5 octaves, that utilizes a tapping technique on the strings.

sticking: On drums, the specific rhythmic patterns laid out for two hands, such as *rudiments.*

Stimme (*Ger., SHTIM-me*) **1:** Voice. **2:** Vocal part.

stirato (*It., stee-RAH-toh*)**:** Slowing down; drawing out.

stop, stopped 1: On organs, a device (*flue stop, reed stop*) that controls the air to a *register.* **2:** On string instruments, to depress the string; a depressed (*stopped*) string. **3:** On horns, to insert a hand into the bell.

Strad (*slang abbr.*)**:** A "Stradivarius"—a violin made by Antonio Stradivari.

straight eighths, straight time: Eighth notes that are not played in a swing style.

strain: A musical phrase, section, or entire tune.

Strat (*slang abbr.*)**:** A Fender Stratocaster electric guitar.

strathspey (*STRATH-spee*)**:** A Scottish dance, slower than a reel, in 4/4 time using the *Scotch snap* rhythm.

street organ: Portable hand-cranked or steam-driven organ used to entertain people on the street or at fairs.

stretta (*It., STRET-tah*)**:** *Stretto* (2).

stretto (*It., STRET-toh*)**:** "Tight." **1:** In the *fugue,* the overlapping of successive entries of the *subject.* **2:** A concluding passage or coda with a faster tempo.

stride: A pop keyboard style derived from *ragtime*. The left hand style "strides" in 4/4 from a single note, octave, or tenth interval on the first and third beats to middle register chords on the second and fourth beats.

string bass: In the violin family, the lowest instrument. See *double bass.*

stringendo (*It., streen-JEN-doh*)**:** "Tightening." Hurrying the tempo; increasing the tension.

string instrument family: Instruments with strings that produce sound when *plucked, bowed,* or struck (*hammered*).

string quartet: Two violins, viola, and cello.
string quintet: Usually two violins, two violas, and cello.
string trio: Violin, viola, and cello.
stroke 1: On drums, the movement made with drum sticks or mallets. **2:** On bowed string instruments, the back and forth movement of the bow.
stromento (*It., stroh-MEN-toh*)**:** Instrument.
strophic (*STROHF-ik*)**:** A song in which all the verses are sung to the same melody.
strum: On string instruments, to stroke a pick or a finger rapidly over the strings.
struts: On guitars, the bars braced inside to give it strength, and stability and to control the direction of the vibrations.
Stück (*Ger., sht[u]ek*)**:** Piece, composition.
studio musician: In the music business, a free-lance musician who works primarily in recording studios.
study score: *Miniature score.*
Stufe (*Ger., SHTOO-fe*)**:** Step or degree of the scale.
subdominant: The fourth *degree* of the *diatonic* scale.
subito (*It., SOO-bee-toh*)**:** Suddenly, immediately.
subject: A *theme* or *motif* that is the basis for a musical form, as in the *fugue* or *sonata.*
submediant: The sixth *degree* of the *diatonic* scale.
suboctave 1: The octave below a given note. **2:** An organ *coupler* producing the octave below.
subtonic: The flatted seventh *degree* of the *diatonic* scale, a whole step below the *tonic.* See *leading note/tone.*
suite (*Fr., s[u]eet, sweet*)**:** A group of short instrumental movements, usually in the same key and in dance forms.
sul (*It., sool*)**:** "On the."
sul ponticello (*It., sool pohn-tee-CHEL-loh*)**:** On bowed string instruments, bowing on or next to the bridge, producing a glassy sound.
sul tasto (*It., sool TAHS-toh*)**:** On the *fingerboard.*
superdominant: The sixth *degree* of the *diatonic* scale. Same as *submediant.*
supertonic: The second *degree* of the *diatonic* scale.
sur (*Fr., s[u]er*)**:** On, over.

suspension: In counterpoint, when a *consonant* note is sustained while another voice moves, resulting in a *dissonance* that is then resolved.
sussurando (*It., soos-soor-RAHN-doh*)**:** Whispering, murmuring.
sustain pedal: On the piano, the pedal depressed by the right foot that raises the *dampers,* allowing the strings to vibrate freely. Also called *damper pedal.*
svelto (*It., ZVEL-toh*)**:** Quick, light.
sweetening (*slang*)**:** In recording, to add instrumental parts (such as strings) or effects (such as *reverb*) to create a more lush sound.
sweet potato (*slang*)**:** *Ocarina.*
swell 1: Gradual *crescendo.* **2:** On organ, a *manual* that controls registers capable of *crescendo* or *diminuendo.*
swing 1: Jazz-flavored big band music of the 1930s. **2:** The essence of jazz, denoting its improvisational, rhythmic feel.
swing time: In jazz, when eighth notes are given a *long-short* rhythmic emphasis.
switch: A percussion instrument, made up of wires bound at one end, that is struck against the hand.
sympathetic string: On string instruments, a string that vibrates without being bowed or plucked, in response to the vibrations of strings that are bowed or plucked.
symphonic band: *Concert band.*
symphonic poem: An orchestral piece based on an extramusical idea—a tone picture.
symphony 1: A piece for large orchestra, usually in four movements, in which the first movement often is in *sonata* form. **2:** A large orchestra.
synchronize: To operate something in time with something else.
syncopation: The placement of rhythmic accents on weak beats or weak portions of beats.
synthesis (*Gr.*)**:** "To put together." Manipulating sound electronically.
synthesizer: An instrument that can produce and manipulate sound electronically.
syrinx (*SEER-inks*)**:** *Panpipes.*
system: Two or more staves connected together.

T

t. (*abbr.*)**:** *Tasto, tempo, trill, tre, tutti.*

T. (*abbr.*)**:** *Tenor, tonic.*

TAB (*abbr.*)**:** *Tablature.*

tabla (*TAH-blah*)**:** A conical wooden Indian drum with three skins on the head. Beaten with the hands; usually played in multiples tuned chromatically.

tablature: A type of notation developed for fretted string instruments in the 16th century. Lines indicate strings and numbers indicate frets. See *Guitar Tablature Notation Guide.*

tabor (*TAY-bor*)**:** In the percussion family, the earliest form of the snare drum, which evolved into a military instrument.

tacet (*Lat., TAH-chet, TA-set*)**:** "Be silent." In instrumental or choral parts, a direction to refrain from playing or singing.

tactus (*Lat., TAHK-toos*)**:** In the 15th century, prior to bar lines, the measurement of the length of a beat.

tag: The ending of a piece, often the *coda.*

taking fours/eights: *Trading fours/eights.*

talking drum: West African *waisted* drums, beaten with a curved stick, whose pitch is varied by adjusting the tension of the lacing. They imitate the tonal quality of the language.

talon: In the violin family, the *nut* of the bow.

tambour (*Fr., taw[n]-BOOR*)**:** Drum.

tambourine: In the percussion family, a small, hand-held frame fitted with *jingles* and with our without a single head of parchment or plastic.

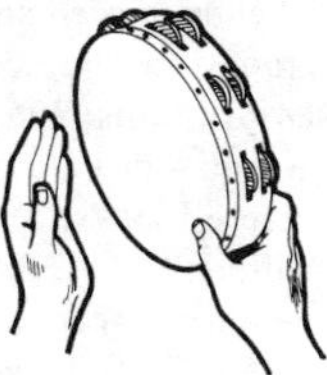

tambourine

tambur, tambura (*tahm-BOOR, tahm-BOO-rah*)**:** Long-necked, round-bodied lutes. Indian *tambura* have four strings, drones and a movable ivory bridge to adjust pitch. Balkan *tambura* are fretted.

tamburo (*It., tahm-BOO-roh*)**:** Drum.

tam-tam: In the percussion family, a large, flat, thin metal saucer suspended on a frame and struck with a soft beater; produces a slightly dissonant sound. See *gong.*

tangent: On the clavichord, the brass blade that presses the string and determines the pitch of the note.

tango (*Sp., TAHN-goh*)**:** A sensual Argentinian dance in syncopated 2/4 time, with the following rhythm:

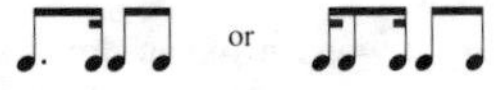

tanto (*It., TAHN-toh*)**:** Much, so much.

Tanz (*Ger., tahnts*)**:** Dance.

tapping-on: On guitar or electric bass, sounding a note by *hammering-on* a string with the *picking* hand.

tarantella (*It., tah-rahn-TEL-lah*)**:** A fast Italian dance in 6/8 time.

tardando (*It., tar-DAHN-doh*)**:** Becoming slower.

tardo, tardamente (*It., TAR-doh, tar-dah-MEN-teh*)**:** Slow, slowly.

Taste (*Ger., TAHS-te*)**:** Key of keyboard instrument.

tasto (*It., TAHS-toh*) **1:** Keyboard. **2:** Fingerboard or fretboard.

technic, technique (*TEK-nik, tek-NEEK*)**:** The skill of performance.

Te Deum (*Lat., teh DEH-oom*)**:** "To You, God." A Christian hymn of praise, based on Psalm 95.

tema (*It., TEH-mah*)**:** Theme.

temperament: A system of tuning where pure intervals are altered slightly to accommodate playing in different keys.

tempestoso (*It., tem-pes-TOH-zoh*)**:** Stormy.

temple bells: Large Far Eastern suspended bells, usually housed in temples, that are struck with a wooden beam or mallet.

temple blocks: In the percussion family, Far Eastern hollow blocks of different sizes, made of camphor wood and suspended on a rack in sets of three, five, or seven, and struck with mallets.

tempo (*It., TEM-poh*)**:** "Time." The pace of a piece of music.

tempo markings: The indications of the pace of the music, such as *largo, moderato, allegro,* and the metronome marking (see *M.M.*).

temps (*Fr., tah[n]*)**:** Beat.

tenor: "Holder." **1:** A high male voice between alto and baritone. (In early polyphonic music, it sang the *cantus firmus* in long, "held" notes.) It has the following range:

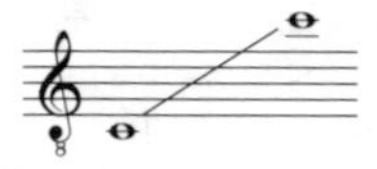

2: Instruments in the tenor range.

tenor banjo: See *banjo.*

tenor clef: A *C clef* falling on the fourth line of the staff:

tenor drum: An snareless orchestral drum, in between a snare or side drum and bass drum in size.

tenor saxophone: See *saxophone.*

tenor trombone: See *trombone.*

tenth: An *interval* of an octave and a third.

tenuto, ten. (*It., teh-NOO-toh*)**:** "Held." **1:** Hold a note for full value. **2:** The tenuto symbol .

ternary form: A compositional form in which an initial section is followed by a contrasting section, which is followed by a return of the initial section (ABA). See *song forms.*

tertian harmony (*TER-shan*)**:** Standard western harmony based on *thirds* or *triads.*

tessitura (*It., tes-see-TOO-rah*)**:** The average highness or lowness in pitch of a vocal piece.

tetrachord (*TET-rah-kord*)**:** A scale of four notes. The *diatonic* scale is made up of two tetrachords; a *twelve-tone row* is made up of three tetrachords.

texture: The number of parts (voices) in a piece and their relation to one another. Thus, there can be *monophonic, homophonic,* and *polyphonic* textures.

theme 1: The musical *subject* of a piece (usually a melody), as in *sonata form* or a *fugue.* **2:** An extramusical concept behind a piece.

theme and variations: A statement of a musical subject followed by restatements in different guises.

theorbo (*thee-OR-boh*)**:** In the lute family, a 16th-century *archlute* or bass lute with numerous *stopped* and *unstopped strings* attached to a separate *pegbox.*

theory: The study of how music is put together.

Theremin (*THEHR-e-min*)**:** An electronic instrument played by moving the hands relative to two antennas.

thesis (*Gr., THEE-sis*)**:** Downbeat or strong beat.

third: An *interval* of three *diatonic* scale degrees.

third-stream: Music that combines elements of jazz and classical styles.

thirty-second note/rest: A note/rest that is half the length of a sixteenth note, and one thirty-second the length of a whole note: 𝅘𝅥𝅰 𝅀

thoroughbass: *Basso continuo.*

three-part form: *Ternary form.*

through-composed: Songs in which the music for each *stanza* differs; in contrast to *strophic.*

thumb piano: See *m'bira.*

thumb-string: On a banjo, the string that carries the melody.

ti (*tee*)**:** The seventh degree of the *diatonic* scale. The same as *si* (1).

tibia (*TIB-ee-ah*) **1:** An organ *stop*. **2:** A Greek *aulos* made out of bone.

tie: A curved line ⁀ connecting two notes of the same pitch, indicating they are to be played as one note.

tied bridge: On guitar, a bridge to which strings can be tied.

timbale, timbales, timballo (*teem-BAH-leh*) **1:** Timpani. **2:** Latin American drums, similar to *bongos,* suspended on a stand in twos or threes, and struck with a stick.

timbral (*TAM-brul*)**:** Having to do with *timbre.*

timbre (*TAM-br*)**:** Tone color or quality.

timbrel (*TIM-brel*)**:** Middle eastern *tambourine.*

time 1: Meter—the number of beats in a measure. **2:** The duration of notes.

time signature: The numbers at the beginning of a piece:

The top number indicates the number of beats in a measure; the bottom number indicates the type of note that receives one beat.

timing clock: In synthesis, a *MIDI real time message* that sends out a code for synchronizing *sequencers*, drum machines, and other devices.

timpani: In the percussion family, large kettle-shaped drums of copper or brass, mounted on legs. The heads are tuned with large screws and beaten with *mallets.*

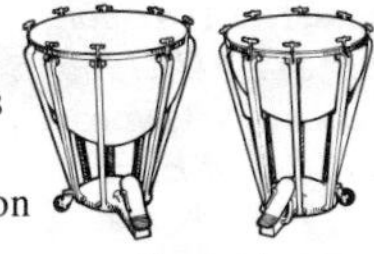
timpani

tine: A metal tuning fork that produces a note on electric pianos such as the *Rhodes piano.*

Tin Pan Alley: Early 20th-century location for the pop music business in the area around 28th Street in New York City.

tin whistle: A high-pitched, end-blown Irish flute with six holes, made out of metal.

toccata (*It., tohk-KAH-tah*)**:** "Touched." A piece, usually for keyboard instruments, featuring fast scales or arpeggios.

tolling: The sound of ringing church bells.

tom-tom: A barrel-shaped double-headed drum, tuned by rings that are moved up and down the lacing holding the heads.

Ton (*Ger., tohn*)**:** Sound, note.

tonal: Pertaining to *tone*, *key,* or *mode.*

tonality: The relationship of a piece to a *tonic* note.

tone 1: A note; the basis of music. **2:** The interval of a second, see *whole tone.*

tonebars: *Drawbars.*

tone cluster: A group of notes—seconds or dissonants—played simultaneously, often with the fist or arm.

tone color: The quality of sound of an instrument or voice.

tone poem: An orchestral work, usually in one continuous movement. See *symphonic poem.*

tone row: In *serial* and *twelve tone* music, the order of twelve notes in a piece as chosen by the composer.

Tonette: In the wind family, a wood or plastic end-blown flute with finger holes.

tone wheel: A spinning disk that generates sound electromagnetically in early electric organs.

tonguing: On wind instruments, articulation with the tongue.

tonic: The first *degree* (I) of the scale; the *keynote.*

tonic accent: Emphasis placed on a note by placing it at a higher pitch than those around it. See *agogic accent, dynamic accent.*

tono (*It., TOH-noh*)**:** Tone, key, pitch.

tosto (*It., TOHS-toh*)**:** Quick.

touch: On keyboards, the manner in which the keys are depressed.

touche (*Fr., toosh*) **1:** A key of a keyboard instrument. **2:** A fret. **3:** Fingerboard.

touch sensitivity: In synthesis, response of a MIDI keyboard*controller* to how quickly the keys are depressed (*velocity sensitivity*) or how much pressure is applied after they are depressed (*pressure sensitivity*).

tr (*abbr.*)**:** Trill.

track: In recording, the electronic "pathways" on which sound is recorded.

tracking: On MIDI guitars or guitar synthesizers, the accuracy and speed with which they can follow the player.

trading fours/eights: In jazz during improvisational passages, when the various performers each take four or eight measures of solo.

train wreck (*slang*)**:** When the parts in an ensemble "collide" because the musicians are not playing together.

tranquillo (*It., trahn-KWEEL-loh*)**:** Calm.

transcription 1: An arrangement of piece written for one music medium into another. **2:** A note-for-note arrangement of a piece off a recording.

transition: The change of key or theme within a passage or entire piece.

transpose, transposition (*v., n.*)**:** Changing a piece from one key to another.

transposing instruments: Instruments that sound different notes than written.

transverse flute: The modern flute, held horizontally (see *flute*).

Travis picking: Guitar *fingerpicking* style developed by Merle Travis, featuring syncopated melodic arpeggios over an evenly alternating bass.

re (*It., treh*)**:** Three.

reble: The highest voice, instrument, or part.

reble clef: The G clef 𝄞 falling on the second line of the staff.

remolando (*It., treh-moh-LAHN-doh*)**:** Trembling, with tremolo.

remolo (*It., TREH-moh-loh*)**:** "Tremulous." **1:** On keyboards, the rapid alternation of two or more notes. **2:** On string instruments, the rapid alternation of very short up and down bows on a single note. **3:** On brass instruments, reiteration of a note with *flutter tonguing.* **4:** In synthesis and on the pipe organ, a special effect achieved via a change in the *amplitude* of the sound. **5** (*slang*)**:** *Vibrato.*

remolo arm: See *whammy bar.*

repak (*TREH-pahk*)**:** A quick Russian (Cossak) dance in 2/4 time.

rès (*Fr., treh*)**:** Very.

riad: A chord of three notes: root, third, fifth.

riangle: In the percussion family, a thin round steel bar bent in the shape of a triangle, struck with a steel beater or wooden stick.

rill: An ornament consisting of the rapid alternation of two adjacent notes—the main note and the note a half or a whole step above it:

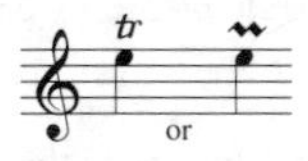

rio 1: A piece for three instruments or voices. **2:** Three performers. **3:** The middle section in minuets, scherzos, and marches, often written in three-part harmony.

rio sonata: A *baroque* form of *chamber music* consisting of two melodic parts plus *basso continuo.*

riple meter: Time signatures with three beats to a measure.

riplet: Three notes that are played in the time of two notes of equal value.

riplet feel: *Shuffle.*

riple tonguing: On flute and brass instruments, a technique of rapidly articulating notes using the front and the back of the tongue ("t-t-k-t-t-k").

ritone (*TREI-tohn*)**:** The interval of an *augmented* fourth or *diminished* fifth—three *whole tones.*

trois (*Fr., trwah*)**:** Three.

tromba (*It., TROHM-bah*)**:** Trumpet.

trombone: In the brass family, a large resonant instrument of the trumpet family with a straight and cyclindrical *bore,* a flared bell, a cup-shaped mouthpiece, and either a U-shaped slide that lengthens the tube (slide trombone) or a set of valves (valve trombone).

trombone

Tenor:

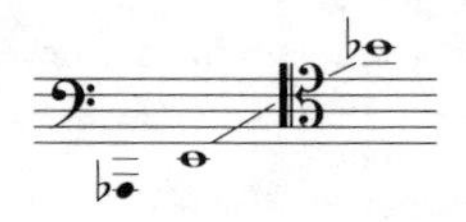

B-flat Bass:

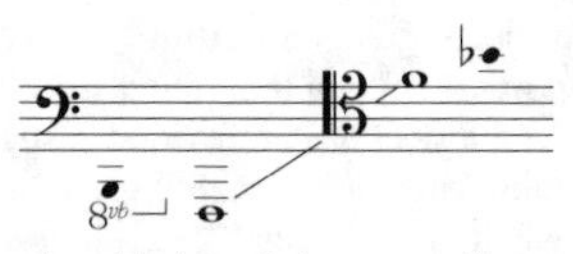

trope: Words and music added to *plainsong* or liturgy.

troppo (*It., TROHP-poh*)**:** Too much.

troubadour: A wandering minstrel—combination poet and musician—who travelled through western Europe in the Middle Ages.

trumpet: In the brass family, an instrument with a straight and cyclindrical *bore* (*tube*) and small flared bell, and a cup-shaped mouthpiece. The modern trumpet is curved with valves and produces a brilliant sound.

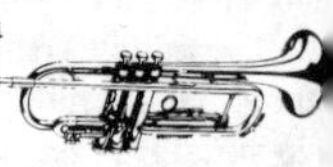

trumpet

B-flat trumpet:

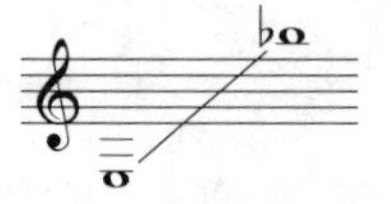

C trumpet:

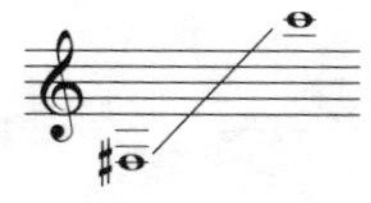

F trumpet:

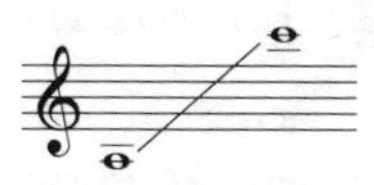

B-flat Piccolo trumpet:

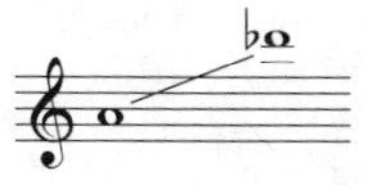

russ rod: In the guitar family, a metal rod set into the neck of the guitar to prevent warping.

TB (*abbr.*)**:** In choral music—tenor, tenor, bass.

TBB (*abbr.*)**:** In choral music—tenor, tenor, bass (or baritone), bass.

uba: In the brass family, a large, deep-sounding, curved valved horn with a wide conical *bore,* a flared *bell,* and a cup-shaped mouthpiece.

tuba

BB-flat:

E-flat:

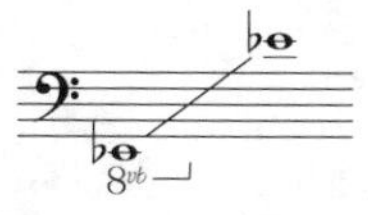

F bass:

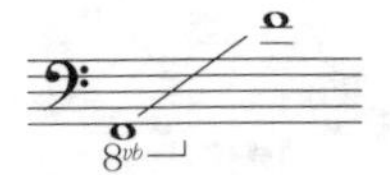

tubular bells, tubular chimes: A set of brass or steel tubes in graduate lengths, tuned chromatically, hanging on a frame with foot dampers, an struck with a mallet.

tune 1: A melody. **2:** The correct pitch (in tune).

tuner: A thumb-screw on the tailpiece of an instrument in the violi family whose purpose is to allow easy fine-tuning of the attached string.

tuning: Adjusting the intonation of an instrument to its desired pitch(es).

tuning fork: A two-tined metal device that, when struck, produces a pur single note.

tuplet (*TUP-let*)**:** A group of notes that, instead of following norm subdivisions of the beat or bar, consists of more or fewer notes of equ value. Examples include the *duplet, triplet,* and *quintuplet.*

turn: An ornament consisting of four to five notes that make a "turn around a note:

tutti (*It., TOOT-tee*)**:** "All." In instrumental music, the term used fo entrance of the full ensemble.

twelve-bar blues: An Afro-American music form using three chords- tonic, subdominant, and dominant—and the blues scale in specific ord within twelve bars. The basis for rock music.

twelve-string guitar: A steel-strung guitar with twelve strings tuned pairs: the bottom four sets are tuned in octaves, the top two sets a tuned in unison.

twelve-tone scale: A scale constructed of all twelve half steps (semitone within an octave organized in a specific order called a *tone row.*

twelve-tone technique: In composition, the arrangement by the composer of the twelve notes of the chromatic scale into a *tone row*, which serves as the basis for composition.
two-part form: *Binary form.*
two step: A quick-tempo Country & Western dance.
tympani: *Timpani.*

U

ud (*ood*)**:** *Oud.*
ukulele (*oo-koo-LEH-leh, yoo-kuh-LAY-lee*)**:** In the guitar family, a small fretted four-string Hawaiian instrument, tuned G, C, E, A.
una corda (*It., oo-nah KOR-dah*)**:** "One string." *Soft pedal.*
unequal temperament: Any system of *temperament* where the octave is divided into twelve intervals that are not all the same size.
unequal voices: Mixed men's and women's voices.
unison: Two or more notes or parts sounding at the same pitch.
un peu (*Fr., uh[n] PE[R]*)**:** A little.
un poco (*It., oon POH-koh*)**:** A little.
unruhig (*Ger., oon-ROO-ee[s]h*)**:** Restless.
upbeat 1: *Pickup, anacrusis.* **2:** The unaccented beat of a measure. **3:** Happy or *up-tempo.*
up bow: In violin family music, stroking the bow upward from the *point.* The symbol is: V
upright 1: In the pianoforte family, a piano in which the strings and soundboard are vertical, rather than horizontal. **2:** Especially such an instrument at least 46" or so tall (distinct from the shorter *console* or *spinet*). **3** (*slang*)**:** The double bass, to distinguish it from the electric bass.

up-tempo: Fast.

Urtext (*Ger., OOR-text*)**:** "Pure text." An edition of a composition that attempts to represent the composer's original notation, without editorial additions—in contrast to so-called performer's, or practical, editions.

ut (*Lat., oot*) **1:** Another name for *do*. **2:** The note C.

ut supra (*Lat., oot SOO-prah*)**:** As before, as above.

V

V. (*abbr.*)**:** *Verse, vide, violin, voice, voce, volti.*

valse (*Fr., vahlss*)**:** Waltz.

valve: On brass instruments, a cylindrical device (piston or rotary) that enables the instrument to produce chromatic notes by shortening or lengthening the column of vibrating air.

valve instruments: Instruments with *valves*.

vamp: *n.*—A short introduction or accompaniment to a song that is repeated until the singer is ready to continue on. *v.*—To play such a repeated passage.

variable: In synthesis, any *controller* or *parameter* that can be altered.

variation: The modification of a theme, figure, or passage by means of melodic, rhythmic, *contrapuntal,* or harmonic changes.

vaudeville (*VAW-de-vil, VAWD-vil*) **1:** In 18th-century France, a popular, often satirical or topical, song. **2:** An opera filled with such songs. **3:** A variety show with music, dancing, and comedy.

VCA (*abbr.*)**:** "Voltage-Controlled Amplifier." In synthesis, a device that controls the level of a signal in proportion to the level of a controlling voltage.

VCF (*abbr.*): "Voltage-Controlled Filter." In synthesis, a device that controls the harmonic content of a signal in proportion to the level of a controlling voltage.

VCO (*abbr.*): "Voltage-Controlled Oscillator." In synthesis, a device that controls the frequency of a signal in proportion to the level of a controlling voltage.

velato (*It., veh-LAH-toh*): Veiled.

velocity: In synthesis, the MIDI code that transmits dynamics.

velocity sensitivity: In synthesis, the ability to respond to how quickly a key is pressed or how hard it strikes the keybed.

Venetian school: Late-Renaissance group of composers in Venice whose style included *polychoral* textures and the foundations of *orchestration.*

vent (*Fr., vah[n]*): Wind.

Ventil, ventile (*Ger., fen-TEEL; It., ven-TEE-leh*): Valve.

verhallend (*Ger., fehr-HAHL-lent*): Fading away.

verismo (*It., veh-REE-zmoh*): "Realism." A style of late-romantic Italian opera that emphasized realistic plots.

verse 1: The solo portion of an *anthem.* **2:** In popular music, the *stanza*, which tells the story of the song, changing with each repeat.

Vespers: In liturgical churches, the daily evening service. See *Matins*.

vessel: In the percussion family, instruments such as pots, cans, bottles, cups, bowls, or gourds, sometimes filled with water, that are tapped with the hand or a stick.

vibes, vibraharp, vibraphone: A *xylophone* with metal bars and a wide tremolo effect produced by electrically operated fans at the upper ends of the resonators.

vibraslap: In the percussion family, a U-shaped metal handle with a ball on one end and a triangular wood box on the other, which, when struck together with the fist, produce a sustained rattle.

vibraphone

vibration: A rapid back-and-forth movement.

vibrato (*It., vee-BRAH-toh*): "Shaking." Repeated fluctuation of pitch.

vibrola (*vee-BROH-lah, vei-BROH-lah*): On electric guitars, a device that alters the pitch of the strings. *Whammy bar.*

vide (*Fr., veed*)**:** "Empty." Open.

vide (*Lat., VEE-deh*)**:** "See." An optional omission or cut, e.g. from "Vi-" to "-de".

vielle (*vee-EL*)**:** A medieval fiddle with three to five strings, one of which was a drone, a flat back, and front or rear tuning pegs. See also *hurdy-gurdy.*

vigoroso (*It., vee-goh-ROH-soh*)**:** Vigorous, strong.

vihuela (*vee-WEH-lah*)**:** In the guitar family, a six-string Spanish Renaissance instrument with a guitar shape, but tuned like a lute.

vina (*VEE-nah*)**:** An Indian string instrument composed of: **1:** a long stick-like, unfretted fingerboard resting on two resonating gourds; or **2:** a wooden body with a wide fretted neck and one gourd.

viola (*vee-OH-lah*)**:** In the violin family, the alto instrument played under the chin, employing the alto (C) or treble (G) clefs with four strings tuned C, G, D, A and with the following range:

viola da braccio (*vee-OH-lah dah BRAH-choh*)**:** "Arm viol." In the viol family, the tenor viol played held on the arm.

viola da gamba (*vee-OH-lah dah GAHM-bah*)**:** "Leg viol." In the viol family, the bass viol played held between the knees.

viola d'amore (*vee-OH-lah dah-MOH-reh*)**:** "Love viol." In the viol family, an unfretted tenor instrument with seven strings and seven to fourteen sympathetic strings.

viol family (*VEI-ohl*)**:** A family of bowed, fretted, six-string instruments from the 16th and 17th centuries, characterized by a flat back and sloping shoulders. The common sizes were treble, tenor, and bass.

violin: In the violin family, the treble instrument played under the chin, employing the treble (G) clef with four strings tuned G, D, A, E and with the following range:

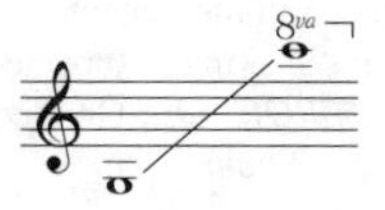

violin

violin family: A family of bowed, four-string instruments from the 17th century, tuned in fifths and characterized by rounded backs and shoulders, f-shaped sound holes, deep middle *bouts.* See *violin, viola, violoncello, string bass.*

violoncello (*vee-oh-lohn-CHEL-loh*)**:** In the violin family, the tenor instrument played held between the knees, employing the bass clef, with four strings tuned C, G, D, A and with the following range:

virginal: In the harpsichord family, a small, soft-sounding, box-shaped 16th-century keyboard.

virtuoso: A brilliant, skillful performer.

vivace (*It., vee-VAH-cheh*)**:** Lively, brisk, quick, bright.

vivo (*It., VEE-voh*)**:** Lively, bright.

Vl., Vln. (*abbr.*)**:** Violin.

Vla. (*abbr.*)**:** Viola.

Vlc. (*abbr.*)**:** Violoncello.

vocalise (*Fr., voh-kah-LEEZ*)**:** A vocal exercise sung to vowels.

vocalization: Practicing singing with exercises.

vocal score: In large vocal works, a complete score, but with the instrumental parts arranged for keyboard. See *vocal selections.*

vocal selections: In large vocal works (especially musicals and operettas), a collection of selected vocal numbers, with the instrumental parts arranged for keyboard. See *vocal score.*

vocal tenor clef: The G clef used for the tenor part in vocal music; pitched an octave below *treble clef*:

voce (*It., VOH-cheh*)**:** Voice.

Vocoder (*VOH-coh-der*)**:** In synthesis, a device that analyzes an incoming signal (usually vocal) and applies the profile of its harmonic spectrum to another signal. It is often used to make instruments "talk" or "sing."

voice 1: The sound produced by human and some animal vocal cords. **2:** In *contrapuntal* music, an instrumental or vocal part. **3:** In synthesis, a note of *polyphony.*

voice leading: In *polyphonic* music, the movement of the individual voices in a harmonic progression.

voicing 1: The vertical (chordal) arrangement of voices or instrumental parts. **2:** On organs, the tonal adjustment of the pipes. On pianos, the adjusment of the hammers for tone quality.

voile (*Fr., vwahl*)**:** Veiled.

voix (*Fr., vwah*)**:** Voice.

Volkslied (*Ger., FOHKS-leet*)**:** Folk song.

volta (*It., VOHL-tah*)**:** Time, occurrence. For example "seconda volta" (or "2a volta") indicates how something is to be played the second time—i.e., upon repeating the passage.

voltage control: A technology used in early synthesizers; functions were controlled by varying voltages.

volti (*It., VOHL-tee*)**:** Turn [the page].

volti subito (*It., VOHL-tee SOO-bee-toh*)**:** Turn [the page] quickly.

volume: Loudness.

voluntary: An organ solo, often extemporaneous, played before or after a church service, or at some other place appropriate for meditation.

Vorschlag (*Ger., FOR-shlahk*)**:** *Appoggiatura.*

Vorspiel (*Ger., FOR-shpeel*)**:** Overture, prelude.

vox (*Lat., vohx*)**:** Voice.

V.S. (*abbr.*)**:** *Volti Subito.*

v.v. (*abbr.*) **1:** Violins. **2:** Verses.

W

Wagner tubas (Tuben) (*Ger., TOO-ben*)**:** Five-valved horns with funnel-shaped mouthpieces designed by Richard Wagner for use in his *The Ring of the Nibelung.*

wah: On brass instruments, an articulation made by opening and closing a cup *mute* over the bell of the horn, producing a full-toned "wah" sound:

wah-wah: On electric guitars and basses, a special effect that produces a "wah" sound by sweeping a resonant filter up and down the frequency spectrum.

waist: A narrowing in the middle of the body of an instrument, resulting in a shape like an hourglass. Typical of most string instruments and some drums.

waits 1: Medieval guards who sounded the hours on instruments (*shawms*). **2:** Itinerant street musicians.

Waldhorn (*Ger., VAHLT-horn*)**:** "Forest horn," hunting horn. A natural horn with a narrow cylindrical *bore* and flaring bell, used in orchestras in the 18th century.

walking bass: A bass line of steady quarter or eighth notes, usually moving stepwise.

waltz: A late-18th-century dance in moderate triple time, and the music written for it.

washboard: A laundry board made of wood or metal and scraped with a rod or played with metal thimbles; used in Afro-American early jazz and English *skiffle*.

waveform: In synthesis, the shape of sound as produced by an *oscillator;* it determines the timbre of the sound. See *sawtooth, sine, square.*

wehmütig (*Ger., veh-M[U]E-tee[s]h*)**:** Sad.

well-temperament, well-tempered: A system of tuning that can be played in all twelve key signatures in which the octave is divided into twelve unequal parts. See *equal temperament.*

Werk(e) (*Ger., VEHRK [-e]*)**:** Work(s); composition(s).

whammy bar: On guitar, a device that changes the pitches of the strings by moving the bridge with a type of spring action. *Vibrola.*

whistle 1: A simple end-blown flute that produces just one shrill sound. **2:** A human musical sound produced by puckering the lips and blowing.

whistle flute: A simple end-blown flute made of bone, wood, metal, clay, cane, or plastic, with a basic mouthpiece and fingerholes, which produces a shrill, high sound.

whole note/rest: A note/rest equal to two half notes or four quarter notes:

o -

whole step: Two half steps; a major second.

whole tone: A whole step.

whole-tone scale: A scale made up solely of whole tones. See *Scale Chart: Other Scales.*

wide lip trill: On brass instruments, a slow trill employing a wider interval than a *lip trill.*

wind chimes: In the percussion family, varied lengths of wood, cane, metal, or stone, strung to hang on a frame, and sounded by striking or by the wind blowing.

wind instrument family: Instruments in which sound is produced by the vibration of air, including *brass* and *woodwind* instruments.

wire brush: In the percussion family, a stick with wire brush at the end used to strike suspended cymbals or drums.

wolf 1: On keyboard instruments, a note or interval that does not sound well due to *unequal temperament.* **2:** On string instruments, a jarring note due to a faulty string or "rogue" vibrations.

WoO (*abbr., Ger.*)**:** "Werk ohne Opuszahl"; "Work without opus number." A system of catalog numbers for identifying works by Beethoven that do not have opus numbers.

wood blocks: In the percussion family, hollow hardwood blocks, either cylindrical (two-tone), tulip-shaped, or rectangular, that are struck with a hard stick.

woodwind family: Instruments, originally made of wood, in which sound is produced by the vibration of air, including *recorders, flutes, clarinets, saxophones, oboes,* and *bassoons.*

woodwind quintet: Flute, clarinet, oboe, French horn, and bassoon.

word painting: In vocal music, when the music reflects the meaning of the words (e.g., fast passages for "running," or dissonances for "anguish").

work song: An Afro-American rhythmic song used to accompany any type of work that required specific rhythms such as picking cotton or laying railroad ties.

world music: In the music business, a *chart* term for recordings featuring foreign music of a folk character.

wuchtig (*Ger., VOO[K]H-tee[s]h*)**:** "Weighty." Ponderous, slow.

würdig (*Ger., V[U]ER-dee[s]h*)**:** "Worthy." Dignified.

X

xylophone: In the percussion family, a set of tuned wooden bars laid horizontally on a frame in the manner of piano keys. The bars are struck with sticks. Many models have tubular *resonators* beneath the bars.

xylophone

Xylotone: Trademarked name for a hand-held electronic musical instrument with a membrane-switch keyboard.

Y

yodel: A type of singing, originally from Switzerland and Austrian Tyrol (also used in American western music), where the voice jumps and glissandos between natural and falsetto.

Z

zapateado (*tsah-pah-teh-AH-doh*)**:** A Spanish dance in triple time characterized by rhythmic heel stamping.

zarzuela (*tsar-TSWEH-lah*)**:** A one- to three-act Spanish play with songs, or a comic opera.

Zeitmass (*Ger., TSEIT-mahss*)**:** Tempo.

ziemlich (*Ger., TSEEM-lee[s]h*)**:** Rather, quite.

Zigeunermusik (*Ger., tsee-GOY-ner-moo-zik*)**:** Gypsy music.

Zink (*Ger., tsink*)**:** *Cornett.*

zither: A family of string instruments where the strings run the entire length of a flat body, such as *Autoharp, dulcimer, Hummel, koto, psaltery.*

zone: In synthesis, a range over which a voice sounds. If zones overlap, the result is *layering*; if they don't, the result is a *split.*

zusammen (*Ger., tsoo-ZAHM-men*)**:** Together.

Zwischenspiel (*Ger., TSVISH-en-shpeel*)**:** Interlude.

zydeco (*ZEI-de-koh*)**:** A style of popular music that mixes Cajun and Afro-Caribbean with rhythm & blues.

Dictionary of Composers and Lyricists

A

Adam, Adolphe (1803–1856)**:** French romantic composer of operas, ballets, and sacred music. He wrote the music for the ballet *Giselle* and the song "Cantique de Noël" ("O Holy Night").

Adams, Stanley (b. 1907)**:** American lyricist, for many years the President of *ASCAP*. His songs include "My Shawl," "Spellbound," and "What a Diff'rence a Day Makes."

Addinsell, Richard (1904–1977)**:** British composer of music for film, stage, and radio. Most famous for the *Warsaw Concerto.*

Adler, Richard (b. 1921)**:** American composer, who collaborated with Jerry *Ross* on the musicals *The Pajama Game* ("Hey There," "Hernando's Hideaway") and *Damn Yankees* ("Whatever Lola Wants," "Heart"), as well as the song "Rags to Riches."

Alberti, Domenico (c. 1710–1740)**:** Italian preclassical composer, harpsichordist, and singer. Wrote harpsichord music and operas. His use of a certain arpeggiated accompaniment figure gave rise to the term *Alberti bass.*

Albéniz, Isaac (1860–1909)**:** Spanish composer and pianist. A central figure in establishing a nationalistic style. Tango in D is one of his best-known works.

Albinoni, Tomaso (1671–1751)**:** Italian baroque composer. The Adagio in G minor for Organ and Strings is his most famous work.

Anderson, Leroy (1908–1975)**:** American composer and arranger of orchestral works, best known for the pieces he wrote for the Boston Pops Orchestra, such as "Syncopated Clock," "Blue Tango," and "Sleigh Ride."

Antheil, George (1900–1959)**:** American composer. His most famous works include the "Airplane" Sonata for piano and the *Ballet Mécanique.*

Arensky, Anton (1861–1906)**:** Russian romantic composer of works in many genres, including opera, orchestral, chamber, and piano music.

Arlen, Harold (1905–1986)**:** American song composer. "Stormy Weather" and "Over the Rainbow" are two of his most popular songs.

Arne, Thomas Augustine (1710–1778)**:** British classical composer of operas, oratorios, and vocal works. He wrote the music to the song "Rule, Britannia."

Arnold, Malcolm (b. 1921)**:** British composer, primarily of instrumental music. He wrote the score for the film *The Bridge on the River Kwai.*

Ashman, Howard (1950–1991)**:** American lyricist and author, collaborator with Alan *Menken*. His works include lyrics for the musical *Little Shop of Horrors* ("Suddenly Seymour") and the animated motion pictures *The Little Mermaid* ("Under the Sea," "Kiss the Girl") and *Beauty and the Beast.*

Auber, Daniel François Esprit (1782–1871)**:** French romantic composer of *opéras comiques.*

Auric, Georges (1899–1983)**:** French composer. Ballets, orchestral works, and piano music form the core of his output. In the 1920s he was a member of the nationalistic group of composers known as "Les Six."

B

Babbitt, Milton (b. 1916)**:** American composer. A proponent of *serial music* and electronic music synthesis, he has written works for instruments, voice, and tape recording, as well as numerous articles about contemporary music.

Bach, Carl Philipp Emanuel (1714–1788)**:** German preclassical composer, keyboardist, and teacher. Son of *Johann Sebastian.* Remembered primarily for his Sonatas, Fantasias, Rondos, and other works for keyboard—especially for *clavichord*—and for his treatise on keyboard playing.

Bach, Johann Christian (1735–1782)**:** German preclassical composer. Son of *Johann Sebastian*. He is remembered most for his operas and orchestral music, which influenced Wolfgang Amadeus *Mozart*.

Bach, Johann Christoph Friedrich (1732–1795)**:** German preclassical composer and keyboardist. Son of *Johann Sebastian*. Keyboard and vocal music contitute his main output.

Bach, Johann Sebastian (1685–1750)**:** German baroque composer, keyboardist, organist, and teacher. As a composer he was distinguished by his mastery of *counterpoint*. Among the many works for which he is remembered are his preludes and fugues for organ (Toccata and Fugue in D Minor), collections of pieces for keyboard (*The Well-Tempered Clavier*, Two- and Three-Part Inventions, *Little Notebook for Anna Magdalena Bach*), instrumental music ("Brandenburg" Concertos), and sacred vocal works (*St. Matthew Passion*, B Minor Mass). His church cantatas contain many movements that have become popular independently ("Jesu, Joy of Man's Desiring," "Sheep May Safely Graze"). The notes B♭-A-C-B (B-A-C-H in the German musical alphabet) have been used by many composers, beginning with Bach himself, as a musical reference to him.

Bach, Wilhelm Friedemann (1710–1784)**:** German preclassical composer and keyboardist. Son of *Johann Sebastian*. He is remembered chiefly for his own keyboard works, and for the "Little Keyboard Book" that his father wrote for him.

Bacharach, Burt (b. 1928)**:** American songwriter. Collaborated with Hal *David* for "Alfie," "Raindrops Keep Fallin' on My Head," and "Do You Know the Way to San Jose?" Wrote "That's What Friends Are For" with Carole Bayer *Sager*.

Bacon, Ernst (b. 1898)**:** American composer, most notably of songs. Also a pianist, conductor, and writer on music.

Balakirev, Mily (1837–1910)**:** Russian romantic composer, chiefly of songs and orchestral works. He led the nationalistic group of composers known as "The Five."

Barber, Samuel (1910–1981)**:** American composer of operas (*Vanessa*), orchestral music ("The School for Scandal" Overture), songs ("Sure on this Shining Night"), and chamber music (Adagio for Strings). His conservative style brought his music uncommon popularity, and his craftsmanship garnered him several prominent awards (including two Pulitzer Prizes).

Bartók, Béla (1881–1945)**:** Hungarian composer, collector of folk music, and pianist. His output consisted mainly of orchestral works (*Music for Strings, Percussion and Celesta*, Concerto for Orchestra, Suite from *The Miraculous Mandarin*), chamber music (six String Quartets), songs and choral works, and piano music ("Evening in the Country," "Allegro Barbaro," *Mikrokosmos*).

Beach, Amy (1867–1944)**:** American romantic composer and pianist. Among her works are a symphony, a piano concerto, and numerous songs.

Beethoven, Ludwig van (1770–1827)**:** German composer and pianist. He bridged the classical and romantic eras. Among his many enduring works are the nine symphonies (No. 3 "Eroica," No. 5, No. 6 "Pastoral," No. 9 "Choral"), 32 piano sonatas ("Moonlight," "Pathétique"), five piano concertos (No. 5 "Emperor"), violin concerto, string quartets and other chamber music ("Kreutzer" Sonata), and the *Missa Solemnis*. Many of these were composed when, during his final years, he was completely deaf.

Bellini, Vincenzo (1801–1835)**:** Italian romantic composer. He is best remembered for his operas, which include *Norma*, *I Puritani*, and *La Sonnambula*.

Benjamin, Arthur (1893–1960)**:** British composer and pianist of Australian origins. He is known primarily for his orchestral works, which include "Jamaican Rumba" and a Harmonica Concerto.

Bennett, Richard Rodney (b. 1936)**:** British composer and pianist. Although he has written a great deal of concert music, his film scores (including *Far from the Madding Crowd*, *Nicholas and Alexandra*, and *Murder on the Orient Express*) are more widely heard.

Bennett, Robert Russell (1894–1981)**:** American orchestrator and composer. He is most widely known for his orchestrations of Broadway musicals, and especially of Richard *Rodgers'* score for the television documentary "Victory at Sea."

Berg, Alban (1885–1935)**:** Austrian composer. A student of Arnold *Schoenberg's*, he adapted his teacher's *serial* technique to his own emotional style in such works as the *Lyric Suite* for string quartet, the Violin Concerto, and the opera *Lulu.* He also wrote the opera *Wozzeck.*

Bergman, Alan (b. 1925) and **Marilyn** (b. 1929)**:** American husband-and-wife lyricists, whose collaborators include Neil *Diamond* ("You Don't Bring Me Flowers"), Marvin *Hamlisch* ("The Way We Were"), and Michel Legrand ("The Windmills of Your Mind," "The Summer Knows," "What are You Doing the Rest of Your Life?").

Berio, Luciano (b. 1925)**:** Italian composer. His works often use electronic and theatrical means. The tape piece *Thema (Omaggio a Joyce)* is one of his best-known works.

Berlin, Irving (1888–1989)**:** American songwriter, born in Russia. Among his many popular songs are "God Bless America," "Easter Parade," "Alexander's Ragtime Band," "White Christmas," "Anything You Can Do," "There's No Business Like Show Business," and "Always." A self-taught musician, he preferred to play on the black keys of the piano and never learned to read or write standard musical notation.

Berlioz, Hector (1803–1869)**:** French romantic composer. In addition to his most popular work, the *Symphonie Fantastique*, he wrote other orchestral works (*The Damnation of Faust*, "Rakoczy" March), several operas (*The Trojans*), and many vocal and choral works (Requiem).

Bernstein, Elmer (b. 1922)**:** American composer, chiefly of film scores (*The Great Escape*, *To Kill a Mockingbird*).

Bernstein, Leonard (1918–1990)**:** American conductor and composer. His works, which include the musicals *On the Town* and *West Side Story*, the operetta *Candide*, the theatrical *Mass*, and the *Chichester Psalms*, often bridge the popular and the serious.

Billings, William (1746–1800)**:** American classical composer of choral music, often regarded as the first important composer born in America. He wrote the Revolutionary War tune "Chester" and the popular *canons* "When Jesus Wept" and "Wake Ev'ry Breath."

Bizet, Georges (1838–1875)**:** French romantic composer, primarily of operas (*Carmen*, *The Pearl Fishers*, *L'Arlésienne*).

Blackwood, Easley (b. 1933)**:** American composer and pianist. His compositions include *microtonal* works.

Bliss, Sir **Arthur** (1891–1975)**:** British post-romantic composer.

Blitzstein, Marc (1905–1964)**:** American composer. His works for the theatre, including *Regina* and *The Cradle Will Rock*, are his best-known.

Bloch, Ernest (1880–1959)**:** Swiss-American composer, known especially for works on Jewish themes (*Schelomo*, *Suite Hébraïque*). Influential as a teacher.

Blow, John (1649–1708)**:** British baroque composer, especially of vocal works.

Boccherini, Luigi (1743–1805)**:** Italian classical composer and cellist. His chamber works and cello concertos are his most important works.

Bock, Jerry (b. 1928)**:** American composer of the musical theatre, working primarily with Sheldon *Harnick*, on musicals including *Mr. Wonderful*, *Fiorello!*, *The Apple Tree*, and *Fiddler on the Roof* ("Sunrise, Sunset," "If I Were a Rich Man").

Bolcom, William (b. 1938)**:** American composer and pianist. His *12 New Etudes for Piano* won a Pulitzer Prize, and several of his ragtime compositions for piano are popular.

Bolling, Claude (b. 1930)**:** French jazz pianist and composer. Works include "Suite for Flute and Jazz Piano" and "Picnic Suite."

Borodin, Alexander (1833–1887)**:** Russian romantic composer, best known for his opera *Prince Igor* (especially the "Polovtsian Dances"), the Nocturne from his String Quartet No. 2, and the orchestral work *In the Steppes of Central Asia*. He was a member of the nationalistic group of composers known as "The Five."

Boublil, Alain (b. 1940)**:** French author and lyricist, whose stage works with composer Claude-Michel *Schönberg* include *Les Misérables* and *Miss Saigon*.

Boulanger, Nadia (1887–1979)**:** French composer and teacher. She is best known for having taught several prominent American composers, including *Copland* and *Piston.*

Boulez, Pierre (b. 1925)**:** French composer and conductor. His chamber work *Le Marteau sans Maître* (*The Hammer without a Master*) is his most influential work.

Boyce, William (1711–1779)**:** British baroque composer and organist, deaf in his later years. He published *Cathedral Music*, an important collection of works by British composers.

Brahms, Johannes (1833–1897)**:** German romantic composer, regarded as a "classicist" (His first symphony was dubbed "Beethoven's Tenth" by some.). In addition to orchestral works (*Academic Festival Overture*, four symphonies), chamber music (string quartets, piano quintet), piano pieces (waltzes, intermezzos, rhapsodies), and choral works (*Liebeslieder Waltzes, A German Requiem*), he is popular for his "Lullaby."

Bricusse, Leslie (b. 1931)**:** British songwriter and lyricist. Has collaborated with Anthony *Newley* ("The Candy Man," *The Roar of the Greasepaint—The Smell of the Crowd*), Henry *Mancini* (*Victor/Victoria*), and John *Williams* ("Can You Read My Mind?"). He also wrote the songs for *Doctor Dolittle*.

Britten, Benjamin (1913–1976)**:** British composer of operas (*Peter Grimes, The Turn of the Screw*), orchestral music (*Simple Symphony*), choral works (*War Requiem, A Ceremony of Carols*), and folksong arrangements.

Brown, Lew (1893–1958)**:** Ukrainian-American lyricist. Collaborated with Ray *Henderson* and B.G. *DeSylva.*

Brubeck, David (b. 1920)**:** American jazz pianist and composer. Recorded *Time Out*, an album of pieces in odd meters, including Paul Desmond's "Take Five" and his own "Blue Rondo à la Turk." Has composed much sacred music.

Bruch, Max (1838–1920)**:** German romantic composer, best-known for his violin concertos.

Bruckner, Anton (1824–1896)**:** Austrian romantic composer of sacred music (*Te Deum*) and nine symphonies (No. 4 "Romantic") noteworthy for their great length.

Bull, John (c. 1562–1628)**:** British late-Renaissance composer and keyboardist, most famous for his works for *virginal*.

Bülow, Hans von (1830–1894)**:** German romantic conductor, pianist, and composer. Associated with the progressives *Liszt* and *Wagner* (he married Liszt's daughter, Cosima, who later left him for Wagner).

Burgmüller, Friedrich (1806–1874)**:** German romantic composer, mainly of study pieces for piano.

Burke, Johnny (1908–1964)**:** American lyricist for such songs as "Misty," "Polka Dots and Moonbeams," "Pennies from Heaven," and "Swinging on a Star."

Busoni, Ferruccio (1866–1924)**:** German-Italian late-romantic composer and pianist. Wrote much piano music, including transcriptions of Bach organ works, and the opera *Doktor Faust*. Anticipated modernistic techniques in his music and writings.

Buxtehude, Dietrich (c. 1637–1707)**:** Danish-German baroque composer and organist. His organ music influenced J.S. *Bach*. He also wrote church cantatas.

Byrd, William (1543–1623)**:** British Renaissance composer of keyboard works (*My Ladye Nevells Virginal Booke*) and sacred vocal music.

C

Caccini, Giulio (c. 1545–1618)**:** Italian composer of the late Renaissance and early baroque eras. His operas are among the earliest. His song "Amarilli, mia Bella" is well-known.

Cage, John (1912–1992)**:** American composer, a pioneer in the use of *prepared piano* and *aleatoric* procedures. His *4' 33"* is perhaps his most infamous piece.

Cahn, Sammy (b. 1913)**:** American lyricist. Wrote the words for "Three Coins in the Fountain" and "Let it Snow! Let it Snow! Let it Snow!" (music by Jule *Styne*), as well as "High Hopes" and "Call Me Irresponsible" (music by Jimmy *Van Heusen*).

Caldara, Antonio (c. 1670–1736)**:** Italian baroque composer of operas, oratorios, and other vocal works. He wrote the songs "Alma del Core" and "Sebben, Crudele."

Campion, Thomas (1567–1620)**:** British composer of the Renaissance, known for his songs (*airs*) with lute and viol accompaniment.

Carissimi, Giacomo (1605–1674)**:** Italian baroque composer of vocal music. He was a pioneer in writing oratorios and cantatas.

Carmichael, Hoagy (1899–1981)**:** American song composer, pioneer of the *blues*. His songs include "Star Dust," "Georgia on my Mind," and "Heart and Soul."

Carolan, Turlough (1670–1738)**:** Irish baroque harper and composer, sometimes popularly known as O'Carolan. His songs for Irish folk harp form the cornerstone of the literature for the instrument.

Carpenter, John Alden (1876–1951)**:** American composer, best-known for his ballet *Skyscrapers*.

Carter, Elliott (b. 1908)**:** American composer with a reputation for involved, intellectual works.

Cesti, Antonio (1623–1669)**:** Italian baroque composer of operas (*Il Pomo d'Oro*) and cantatas.

Chabrier, Emmanuel (1841–1894)**:** French romantic composer, whose *España* rhapsody for orchestra remains popular. He also wrote the comic opera *Le Roi Malgré Lui*.

Chaminade, Cécile (1857–1944)**:** French pianist and composer, remembered for her "salon pieces" for the piano, including "Piece in Ancient Style," and for the "Scarf Dance" from her ballet *Callirhoé*.

Charpentier, Gustave (1860–1956)**:** French romantic composer of operas (*Louise*) and vocal music.

Charpentier, Marc-Antoine (c. 1650–1704)**:** French baroque composer, primarily of sacred music.

Chausson, Ernest (1855–1899)**:** French romantic composer. His songs and other vocal music are important.

Chávez, Carlos (1899–1978)**:** Mexican composer of nationalistic music.

Cherubini, Luigi (1760–1842)**:** Italian classical composer of sacred music (two *Requiem Masses*), *opéras comiques*, and instrumental music. Also wrote an important treatise on *counterpoint*.

Chopin, Frédéric (1810–1849)**:** Polish-French romantic composer of piano music, including many well-known *preludes*, *etudes*, *nocturnes*, *polonaises*, *impromptus*, *mazurkas*, and *waltzes*.

Cimarosa, Domencio (1748–1801)**:** Italian classical composer of operas.

Clarke, Jeremiah (1674–1707)**:** British baroque composer. "Trumpet Voluntary" is his most famous work.

Clementi, Muzio (1752–1832)**:** Italian classical composer, keyboard player, and teacher. His sonatas and sonatinas are still used in teaching piano.

Cohan, George M. (1878–1942)**:** American writer of musical comedies. His songs include "Yankee Doodle Boy" (a.k.a. "Yankee Doodle Dandy"),"You're a Grand Old Flag," "Give My Regards to Broadway," and "Over There."

Coleman, Cy (b. 1929)**:** American composer of musicals including *On the Twentieth Century* and *The Will Rogers Follies* (both with lyrics by Betty *Comden* and Adolph *Green*), *Little Me* (lyrics by Carolyn *Leigh*), and *Sweet Charity* (lyrics by Dorothy *Fields*).

Coleridge-Taylor, Samuel (1875–1912)**:** Black British romantic composer. The cantata *Hiawatha's Wedding Feast* is his best-known work.

Comden, Betty (b. 1915)**:** American lyricist and librettist. Long-standing collaboration with Adolph *Green* and Jule *Styne* included the songs "The Party's Over" and "Make Someone Happy." She and Green have also worked with Cy *Coleman*.

Copland, Aaron (1900–1990)**:** American composer. His most popular works include "Fanfare for the Common Man" and the ballets *Billy the Kid*, *Rodeo*, and *Appalachian Spring*.

Corelli, Arcangelo (1653–1713)**:** Italian baroque composer and violinist, most important for his works for strings: solo sonatas, trio sonatas, and concerti grossi.

Couperin, François (1668–1733)**:** French baroque composer, nicknamed "le Grand" ("the Great") to distinguish him from his uncle *Louis*. Wrote keyboard music and a treatise on playing the harpsichord.

Couperin, Louis (c. 1626–1661)**:** French baroque composer of keyboard music, uncle of *François*.

Coward, Sir **Noël** (1899–1973)**:** British songwriter. Wrote "I'll Follow My Secret Heart" and "Mad Dogs and Englishmen."

Cowell, Henry (1897–1965)**:** American composer who helped originate the use of *tone clusters* and playing inside the piano.

Cramer, Johann Baptist (1771–1858)**:** German classical and romantic pianist and composer, remembered for his etudes for piano.

Crumb, George (b. 1929)**:** American composer. Among his works are *Echoes of Time and the River* (which won a Pulitzer Prize), for orchestra, and *Makrokosmos*, for amplified piano (which includes such unusual notation as a spiral-shaped staff).

Cui, César (1835–1918)**:** Russian romantic composer. He was a member of the nationalistic group of composers known as "The Five."

Czerny, Carl (1791–1857)**:** Austrian romantic pianist and composer. Studied piano with *Beethoven*, taught *Liszt*. Remembered for his teaching pieces.

D

Daquin, Louis-Claude (1694–1772)**:** French baroque keyboardist and composer, remembered for his *noëls* for organ.

David, Hal (b. 1921)**:** American lyricist. Co-wrote "What the World Needs Now is Love" and "(They Long to Be) Close to You" with Burt *Bacharach*. Also wrote "It Was Almost Like a Song" and "To All the Girls I've Loved Before."

Davies, Peter Maxwell (b. 1934)**:** British composer. *Eight songs for a Mad King* is one of his best-known works.

Debussy, Claude (1862–1918)**:** French impressionist composer. His piano music includes "Clair de Lune" (from the *Suite Bergamasque*), "Rêverie," two Arabesques, and two books of Preludes (including "The Sunken Cathedral"). He also wrote *La Mer* and the *Prelude to "The Afternoon of a Faun"* for orchestra, and the opera *Pelléas and Mélisande.*

Delibes, Léo (1836–1891)**:** French romantic composer. He wrote the ballets *Coppélia* and *Sylvia* and the opera *Lakmé.*

Delius, Frederick (1862–1934)**:** British late-romantic composer. His works include *Sea Drift*, for baritone, chorus, and orchestra, and the opera *A Village Romeo and Juliet.*

Dello Joio, Norman (b. 1913)**:** American composer. He won a Pulitzer Prize for his *Meditations on Ecclesiastes*, for string orchestra. He also wrote the opera *The Triumph of St. Joan.*

DeSylva, B.G. "Buddy" (1895–1950)**:** American lyricist, best-known for his collaboration with Lew *Brown* and Ray *Henderson*. Songs include "April Showers," "California, Here I Come," and "The Best Things in Life are Free."

Diabelli, Anton (1781–1858)**:** Austrian classical composer and music publisher. Beethoven's *Diabelli Variations* are based on a waltz theme of Diabelli's.

Diamond, Neil (b. 1941)**:** American singer and songwriter. From an early start in the *Brill Building*, he went on to write such hits as "I'm a Believer," "Sweet Caroline," and "Song Sung Blue."

d'Indy, Vincent (1851–1931)**:** French romantic composer, whose works include the "Istar" Variations for orchestra.

Dittersdorf, Carl Ditters von (1739–1799)**:** Austrian classical composer, who helped develop the genre of the *Singspiel.*

Dohnányi, Ernö (Ernst von) (1877–1960)**:** Hungarian composer, pianist, and conductor.

Donaldson, Walter (1893–1947)**:** American songwriter and composer. His songs include "How 'Ya Gonna Keep 'Em Down on the Farm?" "My Mammy," "Makin' Whoopee!," "My Blue Heaven," and "Yes Sir! That's My Baby."

Donizetti, Gaetano (1797–1848): Italian romantic composer of operas, most notably *L'Elisir d'Amore*, *Lucrezia Borgia*, *Lucia di Lammermoor*, *Daughter of the Regiment*, and *Don Pasquale*.

Dorsey, Thomas A. (b. 1899): Black American gospel songwriter (not trombonist and bandleader Tommy Dorsey). He wrote "Peace in the Valley" and "Precious Lord, Take My Hand."

Dowland, John (1563–1626): British Renaissance composer and lutenist, best-known for his songs (such as "Come Again, Sweet Love") and his compositions for lute.

Dufay, Guillaume (c. 1400–1474): French late-medieval and early-Renaissance composer, important for his vocal works, both sacred (especially his settings of the *Mass*) and secular.

Dukas, Paul (1865–1935): French late-romantic composer. He wrote the ballet *La Péri* and the tone poem *The Sorcerer's Apprentice*.

Duke, Vernon (1903–1969): Russian-American composer and songwriter. He wrote "Autumn in New York" and the music for "April in Paris."

Dunstable, John (c. 1390–1453): British composer of the late medieval era, important for his sacred vocal music, including the chanson "O Rosa Bella" and the motet "Veni Creator."

Dupré, Marcel (1886–1971): French organist and composer.

Durey, Louis (1888–1979) French composer. In the 1920s he was a member of the nationalistic group of composers known as "Les Six."

Dussek, Jan Ladislav (1760–1812): Bohemian classical composer. Also a pianist, he wrote much music for his instrument.

Dvorák, Antonín (1841–1904): Czech romantic composer. His many popular works include the Symphony No. 9 ("From the New World"), the Slavonic Dances, the "Humoresque," and a great deal of chamber music ("Dumky" Trio).

Dylan, Bob (Robert Zimmerman) (b. 1941): American songwriter and singer. His songs include "Blowin' in the Wind," "The Times They Are A-Changin'," "Don't Think Twice, It's All Right," "Mr. Tambourine Man," and "Lay Lady Lay."

E

Ebb, Fred (b. 1936)**:** American lyricist and librettist, collaborator with John *Kander* on musicals for the stage and screen including *Cabaret*, *Zorba*, *Chicago*, and *Funny Lady*.

Elgar, Sir **Edward** (1857–1934)**:** British late-romantic composer. His best-known works are the *Pomp and Circumstance* march No. 1 and the "Enigma" Variations, both for orchestra, and the oratorio *The Dream of Gerontius*.

Ellington, Edward Kennedy "Duke" (1899–1974)**:** Black American jazz composer and band leader. A pioneer of large-scale works, such as *Black, Brown and Beige*, he is most widely remembered for his songs, including "Mood Indigo," "It Don't Mean a Thing (If It Ain't Got That Swing)," "Satin Doll," and "Caravan."

Enesco, Georges (1881–1955)**:** Romanian composer, best-known for his *Romanian Rhapsodies* for orchestra.

F

Fain, Sammy (1902–1989)**:** American song composer, whose songs include "Let A Smile Be Your Umbrella," "I Can Dream, Can't I?" "I'll Be Seeing You," and "Love Is A Many-Splendored Thing."

Falla, Manuel de (1876–1946)**:** Spanish composer. He wrote the ballets *El Amor Brujo* and *The Three-Cornered Hat* and the opera *La Vida Breve*.

Farnaby, Giles (c. 1563–1640)**:** British Renaissance composer of keyboard and vocal music.

Fauré, Gabriel (1845–1924)**:** French late-romantic composer, remembered for his Requiem, his many songs ("Après un Rêve," "En Prière") and his piano music.

Fibich, Zdenek (1850–1900)**:** Czech romantic composer of operas and melodramas.

Field, John (1782–1837)**:** Irish romantic composer of piano music. A forerunner of *Chopin.*

Fields, Dorothy (1904–1974)**:** American lyricist and librettist, whose lyrics include "On the Sunny Side of the Street," "I'm in the Mood for Love," and "The Way You Look Tonight."

Flotow, Friedrich von (1812–1883)**:** German romantic composer. He wrote the opera *Martha.*

Floyd, Carlisle (b. 1926)**:** American composer, best-known for his opera *Susannah.*

Forrest, George "Chet" (b. 1915)**:** American songwriter for the musical theatre, collaborator with Robert *Wright* on *Grand Hotel*, *Kismet* ("Stranger in Paradise"; based on the music of *Borodin*), and *Song of Norway* ("Strange Music"; based on the music of *Grieg*).

Foss, Lukas (b. 1922)**:** American composer, conductor, and pianist of German origins. Many of his works make use of controlled *improvisation.*

Foster, Stephen Collins (1826–1864)**:** American song composer. His songs include "My Old Kentucky Home, Good Night," "Old Folks at Home ('Way Down upon the Swanee River)," "Beautiful Dreamer," "Jeanie with the Light Brown Hair," "Oh! Susanna," and "Camptown Races."

Franck, César (1822–1890)**:** French romantic composer and organist of Belgian origins. His Symphony in D Minor (for orchestra), Three Chorales (for organ), and Sonata for Violin and Piano are among his most important works. He also wrote the song "Panis Angelicus" ("Heavenly Manna," a.k.a. "O Lord Most Holy").

Frescobaldi, Girolamo (1583–1643)**:** Italian baroque composer of instrumental *canzonas* and keyboard music.

Friml, Rudolf (1879–1972)**:** Czech-American popular composer. Remembered for his operettas, including *Rose Marie* (popular for the duet "Indian Love Call"), *The Firefly*, and *The Vagabond King*.

Fux, Johann Joseph (1660–1741)**:** Austrian baroque composer and music theorist, best-known for his treatise on counterpoint, *Gradus ad Parnassum.*

G

Gabrieli, Andrea (c. 1510–1586)**:** Italian Renaissance composer, uncle of *Giovanni.*

Gabrieli, Giovanni (c. 1555–1612)**:** Italian Renaissance composer, foremost representative of the *Venetian school.* He explored the use of space (*polychoral* works, both vocal and instrumental) and dynamics (*Sonata Pian e Forte*) as musical dimensions. His works include several *Sacred Symphonies*.

Gade, Niels (1817–1890)**:** Danish romantic composer of symphonic and chamber music.

Gershwin, George (1898–1937)**:** American composer and pianist. Although well known for his popular songs, he attempted to merge popular, jazz, and concert music in works such as *An American in Paris*, *Rhapsody in Blue*, and the opera *Porgy and Bess*.

Gershwin, Ira (1896–1983)**:** American librettist and lyricist, best-known for his collaborations with his brother *George*, including "Fascinating Rhythm," "'S Wonderful," "I Got Rhythm," and "Let's Call The Whole Thing Off."

Gesualdo, Carlo (c. 1561–1613)**:** Italian Renaissance composer of vocal music. His madrigals are often startlingly chromatic and dissonant.

Gibbons, Orlando (1583–1625)**:** British Renaissance composer.

Gilbert, Sir **William S.** (1836–1911)**:** British playwright and lyricist. Collaborated with Sir Arthur *Sullivan* in operettas including *H.M.S. Pinafore*, *The Mikado*, and *The Pirates of Penzance*.

Ginastera, Alberto (1916–1983)**:** Argentine composer. Much of his music contains nationalistic traits.

Giordano, Umberto (1867–1948)**:** Italian post-romantic composer. He wrote the opera *Andrea Chenier*.

Glass, Philip (b. 1937)**:** American composer. His music, often linked with *minimalism*, has attracted fans of both serious and popular music. The opera *Einstein on the Beach* is one of his best-known works.

Glazunov, Alexander (1865–1936)**:** Russian romantic composer, noteworthy for his Saxophone Concerto, symphonies, the tone poem *Stenka Razin*, and the ballet *Raymonda*.

Glière, Reinhold (1875–1956)**:** Soviet post-romantic composer. He wrote the ballet *The Red Poppy*.

Glinka, Mikhail (1804–1857)**:** Russian romantic composer. His nationalistic style is typified in the opera *Ruslan and Lyudmila*.

Gluck, Christoph Willibald (1714–1784)**:** German classical composer of operas, including *Orfeo ed Euridice*, *Alceste*, *Iphigénie en Tauride*, and *Armide*.

Godowsky, Leopold (1870–1938)**:** Polish-American pianist and composer of virtuoso piano pieces.

Goffin, Gerry (b. 1939)**:** American lyricist, employed at the *Brill Building* in the early 1960s with collaborator and then-wife Carole *King*. Their songs include "Will You Love Me Tomorrow," "The Loco-Motion," "Natural Woman," and "One Fine Day."

Gold, Ernest (b. 1921)**:** Austrian-American composer, best-known for the score to the film *Exodus*.

Goldmark, Karl (1830–1915)**:** Hungarian romantic composer, best-known for the opera *The Queen of Sheba*.

Goldmark, Rubin (1872–1936)**:** American late-romantic composer of Austro-Hungarian descent, nephew of *Karl*. He was a prominent teacher.

Gossec, François-Joseph (1734–1829)**:** Dutch-French classical composer, especially of operas. A Gavotte of his remains a popular light classic.

Gottschalk, Louis Moreau (1829–1869)**:** American romantic composer and pianist. His piano works, such as "Bamboula" and "Le Banjo," often evoke his native New Orleans.

Gould, Morton (b. 1913)**:** American composer and conductor. Orchestral works form the core of his output.

Gounod, Charles (1818–1893)**:** French romantic composer of operas, including *Faust* and *Roméo et Juliette*, as well as other vocal music. He added a melody (and later, traditional Latin words) to J.S. *Bach*'s Prelude in C to create his setting of "Ave Maria."

Grainger, Percy (1882–1961)**:** Australian-American composer and pianist. Although he is remembered primarily for light pieces such as "Country Gardens" and settings of folk songs, much of his music was experimental and forward-looking.

Granados, Enrique (1867–1916)**:** Spanish romantic composer and pianist. His works, including the opera *Goyescas*, are often nationalistic in style.

Green, Adolph (b. 1915)**:** American lyricist, known mainly as a collaborator with Betty *Comden*.

Green, Johnny (b. 1908)**:** American popular composer. He scored the movie *Easter Parade* and wrote songs including "Body and Soul" and "I Cover the Waterfront."

Grieg, Edvard (1843–1907)**:** Norwegian romantic composer whose popular works include incidental music for the play *Peer Gynt* ("In the Hall of the Mountain King," "Anitra's Dance," "Solvejg's Song"), a Piano Concerto, the song "Ich liebe dich," and several collections of *Lyric Pieces* for piano.

Griffes, Charles Tomlinson (1884–1920)**:** American composer. Many of his works, including "The White Peacock," make use of *impressionism*.

Grofé, Ferde (1892–1972)**:** American composer and arranger. He orchestrated Gershwin's *Rhapsody in Blue* and composed the *Grand Canyon Suite*.

Guthrie, Woodrow Wilson "Woody" (1912–1967)**:** American singer and songwriter, father of Arlo. His most popular songs are "So Long (It's Been Good to Know Yuh)" and "This Land is Your Land."

H

Hába, Alois (1893–1973)**:** Czech composer, pioneer in *microtonal* music.

Halévy, Jacques François (1799–1862)**:** French romantic composer, primarily of operas.

Hamlisch, Marvin (b. 1944)**:** American composer, pianist, and conductor. His film scores include *The Sting* and *The Way We Were*; Broadway musicals include *A Chorus Line* and *They're Playing Our Song*. Among his songs is "Through the Eyes of Love" (Theme from *Ice Castles*).

Hammerstein, Oscar II (1895–1960)**:** American lyricist, collaborator with Sigmund Romberg (*The Student Prince*), Jerome Kern (*Show Boat*), and for many years with Richard Rodgers (*Oklahoma!*, *Carousel*, *South Pacific*, *The King And I*, and *The Sound of Music*).

Handel, George Frideric (1685–1759)**:** British baroque composer, born in Germany and educated in Italy. He was renowned for his operas (*Agrippina*, *Rinaldo*, *Il Pastor Fido*, *Giulio Cesare*, *Rodelinda*, *Berenice*, *Serse*, *Acis and Galatea*) and oratorios (*Messiah*, *Judas Maccabaeus*, *Joshua*, *Jephtha*, *Semele*). He also wrote harpsichord suites (including the variations known as "The Harmonious Blacksmith") and other instrumental works (*Music for the Royal Fireworks*, *Water Music*, sonatas, concertos).

Handy, W.C. (1873–1958)**:** Black American song composer, known as the "Father of the Blues." Among his songs are "Memphis Blues" and "St. Louis Blues."

Hanon, Charles-Louis (1819–1900)**:** French romantic pianist, teacher, and composer, whose collection of exercises entitled *The Virtuoso Pianist* is still popular.

Hanson, Howard (1896–1981)**:** American composer and teacher. His symphonies (No. 1 "Nordic," No. 2 "Romantic") are his best-known works.

Harbach (Hauerbach), Otto (1873–1963)**:** American lyricist and librettist. Among his Broadway musicals are *Rose-Marie*; *No, No, Nanette*; and *The Desert Song*. His song lyrics include "Indian Love Call" and "Smoke Gets In Your Eyes."

Harburg, E.Y. "Yip" (1898–1981)**:** American lyricist and librettist, whose works include the musicals *Finian's Rainbow* (Broadway) and *The Wizard of Oz* (movie) and the songs "April in Paris" and "It's Only A Paper Moon."

Harnick, Sheldon (b. 1924)**:** American lyricist and composer, collaborator with Jerry *Bock* on musicals including *The Apple Tree* and *Fiddler on the Roof* ("Sunrise, Sunset," "If I Were a Rich Man").

Harris, Roy (1898–1979)**:** American composer, whose works (including 13 symphonies) often evoke folk and western themes.

Harrison, George (b. 1943)**:** British singer, guitarist, and songwriter. As a member of the Beatles in the 1960s, he wrote such songs as "Something" and "While My Guitar Gently Weeps." On his own he wrote "My Sweet Lord" and "Give Me Love (Give Me Peace on Earth)."

Hart, Lorenz (1895–1943)**:** American lyricist and librettist, famed collaborator with Richard *Rodgers*. Musicals include *The Boys from Syracuse* ("This Can't Be Love"), *Pal Joey* ("Bewitched"), *Babes in Arms* ("My Funny Valentine," "The Lady Is a Tramp"), and *A Connecticut Yankee* ("Thou Swell").

Haydn, Franz Joseph (1732–1809)**:** Austrian classical composer. He wrote the oratorio *The Creation* and the Austrian National Hymn. Many of his instrumental works have earned popular nicknames, including the "Surprise," "Clock," and "Farewell" Symphonies, the "Lark" String Quartet, and the "Gypsy" Rondo.

Haydn, Michael (1737–1806)**:** Austrian classical composer, primarily of sacred and symphonic music. Younger brother of *Franz Joseph*. He wrote the music that became the hymn tune "O Worship the King," and may have written the popular "Toy" Symphony.

Henderson, Ray (1896–1971)**:** American song composer, collaborator with B.G. *DeSylva* and Lew *Brown*. Songs include "Five Foot Two, Eyes of Blue," "The Varsity Drag," and "Life Is Just a Bowl of Cherries."

Henry, Pierre (b. 1927)**:** French composer who, with Pierre *Schaeffer*, originated *musique concrète*.

Herbert, Victor (1859–1924)**:** Irish-American composer of operettas, including *Babes in Toyland*, *Naughty Marietta*, *Mademoiselle Modiste*, *Sweethearts*, and *The Red Mill*.

Herman, Jerry (b. 1933)**:** American writer of musicals including *Mame*, *La Cage aux Folles*, and *Hello, Dolly!*

Herrmann, Bernard (1911–1975)**:** American composer and conductor. His many well-known film scores include *Citizen Kane*, *The Day the Earth Stood Still*, and *Psycho*.

Heyward, DuBose (1885–1940)**:** American author and librettist. Collaborated with George and Ira *Gershwin* in writing the opera *Porgy and Bess*, based on his novel *Porgy*.

Hindemith, Paul (1895–1963)**:** German composer best known for the symphonies drawn from his operas *Mathis der Maler* and *Die Harmonie der Welt*, and for his theoretical writings on *tonality* in modern music. He is often associated with the term *Gebrauchsmusik*.

Holst, Gustav (1874–1934)**:** British late-romantic composer of the symphonic work *The Planets*, the band composition *Hammersmith*, and the music for the hymn "In the Bleak Midwinter."

Honegger, Arthur (1892–1955)**:** Swiss composer. A longtime resident of France, in the 1920s he was a member of the French nationalistic group of composers known as "Les Six." His compositions include the operas *Jeanne d'Arc au Bûcher* and *Judith*, the oratorio *Le Roi David*, and the orchestral work *Pacific 231*.

Hovhaness, Alan (b. 1911)**:** American composer. His Symphony No. 2, "Mysterious Mountain," is one of his best-known works.

Hummel, Johann Nepomuk (1778–1837)**:** Austrian classical composer and pianist. His works for piano are still sometimes used as teaching pieces.

Humperdinck, Engelbert (1854–1921)**:** German romantic composer, remembered for the opera *Hansel and Gretel*.

Husa, Karel (b. 1921)**:** Czech-American composer, known for his String Quartet No. 3 and for the band compositions *Music for Prague* and *The Apotheosis of this Earth*.

I

Ibert, Jacques (1890–1962): French composer whose works include a Flute Concerto and the opera *Angélique*.

Ippolitov-Ivanov, Mikhail (1859–1935): Russian late-romantic composer. His *Caucasian Sketches* for orchestra are still performed.

Isaac, Heinrich (c. 1450–1517): Flemish composer of the Renaissance. He wrote many settings of the *Mass*.

Ives, Charles (1874–1954): American composer, whose bold and eclectic works include the Third and Fourth Symphonies, the "Concord" Sonata for piano, and *The Unanswered Question* for small orchestra.

J

Jackson, Michael (b. 1958): American popular singer, dancer, songwriter, and producer. His songs include "Beat It," "Billie Jean," "Bad," and "Black or White."

Jacob, Gordon (1895–1984): British composer of orchestral, vocal, and chamber music.

Janácek, Leos (1854–1928): Czech late-romantic composer whose works include the operas *Jenufa* and *The Cunning Little Vixen* and the orchestral Sinfonietta and *Taras Bulba* rhapsody.

Jobim, Antonio Carlos (b. 1927): Brazilian pianist, guitarist, and composer of bossa novas, including "The Girl from Ipanema," "How Insensitive," and "Quiet Nights of Quiet Stars."

Joel, Billy (b. 1949)**:** American pop singer, pianist, and songwriter. His hit songs include "Piano Man," "Just The Way You Are," "She's Always a Woman," "Uptown Girl," "Honesty," and "We Didn't Start the Fire."

John, Elton (Reginald Dwight) (b. 1947)**:** British pop singer, pianist, and songwriter, whose songs include "Rocket Man," "Crocodile Rock," "Goodbye Yellow Brick Road," "Sad Songs (Say So Much)," and "Your Song."

Jones, Tom (b. 1928)**:** American lyricist and librettist, collaborator with Harvey *Schmidt* on the musicals *The Fantasticks* ("Try to Remember"), *110 in the Shade*, and *I Do! I Do!* ("My Cup Runneth Over").

Joplin, Scott (1868–1917)**:** Black American popular composer, known as the "King of Ragtime." His many *ragtime* compositions for piano include the "Maple Leaf Rag," "The Entertainer," and "Elite Syncopations." He also wrote the opera *Treemonisha*.

Jósquin Des Pres (Desprez) (c. 1440–1521)**:** French composer of the Renaissance—one of the most important of that era. Among his most enduring works are the secular motet "El Grillo" ("The Cricket") and two masses based on the popular song "L'Homme Armé" ("The Armed Man").

K

Kabalevsky, Dmitri (1904–1987)**:** Russian composer, best-known for his teaching pieces for piano and for the orchestral suite *The Comedians*.

Kahn, Gus (1886–1941)**:** German-American lyricist for songs including "Ain't We Got Fun," "Pretty Baby," "Carolina in the Morning," "Dream a Little Dream of Me," "It Had to be You," and "Makin' Whoopee!"

Kander, John (b. 1927): American composer, collaborator with Fred *Ebb* on musicals for the stage and screen including *Cabaret*, *Zorba*, *Chicago*, and *Funny Lady*.

Kern, Jerome (1885–1945): American popular composer. His scores for musicals such as *Show Boat* and *Roberta* include the songs "Ol' Man River," "I've Told Ev'ry Little Star," "Smoke Gets in Your Eyes," and "All the Things You Are."

Khachaturian, Aram (1903–1978): Russian composer. He wrote the ballet *Gayane*, from which comes the popular "Sabre Dance."

King, Carole (b. 1942): American songwriter and singer, one-time partner and wife of Gerry *Goffin*. On her own she wrote "I Feel the Earth Move," "So Far Away," and "You've Got a Friend," co-wrote "It's Too Late," and recorded the hit album *Tapestry*.

Kodály, Zoltán (1882–1967): Hungarian composer, folk music collector (with Béla *Bartók*), and music educator. His best-known compositions include *Psalmus Hungaricus* and the orchestral suite from the folk-imbued operetta *Háry János*.

Koechlin, Charles (1867–1950): French composer. He wrote a book on *orchestration*.

Köhler, Louis (1820–1886): German romantic composer of methods and teaching pieces for piano.

Korngold, Erich Wolfgang (1897–1957): Austro-Hungarian-American post-romantic composer, remembered for his opera *Die tote Stadt* (*The Dead City*) and scores for films including *Captain Blood* and *Deception*.

Kreisler, Fritz (1875–1962): Austrian-American late-romantic violinist and composer. His works for violin include *Caprice Viennois*, *Tambourin Chinois*, and *Liebesfreud*. He also debuted several works, supposedly by classical composers, which he later confessed that he had composed.

Krenek, Ernst (1900–1991): Austrian-American composer. He wrote the jazz-influenced opera *Jonny spielt auf*.

Kreutzer, Rudolph (1766–1831): German-French classical violinist and composer. He wrote a number of etudes for the violin, as well as operas. He is usually remembered as the dedicatee of *Beethoven*'s "Kreutzer" Sonata.

Kuhlau, Friedrich (1786–1832)**:** German-Danish late-classical and early-romantic composer, remembered for his sonatas, sonatinas, and other teaching pieces for piano.

Kuhnau, Johann (1660–1722)**:** German baroque organist and composer of keyboard and sacred music.

L

Lalo, Edouard (1823–1892)**:** French romantic composer, remembered for the *Symphonie Espagnole* for violin and orchestra.

Landini, Francesco (1325–1397)**:** Italian composer and organist of the *ars nova* (late middle ages). Blind from youth, he wrote a great deal of vocal music, much of which is characterized by a melodic figure now called the *Landini cadence*.

Lane, Burton (b. 1912)**:** American composer and songwriter. Collaborated with E.Y. *Harburg* (*Finian's Rainbow*), Frank *Loesser* (*Some Like It Hot*), and Alan Jay *Lerner* (*On a Clear Day You Can See Forever*).

Lanner, Joseph (1801–1843)**:** Austrian romantic composer of waltzes, a contemporary of Johann *Strauss* Sr.

Lasso, Orlando di (1532–1594)**:** Franco-Flemish Renaissance composer, also known as Roland de Lassus. He wrote a great deal of sacred vocal and choral music.

Lecuona, Ernesto (1896–1963)**:** Cuban popular composer of such pieces as "Malagueña," "Siboney," and "Andalucía."

Lehár, Franz (1870–1948)**:** Hungarian-Austrian late-romantic composer of operettas, most notably *The Merry Widow*.

Leiber, Jerry (b. 1933)**:** American songwriter, partner of Mike *Stoller* in hits such as "Hound Dog," "Jailhouse Rock," and "Spanish Harlem."

Leigh, Carolyn (b. 1926)**:** American lyricist, whose songs include "Young at Heart," "The Best Is Yet to Come," "Hey, Look Me Over," and "Pass Me By."

Leigh, Mitch (b. 1928)**:** American composer, most notable for scoring the musical *Man of La Mancha* ("The Impossible Dream").

Lennon, John (1940–1980)**:** British guitarist, singer, and songwriter, who, with fellow Beatles member Paul *McCartney*, wrote the group's biggest hits, including "Michelle," "Paperback Writer," "Lucy in the Sky with Diamonds," "Penny Lane," "Hey Jude," and "Strawberry Fields Forever." Later, on his own, he wrote "Instant Karma," "Imagine," "Woman," and "(Just Like) Starting Over."

Leoncavallo, Ruggero (1857–1919)**:** Italian romantic opera composer. He wrote *Pagliacci.*

Leonin (c. 1130–c. 1200)**:** French medieval composer specializing in an early form of *polyphony* known as *organum.*

Lerner, Alan Jay (1918–1986)**:** American lyricist and librettist. Collaborated primarily with Frederick *Loewe* (*Brigadoon*, *Paint Your Wagon*, *My Fair Lady*, *Camelot*, *Gigi*) and Burton *Lane* (*On a Clear Day You Can See Forever*).

Liadov, Anatoli (1855–1914)**:** Russian romantic composer of orchestral and piano music.

Ligeti, György (b. 1923)**:** Hungarian-Austrian composer. Much of his music incorporates *tone clusters.*

Liszt, Franz (1811–1886)**:** Hungarian romantic composer and pianist, renowned for his virtuosic piano music (Sonata in B Minor, *Mephisto Waltz*, *Transcendental Etudes*) and symphonic poems (*Les Préludes*). The "Hungarian Rhapsody" No. 2 and "Liebestraum" No. 3 are his most popular works.

Lloyd Webber, Andrew (b. 1948)**:** British popular composer of musicals, including *Joseph and the Amazing Technicolor Dreamcoat*, *Jesus Christ Superstar* ("Everything's Alright," "I Don't Know How to Love Him"), *Evita* ("Don't Cry for Me Argentina"), *Cats* ("Memory"), and *The Phantom of the Opera* ("All I Ask of You").

Loesser, Frank (1910–1969)**:** American songwriter and publisher. His musicals include *Where's Charley?* ("Once in Love with Amy"), *Guys and Dolls* ("Adelaide's Lament," "A Bushel and a Peck"), *The Most Happy Fella* ("Standing on the Corner," "Big D"), and *Hans Christian Andersen* ("Wonderful Copenhagen").

Loewe, Frederick (1901–1988)**:** Austrian-American composer of Broadway musicals, especially in collaboration with Alan Jay *Lerner*. His songs include "Almost Like Being in Love," "They Call the Wind Maria," "I Could Have Danced All Night," "If Ever I Would Leave You," and "Thank Heaven for Little Girls."

Luening, Otto (b. 1900)**:** American composer, who, with Vladimir *Ussachevsky*, was central in the development of tape music in the U.S.

Lully, Jean-Baptiste (1632–1687)**:** Italian-French baroque composer of operas (*Phaéton*, *Roland*) and ballets. He founded the French style of opera composition and developed the *French overture* form.

Lutoslawski, Witold (b. 1913)**:** Polish composer, especially of orchestral works. His Cello Concerto is widely known.

M

MacDowell, Edward (1860–1908)**:** American romantic composer and pianist remembered for his *Woodland Sketches* for the piano, which include "To a Wild Rose."

Machaut, Guilliaume de (c. 1300–1377)**:** French medieval composer of polyphonic vocal music. One of his best-known works is "Ma Fin est Mon Commencement" ("My End is My Beginning"), a *crab canon*.

Mahler, Gustav (1860–1911)**:** Austrian late-romantic composer and conductor, remembered for his 10 symphonies (No. 2 "Resurrection," No. 8 "Symphony of a Thousand") and large works for voice and orchestra such as *Des Knaben Wunderhorn* (*The Youth's Magic Horn*) and *Das Lied von der Erde* (*The Song of the Earth*).

Malotte, Albert Hay (1895–1964)**:** American organist and composer, best remembered for the his musical settings of "The Lord's Prayer" and "The 23rd Psalm," as well as the score for the cartoon "Ferdinand the Bull."

Mancini, Henry (b. 1924)**:** American pianist, composer, arranger, and conductor. Composed music for films including *Breakfast At Tiffany's*, *Charade*, *Days of Wine and Roses*, and *The Pink Panther*; TV themes including "Peter Gunn" and "Newhart"; and songs including "Moon River."

Mandel, Johnny (b. 1925)**:** American arranger and song composer. His songs include "The Shadow of Your Smile" and "The Song from *M*A*S*H* (Suicide Is Painless)."

Mann, Barry (b. 1939)**:** American songwriter, the partner and husband of Cynthia *Weil*, with whom he wrote "Blame it on the Bossa Nova," "Here You Come Again," "On Broadway," and "You've Lost that Lovin' Feelin'."

Marks, Johnny (1909–1985)**:** American songwriter, best-known for his Christmas songs, including "Rudolph the Red-Nosed Reindeer," "A Holly Jolly Christmas," "Rockin' Around the Christmas Tree," and "Silver and Gold."

Martin, Frank (1890–1974)**:** Swiss composer. The *Petite Symphonie Concertante* is his best-known work.

Martinu, Bohuslav (1890–1959)**:** Czech composer. His music is often influenced by Czech folk themes.

Mascagni, Pietro (1863–1945)**:** Italian post-romantic opera composer. He wrote *Cavalleria Rusticana*.

Mason, Lowell (1792–1872)**:** American romantic hymn writer. He wrote or arranged the music for "My Faith Looks Up to Thee," "When I Survey the Wondrous Cross," "Nearer, My God, to Thee," "O For a Thousand Tongues to Sing," and "Joy to the World."

Massenet, Jules (1842–1912)**:** French romantic composer of operas and songs. His best-known works include the operas *Manon* and *Werther*, "Meditation" (from *Thaïs*), and "Elegie" (from *Les Erinnyes*).

McCartney, Paul (b. 1942)**:** British guitarist, bass player, singer, songwriter, and record producer. With fellow Beatles member John *Lennon*, he wrote some of the group's biggest hits, including "Yesterday," "And I Love Her," "Get Back," "Eleanor Rigby," "The Fool on the Hill," "Let It Be," and "The Long and Winding Road." Later, on his own, he wrote "Band on the Run," "Live and Let Die," "My Love," and "Ebony and Ivory."

Mendelssohn, Fanny (1805–1847)**:** German romantic pianist and composer (married name Hensel), sister of *Felix.*

Mendelssohn, Felix (1809–1847)**:** German romantic composer. He wrote the oratorio *Elijah*, incidental music to *A Midsummer Night's Dream* ("Wedding March"), the song "Auf Flügeln des Gesanges" ("On Wings of Song"), piano music (*Songs without Words*), chamber works (Octet), symphonies (No. 3 "Scottish," No. 4 "Italian") and other orchestral music (*Fingal's Cave* Overture, a.k.a *The Hebrides*), two piano concertos, and a violin concerto.

Menken, Alan (b. 1949)**:** American composer, collaborator with Howard *Ashman.* His works include scores for the musical *Little Shop of Horrors* ("Suddenly Seymour") and the animated motion pictures *The Little Mermaid* ("Under the Sea," "Kiss the Girl") and *Beauty and the Beast.*

Mennin, Peter (b. 1923)**:** American composer. He has also served as president of the Juilliard School of Music.

Menotti, Gian Carlo (b. 1911)**:** Italian-American opera composer. He wrote *The Medium*, *The Telephone*, *The Consul*, and *Amahl and the Night Visitors.*

Mercer, Johnny (1909–1976)**:** American lyricist and composer. His songs include "Hooray for Hollywood," "You Must Have Been a Beautiful Baby," "Blues in the Night (My Mama Done Tol' Me)," "That Old Black Magic," "Moon River," and "Days of Wine and Roses."

Merrill, Bob (b. 1921)**:** American songwriter, whose works include the songs "Mambo Italiano," "(How Much is that) Doggie in the Window," and "Honeycomb," and the musicals *Carnival* ("Love Makes the World Go Round") and *Funny Girl* ("People," "Don't Rain on My Parade").

Messiaen, Olivier (1908–1992)**:** French composer of works for orchestra (*Turangalîla-Symphonie*, *Et Exspecto Resurrectionem Mortuorum*), organ (*Nativité du Seigneur*), and piano (*Vingt Regards sur l'Enfant Jésus*, *Catalogue d'Oiseaux*), as well as chamber music (*Quartet for the End of Time*). His highly individual musical language was influenced by birdsong, Indian rhythms, and stained-glass windows.

Meyerbeer, Giacomo (1791–1864)**:** German romantic composer of French operas, including *Robert le Diable*, *Les Huguenots*, and *Le Prophète*.

Milhaud, Darius (1892–1974)**:** French composer. He wrote the ballets *Le Boeuf sur le Toit* and *La Création du Monde* and the piano suites *Saudades do Brasil*. In the 1920s he was a member of the nationalistic group of composers known as "Les Six."

Monk, Thelonious (1918–1982)**:** Black American jazz pianist and composer who helped develop the *bebop* style of jazz. "'Round Midnight" is his best-known song.

Monteverdi, Claudio (1567–1643)**:** Italian composer who bridged the Renaissance (numerous madrigals) and baroque (the opera *L'Orfeo*) eras. His aria "Lasciatemi Morire," from the opera *Ariana*, remains popular among singers.

Moore, Douglas (1893–1969)**:** American composer, notably of the operas *The Devil and Daniel Webster* and *The Ballad of Baby Doe*.

Morley, Thomas (c. 1557–1602)**:** British Renaissance composer of madrigals, including "It Was a Lover and his Lass," "Sing We and Chant It," "April is in My Mistress' Face," and "My Bonnie Lass, She Smileth." He also wrote books of musical instruction.

Morton, Ferdinand "Jelly Roll" (1885–1941)**:** Black American jazz pianist and composer. His compositions include "The Original Jelly Roll Blues," "Wolverine Blues," and "King Porter Stomp."

Mouret, Jean Joseph (1682–1738)**:** French baroque composer of operas and opera-ballets. He is remembered for a Rondeau of his that was used as title music for the television series "Masterpiece Theatre."

Mozart, Leopold (1719–1787)**:** German-Austrian preclassical violinist, composer, and writer, father of *Wolfgang*. He wrote an important treatise on violin playing.

Mozart, Wolfgang Amadeus (1756–1791)**:** Austrian classical composer of operas (*Don Giovanni*, *The Marriage of Figaro*, *The Magic Flute*), symphonies, chamber music (*Eine kleine Nachtmusik*, "Dissonance" String Quartet), piano music (*Sonata Facile*, Variations on "Ah Vous Dirai-je, Maman" [a.k.a. Variations on "Twinkle, Twinkle, Little Star"], "Rondo alla Turca"), concertos (piano, violin, clarinet), and sacred music (*Ave Verum Corpus*, Requiem).

Mussorgsky, Modest (1839–1881)**:** Russian romantic composer, best-known for the opera *Boris Godunov* and the piano suite *Pictures at an Exhibition*. He was a member of the nationalistic group of composers known as "The Five."

N

Nelhybel, Vaclav (b. 1919)**:** Czech-American composer, especially known for his works for symphonic band.

Newley, Anthony (b. 1931)**:** British composer, singer, and actor. Broadway musicals include *The Roar Of The Greasepaint—The Smell Of The Crowd* and *Stop The World—I Want To Get Off* (both with Leslie *Bricusse*).

Nicolai, Otto (1810–1849)**:** German romantic composer. He wrote the opera *The Merry Wives of Windsor*.

Nielsen, Carl (1865–1931)**:** Danish late-romantic composer, most importantly of songs and symphonies.

Niles, John Jacob (1892–1980)**:** American folk singer and song composer. Among the songs he wrote or adapted are "I Wonder as I Wander," "Black is the Color of My True Love's Hair," and "Go 'way from My Window."

Nyro, Laura (b. 1947)**:** American songwriter and singer. Her songs, which have been recorded by numerous artists, include "And When I Die," "Stoney End," "Wedding Bell Blues," "Stoned Soul Picnic," and "Eli's Comin'."

O

Obrecht, Jacob (c. 1450–1505)**:** Dutch Renaissance composer of masses and other sacred polyphonic vocal music.

Ockeghem, Johannes (c. 1410–1497)**:** Franco-Flemish early-Renaissance composer of masses and sacred motets.

Offenbach, Jacques (1819–1880)**:** French romantic composer of operas and operettas. Popular individual numbers from these works include the "Barcarolle" from *The Tales of Hoffmann* and the "Cancan" ("Galop") from *Orpheus in Hades*.

Orff, Carl (1895–1982)**:** German composer, best-known for the oratorio *Carmina Burana*. He was also an important music educator, whose methods incorporated simple percussion instruments now called "Orff instruments."

P

Pachelbel, Johann (1653–1706)**:** German baroque composer and organist. Although he wrote several enduring organ works, his most popular composition in the Canon in D for strings.

Paderewski, Ignace Jan (1860–1941)**:** Polish late-romantic pianist and composer. He wrote a popular Minuet in G, helped edit the works of Chopin, and served as Prime Minister of Poland.

Paganini, Niccolò (1782–1840)**:** Italian romantic violinist and composer. He wrote 24 Caprices for solo violin (No. 24 has been used as a theme for variations by *Brahms*, *Rachmaninoff*, *Lutoslawski*, and *Lloyd Webber*) and several violin concertos (one movement, "La Campanella," was popularized in an arrangement for piano by *Liszt*).

Palestrina, Giovanni Pierluigi da (c. 1525–1594)**:** Italian Renaissance composer of sacred polyphonic vocal music, including the *Missa Papae Marcelli* (*Pope Marcellus Mass*), *Lamentations*, and the motet *Hodie Christus Natus Est*. His setting of the liturgical text "Gloria Patri" later became the music for the hymn "The Strife Is O'er, the Battle Done."

Parish, Mitchell (b. 1900)**:** American lyricist, who wrote English lyrics for a number of foreign songs and instrumental numbers, including "Volare," "La Cucaracha," "Moonlight Serenade," "Sleigh Ride," and "Star Dust."

Parry, Sir **Hubert** (1848–1918)**:** British late-romantic composer, especially of choral music.

Partch, Harry (1901–1976)**:** American composer specializing in *microtonal* music. He built many special instruments, including the "harmonic cannon" and "cloud chamber bowls," to play his compositions.

Peeters, Flor (1903–1986)**:** Belgian composer and organist. He wrote many works for organ, including teaching methods, as well as sacred vocal music.

Penderecki, Krzysztof (b. 1933)**:** Polish composer. He wrote the *Threnody for the Victims of Hiroshima*, for 52 strings, as well as a setting of the *St. Luke Passion*.

Pergolesi, Giovanni Battista (1710–1736)**:** Italian baroque composer of operatic works (including the intermezzo *La Serva Padrona*) and sacred music (especially the *Stabat Mater*). Igor *Stravinsky* used themes of Pergolesi's in his ballet *Pulcinella*.

Peri, Jacopo (1561–1633)**:** Italian composer of the early baroque. His *Euridice* is considered by some to be the first opera.

Pérotin (c. 1150–c. 1230)**:** French medieval composer specializing in an early form of *polyphony* known as *organum*.

Persichetti, Vincent (1915–1987)**:** American composer, especially of sacred and piano music.

Piccinni, Niccolò (1728–1800)**:** Italian classical opera composer. He is best-known for his rivalry with Christoph Willibald *Gluck*.

Piston, Walter (1894–1976)**:** American composer and teacher. He is remembered for the orchestral suite from the ballet *The Incredible Flutist*, as well as for a series of textbooks on music theory.

Ponchielli, Amilcare (1834–1886)**:** Italian romantic opera composer, remembered for *La Gioconda*, which contains the "Dance of the Hours."

Porter, Cole (1892–1964)**:** American songwriter who wrote musicals including *Anything Goes* and *Kiss Me, Kate*, and songs including "Wunderbar," "I Love Paris," "Begin the Beguine," "Night and Day," and "It's De-Lovely."

Poulenc, Francis (1899–1963)**:** French composer. He wote the opera *Dialogues des Carmélites* and a setting of the *Gloria*. In the 1920s he was a member of the nationalistic group of composers known as "Les Six."

Praetorius, Michael (c. 1571–1621)**:** German Renaissance composer and writer. He harmonized the Christmas carol "Lo, How a Rose E'er Blooming" and wrote detailed descriptions of the musical instruments of his day.

Presley, Elvis (1935–1977)**:** American singer and songwriter. He co-wrote such songs as "Love Me Tender," "Don't Be Cruel," "All Shook Up," and "Heartbreak Hotel."

Prokofiev, Sergei (1891–1953)**:** Russian composer. Popular works of his include *Peter and the Wolf*, the March from the opera *The Love for Three Oranges*, the *Visions Fugitives* for piano, the Symphony No. 5, and the ballet *Romeo and Juliet*. His film music, including scores for *Alexander Nevsky* and *Lieutenant Kijé*, is often presented in concert form.

Puccini, Giacomo (1858–1924)**:** Italian late-romantic opera composer. He wrote *La Bohème*, *Tosca*, *Madama Butterfly*, *Manon Lescaut*, and *Gianni Schicchi*.

Purcell, Henry (1659–1695)**:** British baroque composer of opera (*Dido and Aeneas*), vocal music, and pieces for harpsichord and organ ("Trumpet Tune").

Q

Quantz, Johann Joachim (1697–1773)**:** German baroque and preclassical flutist, composer, and writer. He composed many sonatas and concertos for flute, and wrote an important treatise on flute playing.

R

Rachmaninoff, Sergei (1873–1943)**:** Russian late-romantic composer and pianist. His best-known works include the Prelude in C# Minor for piano, the *Rhapsody on a Theme of Paganini* for piano and orchestra, the Piano Concerto No. 2, and the Symphony No. 2.

Rameau, Jean-Philippe (1683–1764)**:** French baroque composer and theorist. He wrote many operas and ballets, and an important book on *harmony*.

Raposo, Joe (1937–1989)**:** American songwriter, best-known for his children's songs, including "Sing," "C is for Cookie," "Bein' Green," and "Sesame Street Theme."

Ravel, Maurice (1875–1937)**:** French composer, sometimes linked with *Debussy* and *impressionism*. He wrote *Boléro*, the ballet *Daphnis and Chloé*, the *Mother Goose* Suite, and *Rapsodie Espagnole*. His piano music includes *Valses Nobles et Sentimentales*, *Gaspard de la Nuit*, and *Pavane for a Dead Infant*. He also orchestrated *Pictures at an Exhibition*, by Modest *Mussorgsky*.

Reger, Max (1873–1913)**:** German late-romantic composer. He wrote the *Variations and Fugue on a Theme of Mozart* for orchestra, and a great deal of organ music.

Respighi, Ottorino (1879–1936)**:** Italian post-romantic composer. His best-known works include *The Fountains of Rome* and *The Pines of Rome* for orchestra and the orchestral arrangements of *Ancient Airs and Dances*.

Rice, Tim (b. 1944)**:** British lyricist, collaborator with Andrew *Lloyd Webber* in musicals including *Jesus Christ Superstar* and *Evita*. Also co-wrote *Chess* ("One Night in Bangkok").

Rimsky-Korsakov, Nikolai (1844–1908)**:** Russian romantic composer. He wrote the symphonic suite *Sheherazade*, the *Russian Easter Festival* Overture, *Capriccio Espagnol*, "Flight of the Bumble Bee," and the operas *Snow Maiden*, *Sadko*, *The Golden Cockerel*, and *Mozart and Salieri*. His brilliant orchestral style (and his book on *orchestration*) influenced generations of Russian and French composers. He was a member of the nationalistic group of composers known as "The Five."

Rodgers, Richard (1902–1979): American popular composer, collaborator with Lorenz *Hart* and Oscar *Hammerstein* II. He wrote musicals including *Oklahoma!*, *South Pacific*, *Carousel*, *The King and I*, and *The Sound of Music*, and songs including "The Lady is a Tramp," "My Funny Valentine," and "Bewitched." He also scored the television documentary "Victory at Sea."

Romberg, Sigmund (1887–1951): Hungarian-American popular composer. He wrote operettas including *The Student Prince*, *Maytime*, and *The Desert Song*.

Rome, Harold (b. 1908): American composer for the stage, whose musicals include *Wish You Were Here*, *I Can Get it for You Wholesale*, *Destry Rides Again*, and *Fanny*.

Rorem, Ned (b. 1923): American composer, chiefly of songs. His *Air Music* for orchestra won the Pulitzer Prize for music.

Ross, Jerry (1926–1955): American lyricist, who collaborated with Richard *Adler* on the musicals *The Pajama Game* ("Hey There," "Hernando's Hideaway") and *Damn Yankees* ("Whatever Lola Wants," "Heart"), as well as the song "Rags to Riches."

Rossini, Gioachino (1792–1868): Italian classical composer of operas, including *William Tell*, *La Cenerentola* (*Cinderella*), *Semiramide*, *The Italian Girl in Algiers*, and *The Barber of Seville*. His sacred *Stabat Mater* is also well-known.

Rota, Nino (1911–1979): Italian composer, best-known for his film scores, including *Romeo and Juliet* and *The Godfather*.

Roussel, Albert (1869–1937): French composer of works for piano, orchestra, and chamber ensembles (especially winds).

Rózsa, Miklós (b. 1907): Hungarian-American composer of film music, including *Spellbound*, *Ben Hur*, and *El Cid*.

Rubinstein, Anton (1829–1894): Russian romantic composer and pianist. He is best-known for piano pieces such as "Kamennoi-Ostrov" and "Melody in F."

S

Sager, Carole Bayer (b. 1946)**:** American songwriter, who has collaborated with Marvin Hamlisch (*They're Playing Our Song*) and one-time husband Burt Bacharach ("Arthur's Theme," "That's What Friends are For").

Saint-Saëns, Camille (1835–1921)**:** French romantic composer of the opera *Samson and Delilah*, the tone poem *Danse Macabre*, the "Organ" Symphony, and *The Carnival of the Animals*.

Salieri, Antonio (1750–1825)**:** Italian classical composer, especially of operas and sacred vocal music. He is infamous for his supposed rivalry with Wolfgang Amadeus *Mozart*.

Sammartini, Giovanni Battista (c. 1700–1775)**:** Italian preclassical composer of symphonies, concertos, and other instrumental music.

Satie, Erik (1866–1925)**:** French composer of *Three Gymnopédies*, *Three Pieces in the Form of a Pear*, *Vexations*, and *Parade*.

Scarlatti, Alessandro (1660–1725)**:** Italian baroque composer, father of *Domenico*. Although mainly known for his operas (*Il Tigrane*, *Il Trionfo dell'Onore*), his output also included masses, cantatas, and toccatas for harpsichord.

Scarlatti, Domenico (1685–1757)**:** Italian baroque and preclassical composer of some 600 harpsichord sonatas. A longtime resident of Spain, he influenced Antonio *Soler*.

Schaeffer, Pierre (b. 1910)**:** French composer who, with Pierre *Henry*, originated *musique concrète*.

Schmidt, Harvey (b. 1929)**:** American composer, collaborator with Tom *Jones* on the musicals *The Fantasticks* ("Try to Remember"), *110 in the Shade*, and *I Do! I Do!* ("My Cup Runneth Over").

Schoenberg, Arnold (1874–1951)**:** Austro-Hungarian composer of *Verklärte Nacht*, *Moses and Aaron*, *Gurrelieder*, *De Profundis*, four string quartets, *Ode to Napoleon*, and *Pierrot Lunaire*. His innovations included *twelve-tone technique*, Klangfarbenmelodie ("tone-color melody"), and *Sprechstimme*.

Schönberg, Claude-Michel (b. 1941)**:** French composer of Hungarian descent, whose stage works with author and lyricist Alain *Boublil* include *Les Misérables* and *Miss Saigon.*

Schubert, Franz (1797–1828)**:** Austrian early-romantic composer. His best-known works include symphonies (No. 5, No. 8 "Unfinished," No. 9 "Great C Major"), chamber music, piano pieces ("Marche Militaire," *Moments Musicaux*, Impromptus), the Mass in G, the Overture to the play *Rosamunde*, and the songs (*Lieder*) "Erlkönig" ("The Erl-King"), "Die Forelle" ("The Trout"), "Gretchen am Spinnrade" ("Gretchen at the Spinning-Wheel"), "Der Tod und das Mädchen" ("Death and the Maiden"), "Ständchen" ("Serenade"), and "An die Musik" ("To Music").

Schuller, Gunther (b. 1925)**:** American composer, originator of *third-stream* music. He wrote *Seven Studies on Themes of Paul Klee* and *American Triptych.*

Schuman, William (b. 1910)**:** American composer of orchestral music (symphonies, *Credendum*, *New England Triptych*).

Schumann, Robert (1810–1856)**:** German romantic composer and journalist. His best-known works include the Piano Concerto in A Minor, the songs "Du Ring an meinem Finger" and "Widmung" ("Dedication"), the Symphony No. 4, and the piano works *Papillons*, *Carnaval*, *Album for the Young* ("The Wild Horseman," "The Happy Farmer"), and *Scenes from Childhood* ("Träumerei").

Schütz, Heinrich (1585–1672)**:** German baroque composer of sacred vocal polyphonic music, including settings of the Psalms and collections entitled *Sacred Symphonies.*

Schwartz, Arthur (1900–1984)**:** American popular composer, whose works include the musical *The Band Wagon* ("Dancing in the Dark") and the songs "By Myself" and "That's Entertainment."

Scriabin, Alexander (1872–1915)**:** Russian post-romantic composer. He wrote the orchestral works *The Poem of Ecstasy* and *Prometheus, the Poem of Fire*, as well as many preludes, etudes, sonatas, and other works for piano.

Sedaka, Neil (b. 1939)**:** American song composer and singer, whose songs include "Breaking up is Hard to Do," "Calendar Girl," "Happy Birthday, Sweet Sixteen," "Love will Keep Us Together," and "Solitaire."

Seeger, Pete (b. 1919)**:** American folk singer and songwriter, son of *Ruth Crawford* Seeger. His songs include "Kisses Sweeter than Wine," "Where Have All the Flowers Gone?," and "If I Had a Hammer."

Seeger, Ruth Crawford (1901–1953)**:** American composer. Her String Quartet is her best-known work. She also collected folk songs.

Sessions, Roger (1896–1985)**:** American composer of symphonies, concertos, music for stage (*The Black Maskers*, *Montezuma*), vocal works (*When Lilacs Last in the Dooryard Bloom'd*), and piano music (*From My Diary*).

Shchedrin, Rodion (b. 1932)**:** Russian composer of dramatic and orchestral music, but perhaps best-known for his compositions for piano (Preludes and Fugues, *Polyphonic Album*).

Sherman, Richard M. (b. 1928) and **Robert B.** (b. 1925: American songwriting brothers associated with the Walt Disney studios in projects such as *Mary Poppins* ("Supercalifragilisticexpialidocious," "Feed the Birds"), *Winnie the Pooh* ("The Wonderful Thing about Tiggers"), and Disneyland ("It's a Small World"). They also wrote "You're Sixteen," as well as songs for *Chitty Chitty Bang Bang* and *Charlotte's Web*.

Shostakovich, Dmitri (1906–1975)**:** Russian composer of symphonies, string quartets and other chamber music, and operas (*The Nose*, *Lady Macbeth of Mtsensk*).

Sibelius, Jean (1865–1957)**:** Finnish late-romantic composer of orchestral music, including symphonies, the "Valse Triste," *Finlandia* (a theme of which was used for the hymn "Be Still, My Soul"), the *Karelia* Overture and Suite, the *Lemminkäinen* Suite (a.k.a. *Four Legends from the Kalevala*; includes "The Swan of Tuonela"), *En Saga*, and *Tapiola*.

Siegmeister, Elie (1909–1992)**:** American composer of orchestral and band music. He also wrote the musical *Sing Out, Sweet Land*.

Simon, Paul (b. 1942)**:** American pop singer, guitarist, and songwriter, half of folk-rock duo Simon and Garfunkel in the 1960s. His songs include "Bridge over Troubled Water" and "Me and Julio Down by the Schoolyard." His album *Graceland* broke new ground in its use of African musicians.

Smetana, Bedrich (1824–1884)**:** Czech romantic composer of operas (*The Bartered Bride*), orchestral music (*My Fatherland*, including "The Moldau"), chamber music (the String Quartet "From My Life"), and piano pieces.

Smyth, Dame **Ethel** (1858–1944)**:** British late-romantic composer of operas (*The Wreckers*), vocal music (Mass in D), and orchestral music (*Antony and Cleopatra* Overture, *March of the Women*).

Soler, Antonio (1729–1783)**:** Spanish baroque composer and organist, known for his keyboard sonatas.

Sondheim, Stephen (b. 1930)**:** American composer and lyricist, best-known for his musicals, including *A Funny Thing Happened on the Way to the Forum* ("Comedy Tonight"), *Company* ("Being Alive"), *A Little Night Music* ("Send in the Clowns"), *Sweeney Todd* ("Pretty Women"), *Sunday in the Park with George*, and *Into the Woods*. He also wrote the lyrics to *West Side Story* and *Gypsy*.

Sor, Fernando (1778–1839)**:** Spanish classical composer and guitarist, remembered for his compositions for guitar.

Sousa, John Philip (1854–1932)**:** American popular composer and band leader, known as the "March King." His compositions include the operettas *El Capitan* and *The Free Lance*, and the marches "The Stars and Stripes Forever," "Semper Fidelis," "King Cotton," and "The Washington Post." He also specified the design of the *sousaphone*.

Spohr, Ludwig (1784–1859)**:** German romantic composer of violin concertos, symphonies, and chamber music (string quartets, Octet, Nonet).

Stamitz, Johann (1717–1757)**:** Bohemian preclassical composer of symphonies and the central figure of the *Mannheim school*.

Stamitz, Carl (1745–1801)**:** German early-classical composer of symphonies, son of *Johann*.

Still, William Grant (1895–1978)**:** Black American composer. The "Afro-American" Symphony is one of his best-known works.

Sting (Gordon Sumner) (b. 1952)**:** British singer, guitarist, bassist, and songwriter. Leader of the rock trio The Police in the early 1980s. Later incorporated jazz into his solo albums, including *Dream of the Blue Turtles* and *Nothing Like the Sun.*

Stockhausen, Karlheinz (b. 1928)**:** German composer. Among his most influential works are *Kontrapunkte* and *Kontakte*, the tape piece *Gesang der Jünglinge*, and numerous *Klavierstücke* (Piano Pieces).

Stoller, Mike (b. 1933)**:** American songwriter, partner of Jerry *Leiber* in hits such as "Hound Dog," "Jailhouse Rock," and "Spanish Harlem."

Stradella, Alessandro (1644–1682)**:** Italian baroque composer of dramatic, vocal, and instrumental music, the latter often employing *concerto grosso* form. He wrote the sacred song "Pietà, Signore."

Strauss, Johann Jr. (1825–1899)**:** Austrian romantic composer and conductor, known as the "Waltz King." His compositions include the operettas *Die Fledermaus* and *The Gypsy Baron* and the waltzes "By the Beautiful Blue Danube," "Voices of Spring," "Vienna Life," "Artist's Life," "Emperor Waltz," and "Tales from the Vienna Woods." With his brother Josef he wrote the "Pizzicato Polka."

Strauss, Johann Sr. (1804–1849)**:** Austrian romantic composer and conductor, father of *Johann Jr.* In addition to many waltzes, he wrote the "Radetzky" March.

Strauss, Richard (1864–1949)**:** German post-romantic composer of songs, operas (*Elektra*, *Salome*, *Der Rosenkavalier*, *Ariadne auf Naxos*), and tone poems (*Ein Heldenleben*, *Don Quixote*, *Till Eulenspiegel's Merry Pranks*, and *Also sprach Zarathustra*).

Stravinsky, Igor (1882–1971)**:** Russian composer of ballets (*Petrushka*, *The Firebird*, *Pulcinella*, *Les Noces*), opera and music drama (*Oedipus Rex*, *The Rake's Progress*, *The Soldier's Tale*), concertos (violin, clarinet), and vocal music (*Symphony of Psalms*). His style ranged from extreme dissonance and rhythmic complexity (The premiere of his ballet *The Rite of Spring* in 1913 incited a well-known riot.) to *neoclassicism* ("Dumbarton Oaks" Concerto, Symphony in C) to *twelve-tone technique* (*Agon*, *Canticum Sacrum*).

Strayhorn, William "Billy" (1915–1967)**:** Black American jazz composer. He collaborated with Duke *Ellington* on several songs, including "Satin Doll," and by himself wrote "Take the 'A' Train" and "Lush Life," among others.

Strouse, Charles (b. 1928)**:** American composer who scored the movie *Bonnie and Clyde*, as well as the musicals *Bye Bye Birdie* ("Put on a Happy Face," "Kids"), *Applause*, and *Annie* ("Tomorrow").

Styne, Jule (b. 1905)**:** American composer, chiefly of songs for the stage and screen. His songs include "Let It Snow! Let It Snow! Let It Snow!," "Diamonds Are a Girl's Best Friend," "Three Coins in the Fountain," "Everything's Coming Up Roses," and "People."

Subotnick, Morton (b. 1933)**:** American composer of electronic music, including *Silver Apples of the Moon.*

Sullivan, Sir **Arthur** (1842–1900)**:** British romantic composer, best-known for his operettas (to librettos by W.S. *Gilbert*), including *HMS Pinafore*, *The Pirates of Penzance*, and *The Mikado*. He also wrote the music for the hymn "Onward, Christian Soldiers" and the song "The Lost Chord."

Suppé, Franz von (1819–1895)**:** Austrian romantic composer remembered for the overtures to stage works such as *Poet and Peasant*, *Light Cavalry*, and *Morning, Noon and Night in Vienna.*

Süssmayr, Franz Xaver (1766–1803)**:** Austrian classical composer, remembered as the man who completed the unfinished *Requiem* by Wolfgang Amadeus *Mozart.*

Sweelinck, Jan Pieterszoon (1562–1621)**:** Dutch Renaissance composer and organist who wrote vocal music (especially settings of the Psalms) and works for keyboard.

Szymanowski, Karol (1882–1937)**:** Polish post-romantic composer, chiefly of piano music (Sonatas, Mazurkas) and works for voice(s) and orchestra (*Love-Songs of Hafiz*, *Stabat Mater*).

T

Tailleferre, Germaine (1892–1983)**:** French composer of operas, ballets, instrumental works, and vocal music. In the 1920s she was a member of the nationalistic group of composers known as "Les Six."

Takemitsu, Toru (b. 1930)**:** Japanese composer. His works include *Textures* (for piano and orchestra) and *November Steps* (for *biwa*, *shakuhachi*, and orchestra).

Tallis, Thomas (c. 1505–1585)**:** British Renaissance composer of sacred vocal music, especially service music for the Anglican church. He wrote the hymn tune known as "Tallis' Canon," as well as the motet *Spem in Alium*, for eight five-part choirs.

Tartini, Giuseppe (1692–1770)**:** Italian baroque composer and violinist. He wrote many virtuoso sonatas and concertos for violin.

Taupin, Bernie (b. 1950)**:** British lyricist, best-known for his long-standing collaboration with Elton *John*.

Tchaikovsky, Piotr Ilyich (1840–1893)**:** Russian romantic composer of ballets (*Swan Lake*, *The Sleeping Beauty*, *The Nutcracker*), operas (*Eugene Onegin*, *Mazeppa*, *The Queen of Spades*), symphonies, *program music* (*Romeo and Juliet*, *Francesca da Rimini*, *Capriccio Italien*, *1812* Overture), concertos (piano, violin), and piano music ("Song without Words").

Tcherepnin, Alexander (1899–1977)**:** Russian-American composer and pianist. His symphonies and piano concertos are among his best-known works.

Telemann, Georg Philipp (1681–1767)**:** German baroque and preclassical composer. He wrote much sacred music, as well as many operas, concertos, and sonatas. Carl Philipp Emanuel *Bach* was his godson and namesake.

Thomas, Ambroise (1811–1896)**:** French romantic opera composer. *Mignon* and *Hamlet* are his best-known works.

Thompson, Randall (1899–1984)**:** American composer of choral music (*The Testament of Freedom*, *Frostiana*) and symphonies.

Thomson, Virgil (1896–1989)**:** American composer and critic, best-known for the operas *Four Saints in Three Acts* and *The Mother of Us All*, and the film scores *The Plow that Broke the Plains* and *Louisiana Story*.

Tiomkin, Dimitri (1894–1979)**:** Russian-American composer of film music. His scores include *Lost Horizon*, *High Noon*, *The Guns of Navarone*, and *The Fall of the Roman Empire*.

Tippett, Sir **Michael** (b. 1905)**:** British composer of operas (*King Priam*, *The Knot Garden*), choral works (*A Child of Our Time*, *The Vision of St. Augustine*), symphonies, and songs.

Toch, Ernst (1887–1964)**:** Austrian-American composer of symphonies, film scores, program music (*Pinocchio*), and choral works ("Geographical Fugue"), but perhaps best-known for his writings on music.

Torelli, Giuseppe (1658–1709)**:** Italian baroque composer specializing in the trio sonata, solo concerto, and *concerto grosso*. He also wrote the song "Tu Lo Sai."

Türk, Daniel Gottlob (1750–1830)**:** German classical composer, remembered for his sonatas and teaching pieces for keyboard.

U

Ussachevsky, Vladimir (1911–1990)**:** Russian-American composer, who, with Otto *Luening*, was central in the development of tape music in the U.S.

V

Vaccai, Nicola (1790–1848)**:** Italian classical composer, especially of teaching pieces for voice.

Van Heusen, Jimmy (b. 1913)**:** American popular composer. Wrote the music to songs including "Call Me Irresponsible," "Darn That Dream," "Here's That Rainy Day," "High Hopes," and "Swinging on a Star."

Varèse, Edgard (1883–1965)**:** French-American composer. His best-known works include *Poème Électronique* for tape, *Ionisation* for percussion ensemble, and *Density 21.5* for solo flute.

Vaughan Williams, Ralph (1872–1958)**:** British composer of symphonies (No. 2 "London," No. 7 *Sinfonia Antartica*) and other orchestral music (*Fantasia on a Theme by Thomas Tallis*, *The Lark Ascending*, *Fantasia on Greensleeves*), choral works (*A Sea Symphony*), operas and ballets (*The Pilgrim's Progress*, *Job*), and hymn tunes ("Sine Nomine," a.k.a. "For All the Saints").

Verdi, Giuseppe (1813–1901)**:** Italian romantic opera composer. He wrote *Rigoletto* ("La Donna è Mobile"), *Il Trovatore*, *La Traviata* ("Drinking Song"), *Don Carlo*, *Un Ballo in Maschera*, *La Forza del Destino*, *Aïda* ("Triumphal March"), *Otello*, *Macbeth*, and *Falstaff*. His Requiem is also an important work.

Victoria, Tomás Luis de (1548–1611)**:** Spanish Renaissance composer of sacred vocal music, including the motets *O Magnum Mysterium* and *O Vos Omnes*.

Villa-Lobos, Heitor (1887–1959)**:** Brazilian composer, best-known for his series of *Bachianas Brasileiras* (No. 5, for soprano and eight cellos) and *Choros*, and for his piano music.

Vitry, Philippe de (1291–1361)**:** French medieval composer of motets. He applied the term *ars nova* to his style of vocal polyphony, and *ars antiqua* to that of the preceding generation.

Vivaldi, Antonio (1678–1741)**:** Italian baroque composer of some 400 concertos, most for solo violin (*The Four Seasons*), as well as other instrumental works, and vocal music (*Gloria*). By virtue of his vocation and the color of his hair, he was known as "the red priest."

W

Wagner, Richard (1813–1883)**:** German romantic composer of operas, which he came to call *music dramas*. He wrote *Rienzi*, *The Flying Dutchman*, *Tannhäuser* (March, "The Evening Star"), *Lohengrin* ("Bridal Chorus"), *The Ring of the Nibelung* (*The Gold of the Rhein*, *The Valkyries* ["The Ride of the Valkyries"], *Siegfried*, *The Twilight of the Gods*), *Tristan and Isolde* (Prelude and "Liebestod"), *The Master-Singers of Nuremberg*, and *Parsifal*. For his works he created the *Wagner tuba* and required the development of the *Heldentenor*.

Waldteufel, Emil (1837–1915)**:** French romantic composer, best-known for the waltzes *The Skaters*, *Très Jolie*, *Estudiantina* (on themes by Paul Lacome), and *España* (on themes by Emmanuel *Chabrier*).

Waller, Thomas "Fats" (1904–1943)**:** Black American pianist and composer, remembered for the songs "Honeysuckle Rose," "The Joint Is Jumpin'," and "Ain't Misbehavin'."

Walton, Sir **William** (1902–1983)**:** British composer, known for the orchestral suite *Façade* and the choral work *Belshazzar's Feast*.

Warren, Harry (1893–1981)**:** American popular composer, whose songs include "42nd Street," "Lullaby of Broadway," "Chattanooga Choo-Choo," "You Must Have Been a Beautiful Baby," and "We're in the Money."

Webb, Jimmy (b. 1946)**:** American popular songwriter. His songs include "By the Time I Get to Phoenix," "Up, Up and Away," "Wichita Lineman," and "MacArthur Park."

Weber, Carl Maria von (1786–1826)**:** German early-romantic composer. He wrote the operas *Der Freischütz*, *Euryanthe*, and *Oberon*, as well as *Invitation to the Dance* for piano and *Grand Duo Concertant* for clarinet and piano.

Webern, Anton (1883–1945)**:** Austrian composer, pupil of Arnold *Schoenberg* and exponent of *serial* techniques. His *Piano Variations* and other instrumental works are considered important.

Webster, Paul Francis (1907–1984)**:** American lyricist for songs including "Love Is a Many-Splendored Thing," "The Shadow of Your Smile," "Somewhere, My Love," and "The Twelfth of Never."

Weil, Cynthia (b. 1937)**:** American songwriter, the partner and wife of Barry *Mann*, with whom she wrote "Blame it on the Bossa Nova," "Here You Come Again," "On Broadway," and "You've Lost that Lovin' Feelin'."

Weill, Kurt (1900–1950)**:** German-American composer well-known for his theatrical works, including *The Threepenny Opera* ("The Ballad of Mack the Knife"), *Rise and Fall of the City of Mahagonny*, *Lost in the Stars*, *Lady in the Dark*, *Knickerbocker Holiday* ("September Song"), and *One Touch of Venus* ("Speak Low").

Widor, Charles-Marie (1844–1937)**:** French late-romantic composer and organist. He wrote 10 "Symphonies" for solo organ; No. 5 ends with a well-known Toccata. He also, with Albert Schweitzer, edited the organ works of J.S. *Bach*.

Williams, Hank Sr. (1923–1953)**:** American country & western singer and songwriter. His songs include "Cold, Cold Heart," "I'm So Lonesome I Could Cry," "Jambalaya (On the Bayou)," and "Your Cheatin' Heart."

Williams, John (b. 1932)**:** American composer, arranger, and conductor. Film scores include *Jaws*, *Star Wars*, *Superman*, *E.T.*, *Close Encounters of the Third Kind*, and *Raiders of the Lost Ark*.

Willson, Meredith (1902–1984)**:** American composer of Broadway musicals, most notably *The Music Man* ("Goodnight, My Someone," "Seventy Six Trombones") and *The Unsinkable Molly Brown* ("I Ain't Down Yet").

Wolf, Hugo (1860–1903)**:** Austrian romantic composer of art songs (*Lieder*). He set poems by Mörike, Eichendorff, and Goethe, as well as German translations of Italian and Spanish poetry.

Wonder, Stevie (b. 1950)**:** Black American singer, keyboardist, and songwriter. His hit songs include "You Are the Sunshine of My Life," "Signed, Sealed, Delivered, I'm Yours," and "I Just Called to Say I Love You."

Wright, Robert C. (b. 1914)**:** American songwriter for the musical theatre, collaborator with George *Forrest* on *Grand Hotel*, *Kismet* ("Stranger in Paradise"; based on the music of *Borodin*), and *Song of Norway* ("Strange Music"; based on the music of *Grieg*).

Wuorinen, Charles (b. 1938)**:** American composer. He is best-known for the Pulitzer-Prize-winning electronic composition *Time's Encomium*.

X

Xenakis, Iannis (b. 1922)**:** French composer of Greek descent. He is best-known for his mathematical approach to composition.

Y

Yon, Pietro (1886–1943)**:** Italian-American organist and late-romantic composer. He wrote "Gesù Bambino."

Youmans, Vincent (1898–1946)**:** American composer for the Broadway stage, including the musicals *No, No, Nanette* ("Tea for Two," "I Want to Be Happy") and *Hit The Deck!* ("Sometimes I'm Happy," "Hallelujah").

Yradier, Sebastián de (1809–1865)**:** Spanish romantic composer, remembered for his song "La Paloma." Georges *Bizet* adapted a melody by Yradier for the "Habanera" in the opera *Carmen*.

Z

Zappa, Frank (b. 1940)**:** American singer, guitarist, and composer. Led the group The Mothers of Invention in the late 1960s and early 1970s. Noted for his mixture of rock music and the avant garde.

Zelenka, Jan Dismas (1679–1745)**:** Czech baroque composer of chamber music and sacred vocal works.

Zelter, Carl Friedrich (1758–1832)**:** German classical and early-romantic song composer.

Zemlinsky, Alexander (1871–1942)**:** Austrian post-romantic composer and conductor. He was a teacher (and, later, brother-in-law) of Arnold *Schoenberg*.

Zimmermann, Bernd Alois (1918–1970)**:** German composer, noted for quoting music of other composers in his scores. He wrote the opera *Die Soldaten* (*The Soldiers*).

Time Line of Major Composers

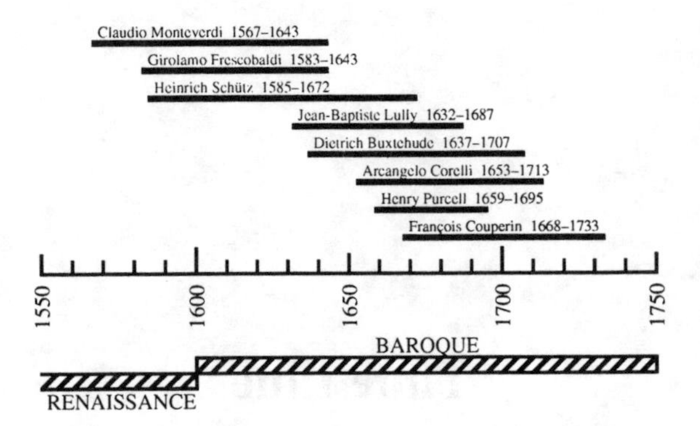

Claudio Monteverdi 1567–1643
Girolamo Frescobaldi 1583–1643
Heinrich Schütz 1585–1672
Jean-Baptiste Lully 1632–1687
Dietrich Buxtehude 1637–1707
Arcangelo Corelli 1653–1713
Henry Purcell 1659–1695
François Couperin 1668–1733
1550
1600
1650
1700
1750
BAROQUE
RENAISSANCE

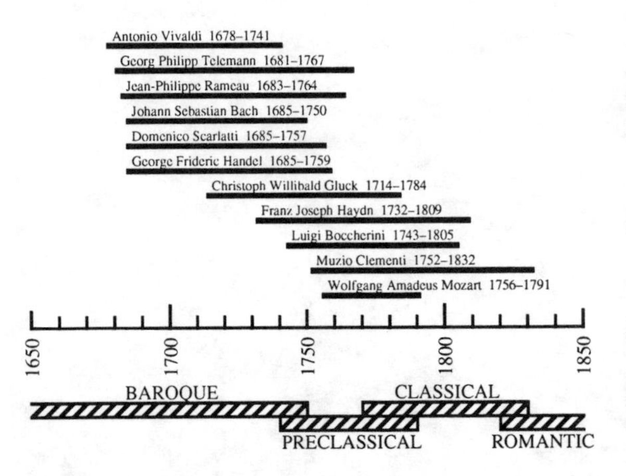

Antonio Vivaldi 1678–1741
Georg Philipp Telemann 1681–1767
Jean-Philippe Rameau 1683–1764
Johann Sebastian Bach 1685–1750
Domenico Scarlatti 1685–1757
George Frideric Handel 1685–1759
Christoph Willibald Gluck 1714–1784
Franz Joseph Haydn 1732–1809
Luigi Boccherini 1743–1805
Muzio Clementi 1752–1832
Wolfgang Amadeus Mozart 1756–1791
1650
1700
1750
1800
1850
BAROQUE
CLASSICAL
PRECLASSICAL
ROMANTIC

Guilliaume de Machaut 1300–1377
1250
1300
1350
1400
1450
MIDDLE AGES

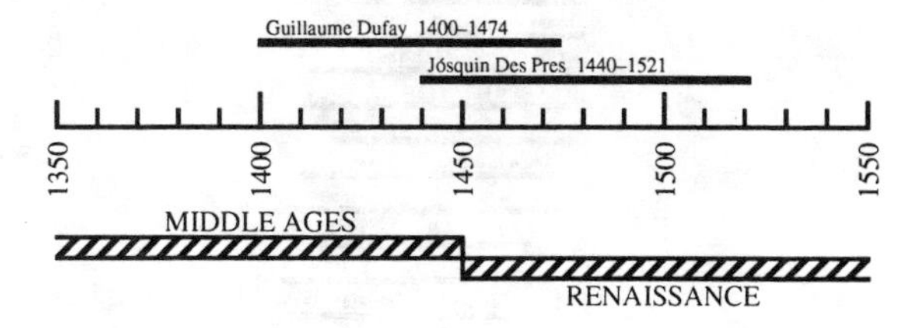
Guillaume Dufay 1400–1474
Jósquin Des Pres 1440–1521
1350
1400
1450
1500
1550
MIDDLE AGES
RENAISSANCE

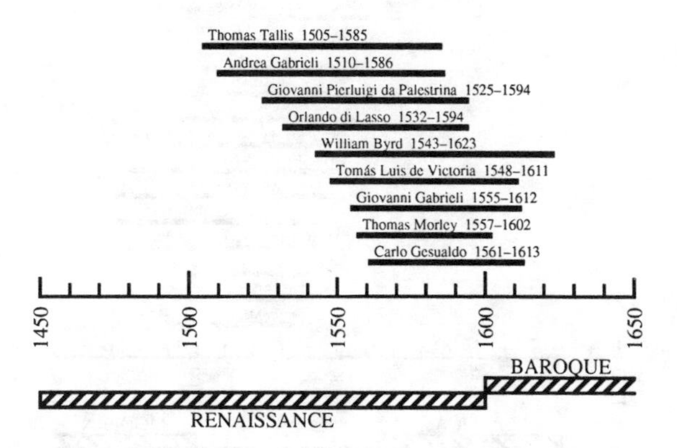
Thomas Tallis 1505–1585
Andrea Gabrieli 1510–1586
Giovanni Pierluigi da Palestrina 1525–1594
Orlando di Lasso 1532–1594
William Byrd 1543–1623
Tomás Luis de Victoria 1548–1611
Giovanni Gabrieli 1555–1612
Thomas Morley 1557–1602
Carlo Gesualdo 1561–1613
1450
1500
1550
1600
1650
BAROQUE
RENAISSANCE

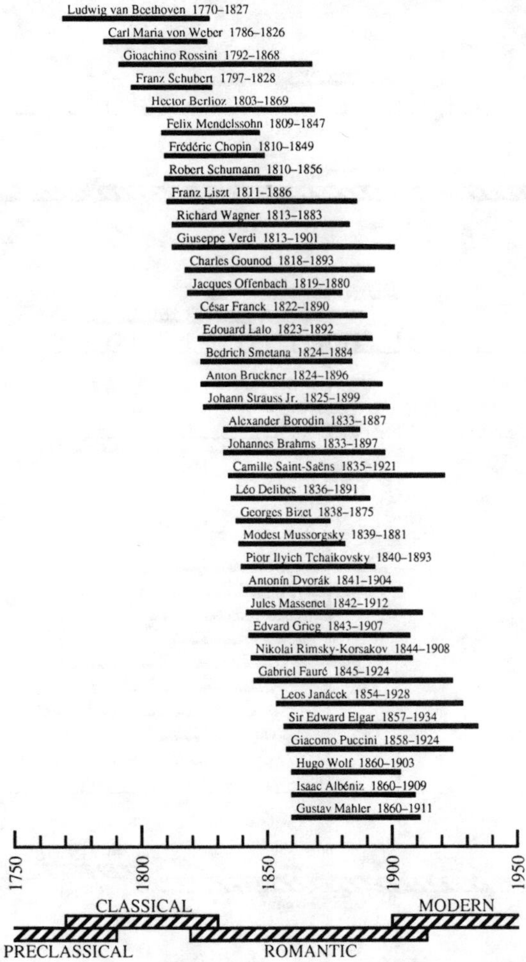

Ludwig van Beethoven 1770–1827

Carl Maria von Weber 1786–1826

Gioachino Rossini 1792–1868

Franz Schubert 1797–1828

Hector Berlioz 1803–1869

Felix Mendelssohn 1809–1847

Frédéric Chopin 1810–1849

Robert Schumann 1810–1856

Franz Liszt 1811–1886

Richard Wagner 1813–1883

Giuseppe Verdi 1813–1901

Charles Gounod 1818–1893

Jacques Offenbach 1819–1880

César Franck 1822–1890

Edouard Lalo 1823–1892

Bedrich Smetana 1824–1884

Anton Bruckner 1824–1896

Johann Strauss Jr. 1825–1899

Alexander Borodin 1833–1887

Johannes Brahms 1833–1897

Camille Saint-Saëns 1835–1921

Léo Delibes 1836–1891

Georges Bizet 1838–1875

Modest Mussorgsky 1839–1881

Piotr Ilyich Tchaikovsky 1840–1893

Antonín Dvorák 1841–1904

Jules Massenet 1842–1912

Edvard Grieg 1843–1907

Nikolai Rimsky-Korsakov 1844–1908

Gabriel Fauré 1845–1924

Leos Janácek 1854–1928

Sir Edward Elgar 1857–1934

Giacomo Puccini 1858–1924

Hugo Wolf 1860–1903

Isaac Albéniz 1860–1909

Gustav Mahler 1860–1911

1750 1800 1850 1900 1950

CLASSICAL MODERN

PRECLASSICAL ROMANTIC

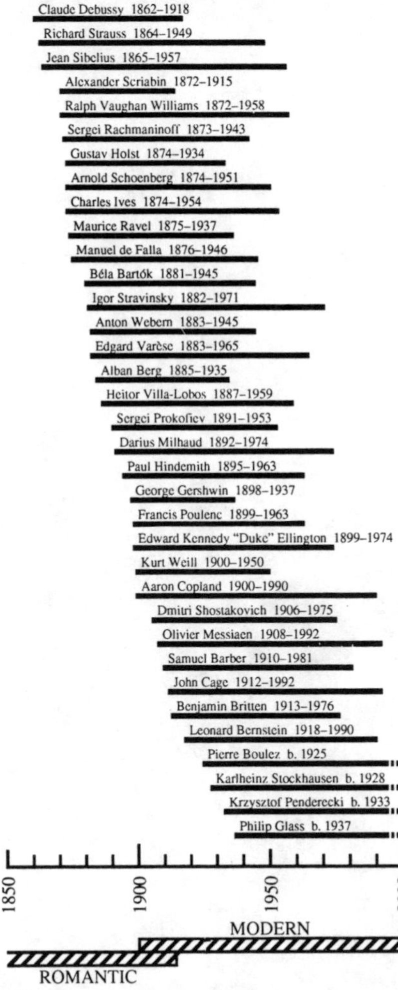

Claude Debussy 1862–1918
Richard Strauss 1864–1949
Jean Sibelius 1865–1957
Alexander Scriabin 1872–1915
Ralph Vaughan Williams 1872–1958
Sergei Rachmaninoff 1873–1943
Gustav Holst 1874–1934
Arnold Schoenberg 1874–1951
Charles Ives 1874–1954
Maurice Ravel 1875–1937
Manuel de Falla 1876–1946
Béla Bartók 1881–1945
Igor Stravinsky 1882–1971
Anton Webern 1883–1945
Edgard Varèse 1883–1965
Alban Berg 1885–1935
Heitor Villa-Lobos 1887–1959
Sergei Prokofiev 1891–1953
Darius Milhaud 1892–1974
Paul Hindemith 1895–1963
George Gershwin 1898–1937
Francis Poulenc 1899–1963
Edward Kennedy "Duke" Ellington 1899–1974
Kurt Weill 1900–1950
Aaron Copland 1900–1990
Dmitri Shostakovich 1906–1975
Olivier Messiaen 1908–1992
Samuel Barber 1910–1981
John Cage 1912–1992
Benjamin Britten 1913–1976
Leonard Bernstein 1918–1990
Pierre Boulez b. 1925
Karlheinz Stockhausen b. 1928
Krzysztof Penderecki b. 1933
Philip Glass b. 1937

1850 1900 1950 2000

MODERN

ROMANTIC

Dictionary of Named and Nicknamed Compositions

This section is a reference for those who want to know "Exactly what is the 'Eroica,' anyway?"

Popular names of compositions are given here in the language(s) in which they are most often encountered; where more than one language is common, each is given its own entry.

Names that begin with an article ("A" or "The" in English; "Das," "Der," "Die," "Il," "L'," "La," "Le," "Les," etc. in other languages) are generally listed with the article at the end (e.g., "Adieux, Les" or "Lark, The").

With few exceptions, the following have *not* been included in this listing:

- Formal names of vocal works—be they songs, cantatas, oratorios, operas, operettas, or musicals.
- Names of programmatic pieces—those that tell a story or paint a picture of some extramusical thing or idea.
- Names of popular songs based on classical melodies.
- Titles of movies, TV shows, or radio programs for which classical pieces have been used as themes.

Even with these necessary restrictions, the list is quite long—over 350 entries! And you may be surprised at how many of the names you've heard or read before.

A

Actus Tragicus: Bach Cantata No. 106, *Gottes Zeit ist die allerbeste Zeit.*

Adieu, L': Chopin Waltz in A-flat for piano, Op. 69, No. 1.

Adieux, Les: Beethoven Piano Sonata No. 26 in E-flat, Op. 81a.

Aeolian Harp Etude: Chopin Etude in A-flat for piano, Op. 25, No. 1.

Age of Anxiety: Bernstein Symphony No. 2.

Air on the G String: Bach Suite for orchestra No. 3 in D, second movement.

Alla Tedesca: Beethoven Piano Sonata No. 25 in G, Op. 79.

Alleluia Symphony: Haydn Symphony No. 30 in C.

Alto Rhapsody: Brahms *Rhapsodie aus Goethes 'Harzreise im Winter'* for alto, male chorus, and orchestra, Op. 53.

American Quartet: Dvorák String Quartet in F, Op. 96.

Andante Cantabile: Tchaikovsky Symphony No. 5 in E Minor, second movement.

Andante Favori: Beethoven Andante in F for piano, WoO 57.

Andantino: Edwin H. Lemare *Andantino in D-flat* for organ.

Antar Symphony: Rimsky-Korsakov Symphony No. 2, Op. 9.

Antartica: Vaughan Williams Symphony No. 7.

Apocalyptic Symphony: Bruckner Symphony No. 8 in C Minor.

Appassionata: Beethoven Piano Sonata No. 23 in F Minor, Op. 57.

Apponyi Quartets: Six Haydn String Quartets, Opp. 71 and 74.

Archduke Trio: Beethoven Piano Trio in B-flat, Op. 97.

Arioso: Bach Harpsichord Concerto No. 5 in F Minor, second movement. Also used in Cantata No. 156, *Ich steh' mit einem Fuss im Grabe.*

Arpeggione: Schubert Sonata for arpeggione (a bowed guitar) and piano in A Minor, D 821; usually performed on cello and piano.

Arte del Violino, L': Locatelli violin collection of Twelve Concerti and Twenty-Four Caprices, Op. 3.

Auf dem Anstand: Haydn Symphony No. 31 in D.

B

Babi Yar: Shostakovich Symphony No. 13 in B-flat Minor, Op. 113.

Bach Chaconne: Bach Partita in D Minor for unaccompanied violin, BWV 1004, fifth movement.

Bach Minuet: Bach Minuet in G for keyboard, *Notebook for Anna Magdalena Bach*, first selection.

Bach Prelude: Bach Prelude in C for keyboard, *Well-Tempered Clavier* Volume 1, first selection.

Basle Concerto: Stravinsky Concerto in D for strings.

Battle Symphony: Beethoven orchestral work *Wellington's Victory*, Op. 91.

Bear, The: Haydn Symphony No. 82 in C.

Bell, The 1: Haydn String Quartet in D Minor, Op. 76, No. 2. **2:** Khachaturian Symphony No. 2 in A Minor.

Bells of Zlonice, The: Dvorák Symphony No. 1, in C Minor, Op. 3.

Bird, The: Haydn String Quartet in C, Op. 33, No. 3.

Black-Key Etude: Chopin Etude in G-flat for piano, Op. 10, No. 5.

Black Mass, The: Scriabin Piano Sonata No. 9 in F, Op. 68.

Brahms Lullaby: Brahms song "Wiegenlied," Op. 49, No. 4.

Brahms Requiem: Brahms *A German Requiem* for soprano, baritone, chorus, and orchestra, Op. 45.

Brandenburg Concertos: Six Bach Concertos for various instruments, BWV 1046–1051.

Bridal Chorus: Wagner chorus "Treulich geführt ziehet dahin," from Act III of his opera *Lohengrin*.

Butterfly Etude: Chopin Etude in G-flat for piano, Op. 25, No. 9.

C

Caccia, La: Vivaldi Violin Concerto in B-flat, Op. 8, No. 10.

Campanella, La: Paganini Violin Concerto No. 2 in B Minor, Op. 7, third movement. Arranged for piano by Liszt in his Paganini Etudes, No. 3.

Camp Meeting, The: Ives Symphony No. 3.

Caroline Te Deum: Handel Te Deum in D.

Cat's Fugue: Domenico Scarlatti Fugue in G Minor for harpsichord.

Cat Waltz: Chopin Waltz in F for piano, Op. 34, No. 3.

Cetra, La 1: Six Allessandro Marcello Concerti Grossi. **2:** Twelve Vivaldi Violin Concerti, Op. 9.

Chandos Anthems: Eleven Handel anthems: "O Be Joyful" (*Chandos Jubilate*), "In the Lord Put I My Trust," "Have Mercy upon Me, O God," "O Sing unto the Lord," "I Will Magnify Thee, O God," "As Pants the Hart," "My Song Shall Be Alway," "O Come Let Us Sing unto the Lord," "O Praise the Lord with One Consent," "The Lord Is My Light," and "Let God Arise."

Chandos Jubilate: Handel *Chandos anthem* No. 1 in D, "O Be Joyful."

Chandos Te Deum: Handel Te Deum in B-flat.

Chasse, La 1: Haydn String Quartet in B-flat, Op. 1, No. 1. **2:** Haydn Symphony No. 73 in D.

Chopin's Nocturne: Chopin Nocturne in E-flat for piano, Op. 9, No. 2.

Choral Fantasy: Beethoven Fantasia in C Minor for Piano, Chorus, and Orchestra, Op. 80.

Choral Symphony: Beethoven Symphony No. 9 in D, Op. 125.

Christmas Concerto: Corelli Concerto Grosso in G Minor, Op. 6, No. 8.

Christmas Symphony: Haydn Symphony No. 26 in D Minor.

Cimento dell'Armonia e dell'Inventione: Twelve Vivaldi Violin Concerti, Op. 8.

Classical Symphony: Prokofiev Symphony No. 1 in D, Op. 25.

Clock Symphony: Haydn Symphony No. 101 in D.

Coffee Cantata: Bach Cantata No. 211, *Schweigt stille, plaudert nicht.*

Colloredo Serenade: Mozart Serenade in D for orchestra, K 203.

Compliment Quartet: Beethoven String Quartet in G, Op. 18, No. 2.

Concerto Accademico: Vaughan Williams Violin Concerto in D Minor.

Concord Sonata: Ives Piano Sonata No. 2, *Concord, Mass., 1840–60.*

Coronation Anthems: Four Handel anthems: "Let Thy Hand Be Strengthened," "My Heart Is Inditing," "The King Shall Rejoice," and "Zadok the Priest."

Coronation Concerto: Mozart Piano Concerto in D, K 537.

Coronation Mass 1: Haydn Mass in D Minor, H XXII:11. **2:** Mozart Mass in C, K 317.

Creation Mass: Haydn Mass in B-flat, H XXII:13.

Credo Mass: Mozart Mass in C, K 257.

Cuckoo and the Nightingale, The: Handel *A Second Set of Six Concertos* for organ and orchestra, No. 1 in F.

D

Death and the Maiden Quartet: Schubert String Quartet in D Minor, D 810.

Dettingen Anthem: Handel anthem in D, "The King Shall Rejoice."

Dettingen Te Deum: Handel Te Deum in D.

Devil's Trill Sonata: Tartini Violin Sonata in G Minor.

Diabelli Variations: Beethoven *Thirty-Three Variations on a Waltz by Diabelli* in C for piano, Op. 120.

Didone Abbandonata 1: Tartini Violin Sonata in G Minor, Op. 6, No. 10. **2:** Clementi Piano in G Minor, Op. 50, No. 3.

Difficult Decision, The: Beethoven String Quartet in F, Op. 135, fourth movement.

Dissonance Quartet: Mozart String Quartet in C, K 465.

Distratto, Il: Haydn Symphony No. 60 in C.

Dog Waltz: Chopin Waltz in D-flat for piano, Op. 64, No. 1.

Dominicus Mass: Mozart Mass in C, K 66.

Donkey Quartet: Haydn String Quartet in D Minor, Op. 76, No. 2.

Dorian Toccata and Fugue: Bach Toccata and Fugue in D Minor for organ, BWV 538. (NOTE: This is not the famous Bach Toccata and Fugue in D Minor.)

Dream, A: Haydn String Quartet in F, Op. 50, No. 5, second movement.

Drumroll Symphony: Haydn Symphony No. 103 in E-flat.

Dumbarton Oaks Concerto: Stravinsky Concerto in E-flat for chamber ensemble.

Dumky Trio: Dvorák Piano Trio in E Minor, Op. 90.

E

Ebony Concerto: Stravinsky Concerto for clarinet and jazz band.

Edward: Brahms Ballade in D Minor for piano, Op. 10, No. 1.

Eine kleine Nachtmusik: Mozart Divertimento in G for strings, K 525.

Eine kleine Trauermusik: Schubert Nonet in E-flat Minor for winds, D 79.

Elegy: Massenet orchestral selection in E Minor from his opera *Les Érinnyes*.

Emperor Concerto: Beethoven Piano Concerto No. 5 in E-flat, Op. 73.

Emperor Quartet: Haydn String Quartet in C, Op. 76, No. 3.

Emperor's Hymn: Haydn song "Gott erhalte Franz den Kaiser," used as the national anthem for Austria and Germany.
English Suites: Six Bach Suites for harpsichord, BWV 806–811.
Erdödy Quartets: Six Haydn String Quartets, Op. 76.
Eroica: Beethoven Symphony No. 3 in E-flat.
Eroica Variations: Beethoven *Fifteen Variations and a Fugue on an Original Theme* in E-flat for piano, Op. 35.
Espansiva: Nielsen Symphony No. 3, Op. 27.
Estro Armonico, L': Twelve Vivaldi Concerti Grossi, Op. 3.
Eyeglass Duo: Beethoven Duo in E-flat for viola and cello.

F

F.A.E. Sonata: Violin Sonata composed of movements written by Albert Dietrich, Schumann, and Brahms.
Fall of Warsaw: Chopin Etude in C Minor for piano, Op. 10, No. 12.
Farewell Symphony: Haydn Symphony No. 45 in F-sharp Minor.
Fate 1: Beethoven Symphony No. 5 in C Minor, Op. 67. **2:** Tchaikovsky Symphony No. 4 in F Minor, Op. 36.
Favorito, Il: Vivaldi Violin Concerto in E Minor, Op. 11, No. 2.
Festive Symphony: Smetana Symphony in E.
Fiddle Fugue: Bach Fugue in D Minor for organ, BWV 539.
Fifths: Haydn String Quartet in D Minor, Op. 76, No. 2.
Fifth Symphony: Beethoven Symphony No. 5 in C Minor, Op. 67.
Fingal's Cave: Mendelssohn Overture for orchestra, Op. 26.
Fire Symphony: Haydn Symphony No. 59 in A.
Flight of the Bumble Bee, The: Rimsky-Korsakov orchestral selection in A Minor from his opera *The Tale of Tsar Saltan*.

Forty-Eight, The: Bach *Well-Tempered Clavier.*

Four Seasons, The: Four Vivaldi Violin Concertos, Op. 8., Nos. 1–4.

Frei aber Einsam: Violin Sonata composed of movements written by Albert Dietrich, Schumann, and Brahms.

French Suites: Six Bach Suites for harpsichord, BWV 812–817.

Frog, The: Haydn String Quartet in D, Op. 50, No. 6.

From My Life: Smetana String Quartets Nos. 1 in E Minor (especially) and 2 in D Minor.

From the New World: Dvorák Symphony No. 5 (No. 9) in E Minor.

Funeral Anthem: Handel anthem in G Minor, "The Ways of Zion Do Mourn."

Funeral March 1: Beethoven Piano Sonata No. 12 in A-flat, Op. 26, third movement. **2:** Beethoven Symphony No. 3 in E-flat, Op. 55, second movement. **3:** Chopin Piano Sonata No. 2 in B-flat Minor, Op. 35, third movement.

Für Elise: Beethoven Bagatelle in A Minor for piano, WoO 59.

G

Gardellino, Il: Vivaldi Flute Concerto in D, Op. 10, No. 3. Originally composed as a concerto grosso.

Gassenhauer Trio: Beethoven Trio in B-flat for Clarinet, Cello, and Piano, Op. 11.

Ghost Trio: Beethoven Piano Trio in D, Op. 70, No. 1.

Gli Scherzi: See *Scherzi, Gli.*

Goldberg Variations: Bach *Aria with Diverse Variations* for harpsichord, BWV 988.

Grande Valse Brillante: Chopin Waltz in E-flat for piano, Op. 18.

Grazer Fantasie: Schubert Fantasy in C for piano, D 605a.
Great C Major Symphony: Schubert Symphony No. 9 in C, D 944.
Great Fugue: Beethoven Fugue in B-flat for String Quartet, Op. 133.
Great G Minor Symphony: Mozart Symphony No. 40 in G Minor, K 550.
Great Organ Mass: Haydn Mass in E-flat, H XXII:4.
Grief: Chopin Etude in E for piano, Op. 10, No. 3.
Grosse Fuge: Beethoven Fugue in B-flat for String Quartet, Op. 133.
Gypsy Rondo: Haydn Piano Trio in G, H XV:25, third movement.

H

Haffner Serenade: Mozart Serenade D for orchestra, K 250 (K 248b).
Haffner Symphony: Mozart Symphony No. 35 in D, K 385.
Hallelujah Chorus: Handel chorus in D from his oratorio *Messiah*, No. 44.
Hallelujah Concerto: Handel Organ Concerto in B-flat, Op. 7, No. 3.
Hammerklavier: Beethoven Piano Sonata No. 29 in B-flat, Op. 106.
Handel's Largo: Handel aria "Ombra mai fù," from his opera *Serse* (*Xerxes*).
Handel Variations: Brahms *Variations and Fugue on a Theme by George Frideric Handel* in B-flat for piano, Op. 24.
Harmonious Blacksmith: Handel Harpsichord Suite No. 5 in E, fourth movement (Air with Five Variations).
Harmony Mass: Haydn Mass in B-flat, H XXII:14.
Harp Etude: Chopin Etude in A-flat for piano, Op. 25, No. 1.
Harp Quartet: Beethoven String Quartet in E-flat, Op. 74.
Haydn Quartets: Six Mozart String Quartets, Op. 10 (K 387–465).
Haydn Variations: Brahms *Variations on a Theme by Joseph Haydn* in B-flat, Opp. 56a (for orchestra) and 56b (for piano duo).

Heavenly Length: Schubert Symphony No. 9 in C, D 944.
Hebrides, The: Mendelssohn Overture for orchestra, Op. 26.
Heiliger Dankgesang: Beethoven String Quartet in A Minor, Op. 132, third movement.
Heiligmesse: Haydn Mass in B-flat, H XXII:10.
Hen, The: Haydn Symphony No. 83 in G Minor.
Hexenmenuet: Haydn String Quartet in D Minor, Op. 76, No. 2, third movement.
Historical Symphony: Spohr Symphony No. 6 in G, Op. 116.
Hoffmeister Quartet: Mozart String Quartet in D, K 499.
Hornpipe Concerto: Handel Concerto Grosso in B Minor, Op. 6, No. 12.
Horn Signal Symphony: Haydn Symphony No. 31 in D.
Horn Trio: Brahms Trio in E-flat for Violin, Horn, and Piano, Op. 40.
How do you do?: Haydn String Quartet in G, Op. 33, No. 5.
Humoresque: Dvorak piano piece in G-flat, Op. 101, No. 7.
Hunt, The 1: Haydn String Quartet in B-flat, Op. 1, No. 1. **2:** Haydn Symphony No. 73 in D. **3:** Mozart String Quartet in B-flat, K 458.
Hunt Cantata: Bach Cantata No. 208, *Was mir behagt, ist nur die muntre Jagd!*
Hymn of Praise: Mendelssohn Symphony No. 2 in B-flat, Op. 52.

I

Imperial Mass: Haydn Mass in D Minor, H XXII:11.
Imperial Symphony: Haydn Symphony No. 53 in D.
Inextinguishable, The: Nielsen Symphony No. 4, Op. 29.
Intimate Pages: Janácek String Quartet No. 2.
Italian Concerto: Bach Concerto for harpsichord alone, BWV 971.
Italian Symphony: Mendelssohn Symphony No. 4 in A, Op. 90.

J

Jeremiah: Bernstein Symphony No. 1.
Jesu, Joy of Man's Desiring: Bach chorale prelude from his Cantata 147, *Herz und Mund und That und Leben.*
Jeunehomme Concerto: Mozart Piano Concerto in E-flat, K 271.
Jig Fugue: Bach Fugue in G for organ, BWV 577.
Joke, The: Haydn String Quartet in E-flat, Op. 33, No. 2.
Jungfernquartette: Six Haydn String Quartets, Op. 33.
Jupiter Symphony: Mozart Symphony No. 41 in C, K 551.

K

Kaddish: Bernstein Symphony No. 3.
Kamennoi-Ostrov: Anton Rubinstein piece for piano in F-sharp, No. 22 from *Kamennoi-Ostrov* ("*Rocky Island*"; 24 Portraits), Op. 10.
Kreutzer Sonata: Beethoven Violin Sonata No. 9 in A Minor, Op. 47.
Kreutzer Sonata Quartet: Janácek String Quartet No. 1.

L

Lamentations Symphony: Haydn Symphony No. 26 in D Minor.
Largo 1: Handel aria "Ombra mai fù," from his opera *Serse* (*Xerxes*). **2:** Dvorák Symphony No. 5 (No. 9) in E Minor, second movement.
Lark, The: Haydn String Quartet in D, Op. 64, No. 5.
Late Quartets: Beethoven String Quartets Opp. 127, 130–133, and 135.
Laudon Symphony: Haydn Symphony No. 69 in C.
Lebewohl, Das: Beethoven Piano Sonata No. 26 in E-flat, Op. 81a.
Leningrad Symphony: Shostakovich Symphony No. 7 in C, Op. 60.
Liebestraum: Liszt piano piece in A-flat, No. 3 of three by that title.
Linz Symphony: Mozart Symphony No. 36 in C, K 425.
Little C Major Symphony: Schubert Symphony No. 6 in C, D 589.
Little Fugue in G Minor: Bach Fugue for organ, BWV 578.
Little G Minor Symphony: Mozart Symphony No. 25 in G Minor, K 183 (K 173dB).
Little Organ Mass: Haydn Mass in B-flat, H XXII:7.
Little Russia Symphony: Tchaikovsky Symphony No. 2 in C Minor, Op. 17.
Lobgesang: Mendelssohn Symphony No. 2 in B-flat, Op. 52.
Lobkowitz Quartets: Two Haydn String Quartets, Op. 77.
London Symphonies: Haydn Symphonies Nos. 93–104.
London Symphony 1: Haydn Symphony No. 104 in D. **2:** Vaughan Williams Symphony No. 2.
Lord Nelson Mass: See *Nelson Mass*.

M

Malinconia, La: Beethoven String Quartet in B-flat, Op. 18, No. 6, fourth movement.

Marche Militaire: Schubert March in D for piano duet, Op. 51 (D 733), No. 1.

Maria Theresia Symphony: Haydn Symphony No. 48 in C.

Mariazell Mass: Haydn Mass in C, H XXII:8.

Mass in Time of War: Haydn Mass in C, H XXII:9.

Matin, Le: Haydn Symphony No. 6 in D.

May 1st: Shostakovich Symphony No. 3 in E-flat, Op. 20.

Mazeppa Etude: Liszt *Transcendental Etudes* for piano, No. 4.

Meditation: Massenet selection in D for violin and orchestra from his opera *Thaïs*.

Melody in F: Anton Rubinstein piano piece, No. 1 of *Two Melodies*, Op. 3.

Mercury Symphony: Haydn Symphony No. 43 in E-flat.

Midi, Le: Haydn Symphony No. 7 in C.

Military Polonaise: Chopin Polonaise in A for piano, Op. 40, No. 1.

Military Symphony: Haydn Symphony No. 100 in G.

Minuet in G 1: Bach *Notebook for Anna Magdalena Bach*, first selection. **2:** Beethoven *Six Minuets,* WoO 10, No. 2. **3:** Paderewski Minuet for piano, Op. 14, No. 1.

Minute Waltz: Chopin Waltz in D-flat for piano, Op. 64, No. 1.

Miracle Symphony: Haydn Symphony No. 96 in D.

Missa Solemnis: Beethoven Mass in D, Op. 123.

Moonlight Sonata: Beethoven Piano Sonata No. 14 in C-sharp Minor, Op. 27, No. 2.

Mount of Olives, The: Beethoven oratorio *Christ on the Mount of Olives*, Op. 85.

Musical Joke, A: Mozart Divertimento in F for chamber ensemble, K 522.

Muss es sein? Es muss sein! Es muss sein!: Beethoven String Quartet in F, Op. 135, fourth movement.

Mysterious Mountain: Hovahness Symphony No. 2, Op. 132.

N

Nelson Mass: Haydn Mass in D Minor, H XXII:11.
New England Symphony, A: Ives *First Orchestral Set.*
New World Symphony: Dvorák Symphony No. 5 (No. 9) in E Minor.
Nicolai Mass: Haydn Mass in G, H XXII:6.
Ninth Symphony: Beethoven Symphony No. 9 in D, Op. 125.
Nordic Symphony: Hanson Symphony No. 1 in E Minor, Op. 21.
Nullte, Die: Bruckner Symphony "No. 0" in D Minor.

O

October: Shostakovich Symphony No. 2 in C, Op. 14.
Ode to Joy: Beethoven Symphony No. 9 in D, Op. 125, fourth movement theme.
Organ Solo Mass: Mozart Mass in C, K 259.
Organ Symphony: Saint-Saëns Symphony No. 3 in C Minor, Op. 78.
Ours, L': Haydn Symphony No. 82 in C.
Oxford Symphony: Haydn Symphony No. 92 in G.

P

Paganini Etudes: Six Liszt Etudes for piano on themes of Paganini.

Paganini Variations: Brahms *Variations on a Theme by Paganini* in A Minor for piano, Op. 35.

Palindrome Symphony: Haydn Symphony No. 47 in G.

Paris Symphonies: Haydn Symphonies Nos. 82–87.

Paris Symphony: Mozart Symphony No. 31 in D, K 297 (K 300a).

Passione, La: Haydn Symphony No. 49 in F Minor.

Pastoral Sonata: Beethoven Piano Sonata No. 15 in D, Op. 28.

Pastoral Symphony 1: Handel interlude from his oratorio *Messiah*, No. 13. **2:** Beethoven Symphony No. 6 in F, Op. 68. **3:** Vaughan Williams Symphony No. 3.

Pastor Fido, Il: Six Vivaldi Solo Sonatas, Op. 13.

Pathétique 1: Beethoven Piano Sonata No. 8 in C Minor, Op. 13. **2:** Tchaikovsky Symphony No. 6 in B Minor, Op. 74.

Paukenmesse: Haydn Mass in C, H XXII:9.

Peasant Cantata: Bach Cantata No. 212, *Mer hahn en neue Oberkeet.*

Philosopher, The: Haydn Symphony No. 22 in E-flat.

Polish Symphony: Tchaikovsky Symphony No. 3 in D, Op. 29.

Pomp and Circumstance: Elgar March in D, from a set of five by that title (Op. 39), No. 1.

Posthorn Serenade: Mozart Serenade in D for orchestra, K 320.

Poule, La: Haydn Symphony No. 83 in G Minor.

Prague Symphony: Mozart Symphony No. 38 in D, K 504.

Prelude in C: Bach *Well-Tempered Clavier* Volume 1, first selection.

Prelude in C-sharp Minor: Rachmaninoff Prelude for piano, Op. 3, No. 2.

Prussian Quartets 1: Six Haydn String Quartets, Op. 50. **2:** Three Mozart String Quartets, K 575, 589, and 590.

Q

Quartetto Serioso: Beethoven String Quartet in F Minor, Op. 95.
Quinten: Haydn String Quartet in D Minor, Op. 76, No. 2.

R

Rage over a Lost Penny: Beethoven *Rondo a Capriccio* in G for piano, Op. 129.
Raindrop Prelude: Chopin Prelude in D-flat for piano, Op. 28, No. 15.
Rain Sonata: Brahms Violin Sonata No. 1 in G, Op. 78.
Ratswahl Cantata: Bach Cantata No. 71, *Gott ist mein König*.
Razor Quartet: Haydn String Quartet in F Minor, Op. 55, No. 2.
Razumovsky Quartets: Three Beethoven String Quartets, Op. 59.
Recitative: Haydn String Quartet in G, Op. 17, No. 5.
Reformation Symphony: Mendelssohn Symphony No. 5 in D, Op. 107.
Reine, La: Haydn Symphony No. 85 in B-flat.
Reliquie Sonata: Schubert Piano Sonata in C, D 840.
Requiem Symphony: Hanson Symphony No. 4, Op. 34.
Resurrection Symphony: Mahler Symphony No. 2 in C Minor.
Rève Angélique: Anton Rubinstein piece for piano in F-sharp, No. 22 from *Kamennoi-Ostrov* ("*Rocky Island*"; 24 Portraits), Op. 10.
Revolutionary Etude: Chopin Etude in C Minor for piano, Op. 10, No. 12.
Rhenish Symphony: Schumann Symphony No. 3 in E-flat, Op. 97.

Rider, The: Haydn String Quartet in G Minor, Op. 74, No. 3.

Romantic Symphony 1: Bruckner Symphony No. 4 in E-flat. **2:** Hanson Symphony No. 2, Op. 30.

Rondo alla Turca: Mozart Piano Sonata in A, K 331 (K300i), third movement.

Roxelane, La: Haydn Symphony No. 63 in C.

Russian Quartets 1: Six Haydn String Quartets, Op. 33. **2:** Three Beethoven String Quartets, Op. 59.

Rustic Wedding: Karl Goldmark Symphony, Op. 26.

S

St. Anne Fugue: Bach (Prelude and) Fugue in E-flat for organ, BWV 552.

St. Anthony Chorale: Haydn Divertimento in B-flat for winds, H II:46, second movement.

St. Cecilia Mass: Haydn Mass in C, H XXII:5.

St. Joseph Mass: Haydn Mass in E-flat, H XXII:4.

Salomon Symphonies: Haydn Symphonies Nos. 93–104.

Salomon Symphony: Haydn Symphony No. 104 in D.

Scherzi, Gli: Six Haydn String Quartets, Op. 33.

Scherzoso: Beethoven String Quartet in B-flat, Op. 130.

Schoolmaster, The: Haydn Symphony No. 55 in E-flat.

Schübler Chorales: Six Bach Chorale Preludes for organ, BWV 645–650.

Scotch (Scottish) Symphony: Mendelssohn Symphony No. 3 in A Minor, Op. 56.

Sea Symphony 1: Vaughan Williams Symphony No. 1 in C. **2:** Hanson Symphony No. 7.
Serenata Notturna: Mozart Serenade in D for strings and timpani, K 239.
Serioso: Beethoven String Quartet in F Minor, Op. 95.
Sheep May Safely Graze: Bach movement from his Cantata 208, *Was mir behagt, ist nur die muntre Jagd!*
Shepherd Boy Etude: Chopin Etude in A-flat for piano, Op. 25, No. 1.
Simple Symphony: Britten Symphony, Op. 4.
Sinfonia Antartica: Vaughan Williams Symphony No. 7.
Sinfonia da Requiem: Britten Symphony, Op. 20.
Six-Four-Time Mass: Haydn Mass in G, H XXII:6.
Soir, Le: Haydn Symphony No. 8 in G.
Solemn Vespers: Mozart *Vesperae Solennes de Confessore* in C, K 339.
Sonata Facile: Mozart Piano Sonata in C, K 545.
Sonata quasi una Fantasia: Beethoven Piano Sonatas Nos. 13 in E-flat and 14 in C-sharp Minor, Op. 27, Nos. 1 and 2.
Spatzenmesse: Mozart Mass in G, K 220 (K 196b).
Spaur Mass: Mozart Mass in C, K 258.
Spring Sonata: Beethoven Violin Sonata No. 5 in F, Op. 24.
Spring Symphony: Schumann Symphony No. 1 in B-flat, Op. 38.
Stravaganza, La: Twelve Vivaldi Violin Concerti, Op. 4.
Street Song Trio: Beethoven Trio in B-flat for Clarinet, Cello, and Piano, Op. 11.
Study Symphony: Bruckner Symphony in F Minor, unnumbered.
Sun Quartets: Six Haydn String Quartets, Op. 20.
Sunrise Quartet: Haydn String Quartet in B-flat, Op. 76, No. 4.
Surprise Symphony: Haydn Symphony No. 94 in G.
Swedish Rhapsody: Hugo Alfvén *Midsommarvaka* for orchestra, Op. 19.
Symphony of a Thousand: Mahler Symphony No. 8 in E-flat.

T

Tempest 1: Haydn Symphony No. 8 in G, fourth movement. **2:** Beethoven Piano Sonata No. 17 in D Minor, Op. 31, No. 2.

Tempora Mutantur: Haydn Symphony No. 64 in A.

Theresia Mass: Haydn Mass in B-flat, H XXII:12.

Three Places in New England: Ives *First Orchestral Set.*

Timpani Mass: Haydn Mass in C, H XXII:9.

Titan Symphony: Mahler Symphony No. 1 in D.

Torrent, The: Chopin Etude in C-sharp Minor for piano, Op. 10, No. 4.

Tost Quartets: Twelve Haydn String Quartets, Opp. 54, 55, and 64.

To the Memory of an Angel: Berg Violin Concerto.

To the Memory of Lenin: Shostakovich Symphony No. 12 in D Minor, Op. 112.

Toy Symphony: Symphony in C variously ascribed to Franz Joseph Haydn, Michael Haydn, or Leopold Mozart.

Tragic Symphony: Schubert Symphony No. 4 in C Minor, D 417.

Trauer-Ode: Bach Cantata No. 198, *Lass, Fürstin, lass noch einen Strahl.*

Trauersinfonie: Haydn Symphony No. 44 in E Minor.

Traum, Ein: Haydn String Quartet in F, Op. 50, No. 5, second movement.

Triangle Concerto: Liszt Piano Concerto No. 1 in E-flat.

Triple Concerto: Beethoven Concerto in C for Piano, Violin, and Cello, Op. 56.

Tristesse: Chopin Etude in E for piano, Op. 10, No. 3.

Triumphal Symphony: Smetana Symphony in E.

Trout Quintet: Schubert Quintet in A for piano, violin, viola, cello, and double bass, D 667.

Trumpet Tune: Purcell harpsichord piece in C.

Trumpet Voluntary: Jeremiah Clarke instrumental piece in D.

Turkish March: Beethoven incidental music to *The Ruins of Athens* for orchestra, Op. 113, fourth number. Also arranged by the composer for piano duet. Previously used in his *Six Variations on an Original Theme* in D for piano, Op. 76.

Turkish Rondo: Mozart Piano Sonata in A, K 331 (K300i), third movement.

Twinkle Twinkle Variations: Mozart Variations on "Ah, vous dirai-je, maman" in C for piano, K 265 (K 300e).

Two-Cello Quintet: Schubert String Quintet in C, Op. 163 (D 956).

U

Ukrainian Symphony: Tchaikovsky Symphony No. 2 in C Minor, Op. 17.

Unfinished Symphony: Schubert Symphony No. 8 in B Minor, D 759.

Utrecht Jubilate: Handel Jubilate in D.

Utrecht Te Deum: Handel Te Deum in D.

V

Villanelle: Chopin Etude in G-flat for piano, Op. 25, No. 9.
Voces Intimae: Sibelius String Quartet in D Minor, Op. 56.

W

Wagner Symphony: Bruckner Symphony No. 3 in D Minor.
Waisenhausmesse: Mozart Mass in C Minor, K 139 (K 47a).
Waldstein: Beethoven Piano Sonata No. 21 in C, Op. 53.
Wanderer Fantasy: Schubert Fantasy in C for piano, D 760.
Wedding March: Mendelssohn incidental music to *A Midsummer Night's Dream* for orchestra, Op. 61, ninth movement.
Wedge Fugue: Bach (Prelude and) Fugue in E Minor for organ, BWV 548.
White Mass, The: Scriabin Piano Sonata No. 7 in F, Op. 64.
Wind-Band Mass: Haydn Mass in B-flat, H XXII:14.
Winter Dreams: Tchaikovsky Symphony No. 1 in G Minor, Op. 13.
Winter Wind Etude: Chopin Etude in A Minor for piano, Op. 25, No. 11.
Witches' Minuet: Haydn String Quartet in D Minor, Op. 76, No. 2, third movement.
WTC: Bach *Well-Tempered Clavier.*

Y

Year 1905, The: Shostakovich Symphony No. 11 in G Minor, Op. 103.
Year 1917, The: Shostakovich Symphony No. 12 in D Minor, Op. 112.

Reference Charts

Accents and Articulation Marks

Symbol	Meaning
>	Accent
sfz / ∧	Sforzando
fp	Forte-Piano
	Legato
	Portato
	Tenuto
	Marcato
	Staccato
	Staccatissimo

Chord Symbols

BASIC SYMBOLS:

Symbol	**Chord Type**
C	Major
Cm, Cmin	Minor
C+, Caug	Augmented
Cdim, Cdim7, C°	Diminished (Seventh)
Cø	Half-Diminished Seventh
Csus	Suspended Fourth
Csus2	Suspended Second
N.C.	No Chord

ADDITIONS AND ALTERATIONS:

Symbol	**Meaning**
6	Sixth
6/9	Sixth and Ninth
7	Flat Seventh
maj7	Major Seventh
9	Flat Seventh and Ninth
maj9	Major Seventh and Ninth
11	Flat Seventh, Ninth, and Eleventh
13	Flat Seventh, Ninth, Eleventh, and Thirteenth
♭,–	Lower the following Note by a Half Step
♯,+	Raise the following Note by a Half Step
add2, add9	Add the Note Specified
no 3rd	Eliminate the Third
C/G	Bass Note other than Root

Circle of Fifths

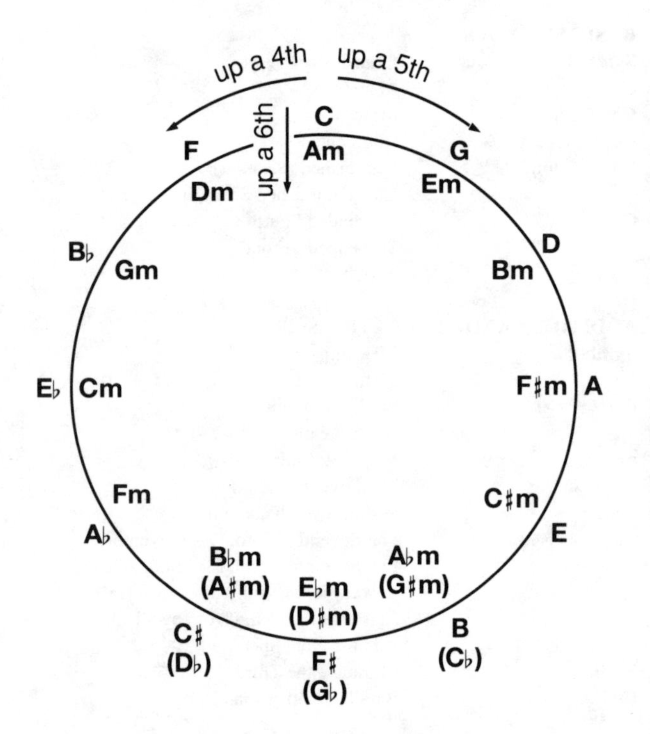

Dynamic Signs and Symbols

Symbol	Term	Meaning
ppp	Pianississimo	Very Very Soft
pp	Pianissimo	Very Soft
p	Piano	Soft
mp	Mezzo Piano	Medium Soft
mf	Mezzo Forte	Medium Loud
f	Forte	Loud
ff	Fortissimo	Very Loud
fff	Fortississimo	Very Very Loud
cresc.	Crescendo	Gradually Becoming Louder
decresc.	Decrescendo	Gradually Becoming Softer
dim.	Diminuendo	Gradually Becoming Softer
	Messa di Voce	Becoming Louder, Then Softer

Guitar Tablature Notation Guide

In tablature ("tab") notation, the lines of the staff represent the strings of the instrument, rather than absolute pitch. For guitar, the tablature staff normally has six lines. The word "TAB" appears at the beginning of this staff:

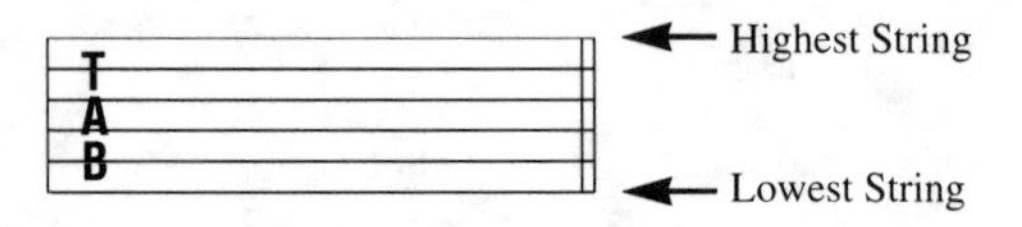

Numbers represent notes played on the strings by indicating what fret is played; the number 0 indicates an open string. These numbers can be placed one after another to represent melodic lines, or "stacked" to represent chords:

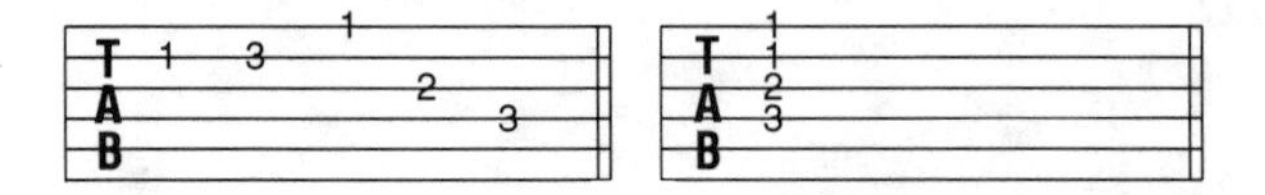

Tablature is often printed in tandem with traditional staff notation. In many cases this allows complex technical maneuvers to be expressed clearly:

Miscellaneous Symbols

Symbol	Meaning
♯	Sharp
♭	Flat
𝄪	Double Sharp
𝄫	Double Flat
𝄴	Common Time
𝄵	Cut Time
M.M.	Maelzel's Metronome (Metronome Marking)
2	Duplet
3	Triplet
8	Vocal Tenor Clef (An Octave Below Treble Clef)

Ornaments

Symbol	Meaning
	Glissando
	Rolled Chord
	Vibrato (Guitar)
	Grace Note
	Mordent
	Inverted Mordent, Trill
tr *tr*	Trill
	Turn
	Tremolo or Roll

Performance Indications

Symbol	Meaning
a2	A Due
𝄐	Fermata
,	Breath
//	Caesura
G.P.	Grand Pause
[pedal bracket lines]	Press and Release Pedal
𝆮	Press Pedal
❉	Release Pedal
⊓	Down Bow
V	Up Bow

Symbol	Meaning
∪	Heel (Organ)
∧	Toe (Organ)
○	Harmonic (Strings); Wah (Brass)
15ma	Play Two Octaves Higher than Written
8va	Play an Octave Higher than Written
8vb / 8va *bassa*	Play an Octave Lower than Written
- - - - - - - - ˥ / - - - - - - - - ˩	Continuation of Octave Higher or Lower
loco	Play at Written Pitch
R.H.	Right Hand
L.H.	Left Hand
[	Play with Same Finger or Hand
V.S.	Volti Subito

Repeat Signs and Symbols

Symbol	Meaning
	Repeat Signs
1 2	First and Second Endings
D.S.	Dal Segno
D.C.	Da Capo
𝄋	Segno
𝄌	Coda
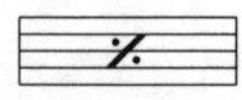	Repeat Previous Measure
	Repeat Previous Two Measures
bis	Repeat Everything in Bracket
	Repeat (Chord) on Beats
	Repeated Notes

Scale Chart: Major and Minor, with Key Signatures

Each system shows the notes of a major scale and its relative minor scale, and the key signature they share.

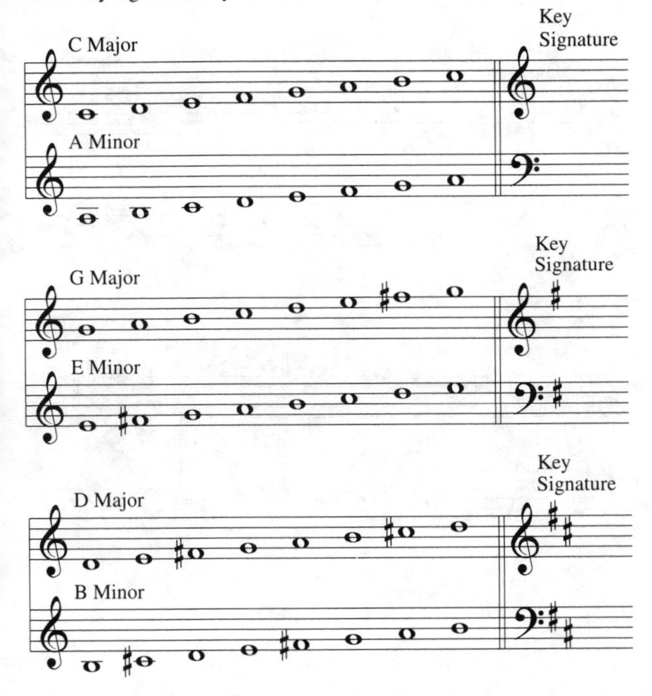

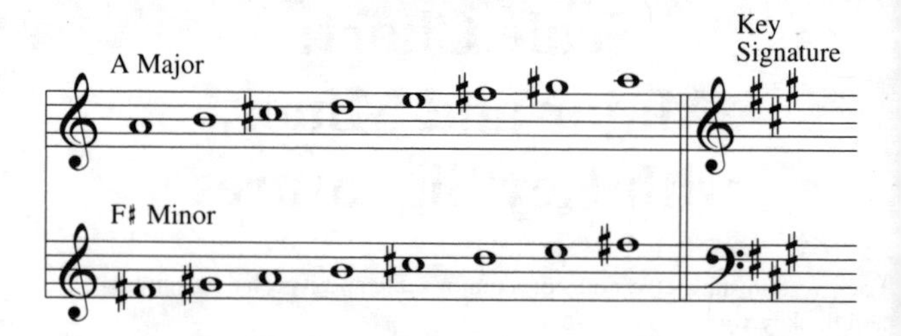
A Major
Key
Signature
F♯ Minor

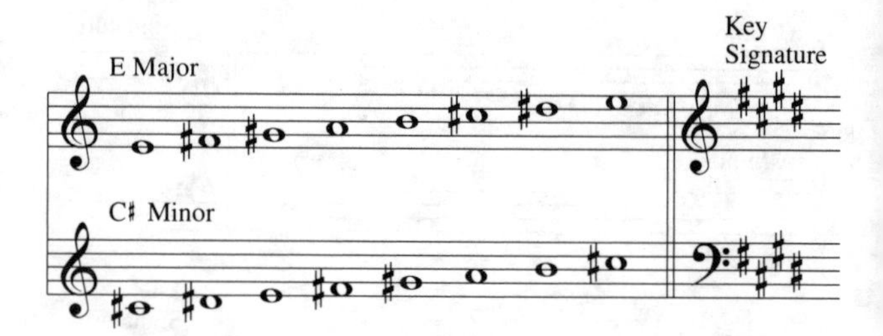
E Major
Key
Signature
C♯ Minor

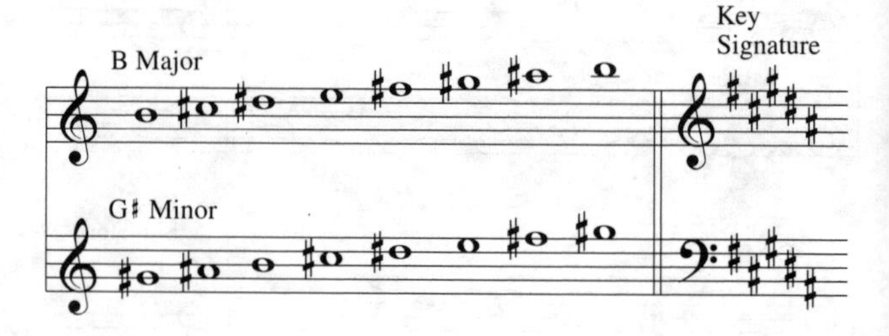
B Major
Key
Signature
G♯ Minor

F♯ Major
Key
Signature
D♯ Minor

C♯ Major
Key
Signature
A♯ Minor

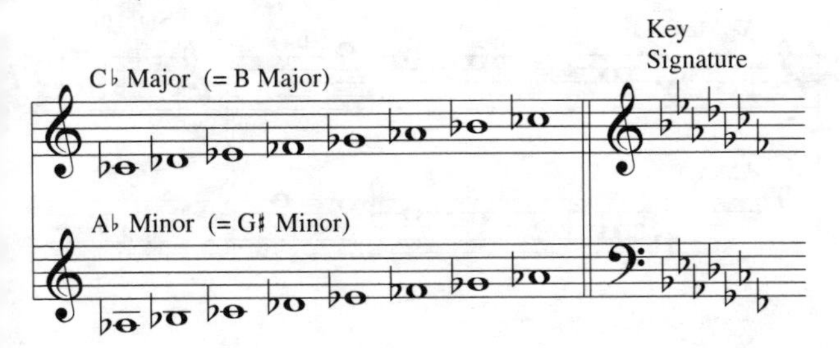
C♭ Major (= B Major)
Key
Signature
A♭ Minor (= G♯ Minor)

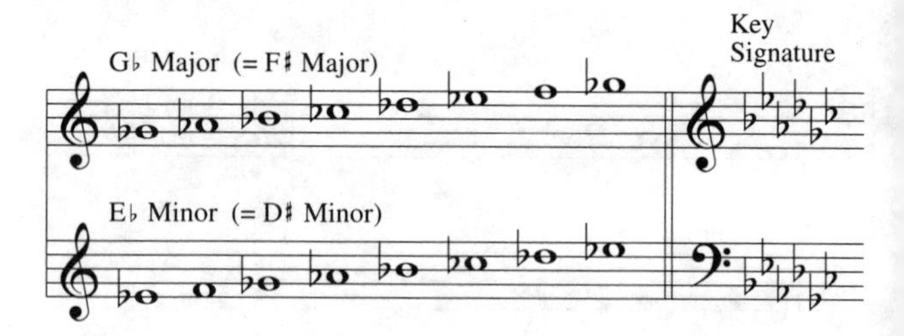
G♭ Major (= F♯ Major)
Key Signature
E♭ Minor (= D♯ Minor)

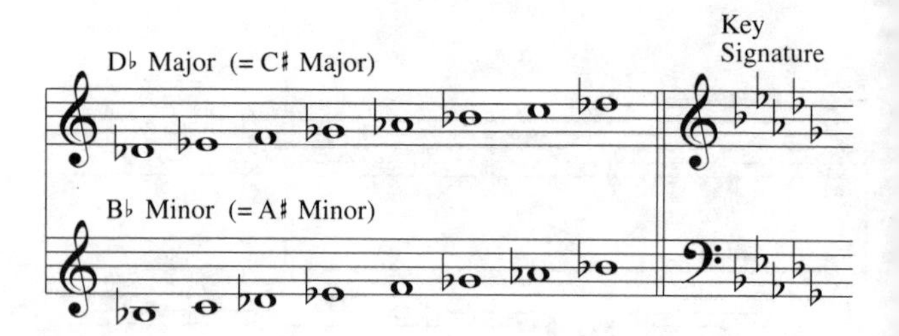
D♭ Major (= C♯ Major)
Key Signature
B♭ Minor (= A♯ Minor)

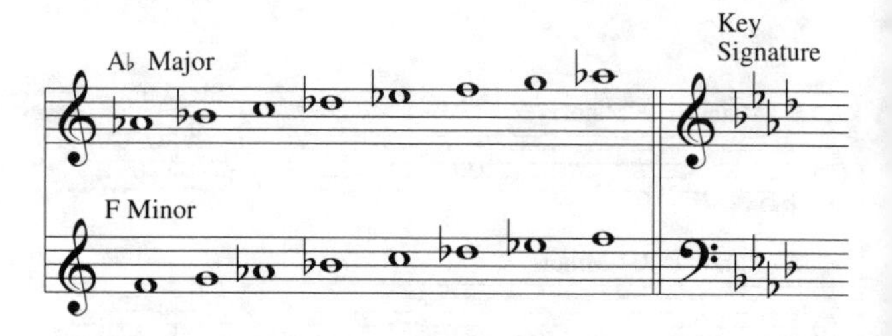
A♭ Major
Key Signature
F Minor

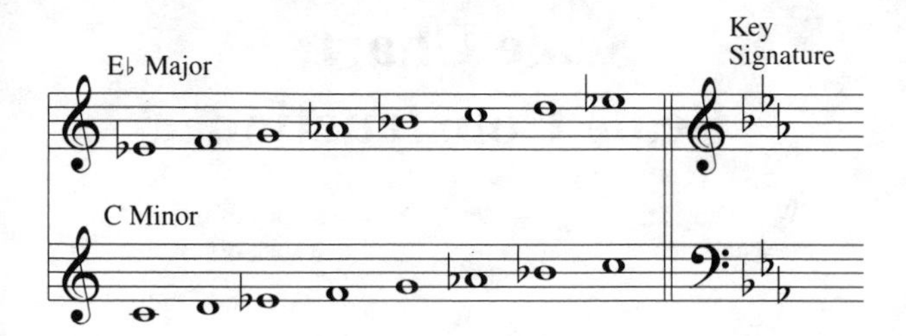
E♭ Major
C Minor
Key
Signature

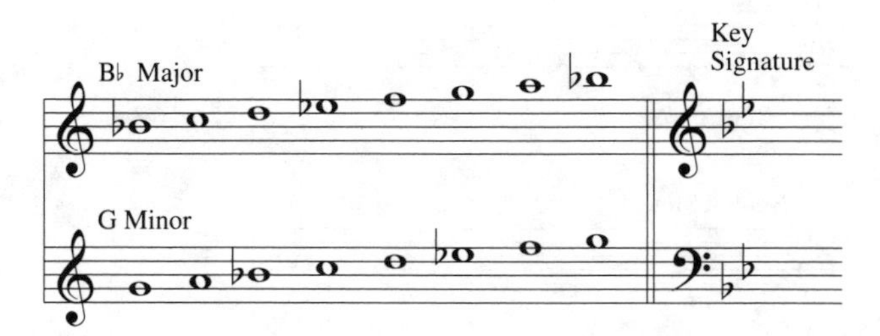
B♭ Major
G Minor
Key
Signature

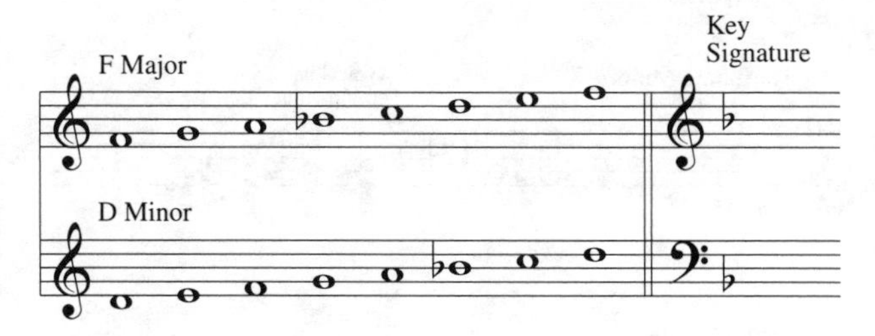
F Major
D Minor
Key
Signature

Scale Chart: Scale Construction

Scale Chart: Modes

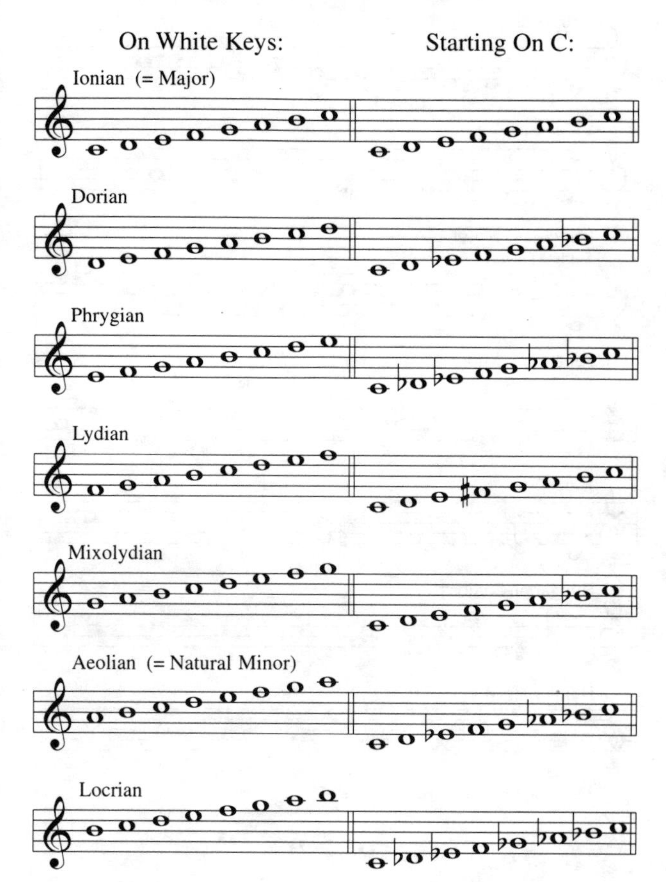

Scale Chart: Other Scales

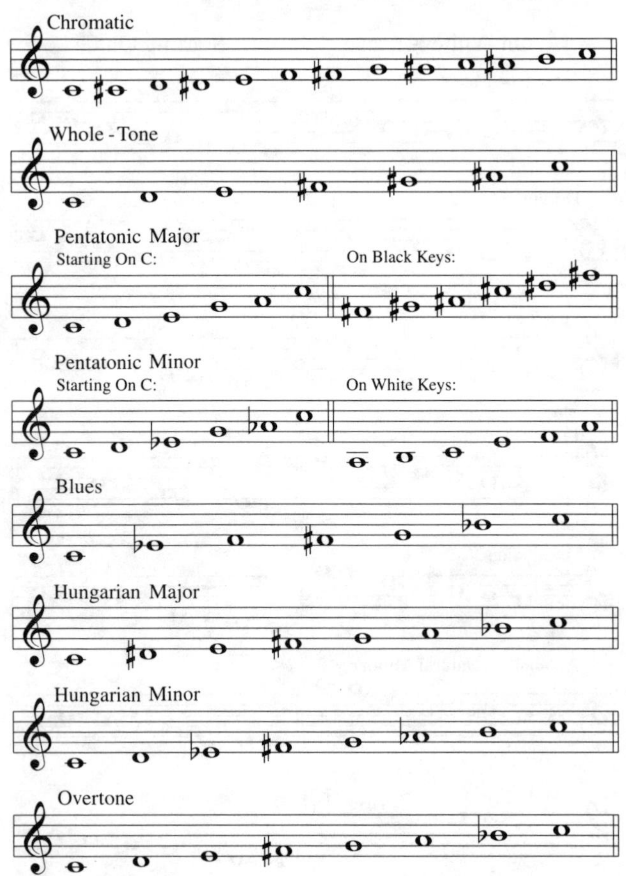

Tempo Terms

Term	Meaning
Grave	Very Slow
Largo, Lento	Slow
Larghetto	A little faster than Largo
Adagio	Moderately Slow
Andante	"Walking" Tempo
Andantino	A little faster than Andante*
Allegretto	A little slower than Allegro
Allegro	Fast
Vivace	Lively
Presto	Very Fast
Prestissimo	Very Very Fast
Moderato	Moderate(ly)
Molto	Very
Accel., Accelerando	Gradually Becoming Faster
Rit., Ritardando	Gradually Becoming Slower

*Andantino rarely means a little *slower* than Andante